Culturally Relevant Pedagogy

Clashes and Confrontations

Edited by
Lisa Scherff and Karen Spector

ROWMAN & LITTLEFIELD EDUCATION

A division of

ROWMAN & LITTLEFIELD PUBLISHERS, INC.
Lanham • New York • Toronto • Plymouth, UK

KH

Published by Rowman & Littlefield Education
A division of Rowman & Littlefield Publishers, Inc.
A wholly owned subsidary of The Rowman & Littlefield Publishing Group, Inc.
4501 Forbes Boulevard, Suite 200, Lanham, Maryland 20706
http://www.rowmaneducation.com

Estover Road, Plymouth PL6 7PY, United Kingdom

British Library Cataloguing in Publication Information Available

Library of Congress Cataloging-in-Publication Data

Culturally relevant pedagogy : clashes and confrontations / [edited by] Lisa Scherff and Karen Spector.
    p. cm.
    Includes bibliographical references and index.
    ISBN 978-1-60709-419-7 (cloth : alk. paper) — ISBN 978-1-60709-420-3 (pbk. : alk. paper) — ISBN 978-1-60709-421-0 (electronic)
    1. Multicultural education—United States. 2. Critical pedagogy—United States. 3. Teaching—United States. 4. Minorities—Education—United States. 5. Learning—Social aspects—Cross-cultural studies. I. Scherff, Lisa, 1968– II. Spector, Karen.
    LC1099.3.C847 2010
    370.11'5—dc22   2010030016

Printed in the United States of America

2/28/12

Contents

Contents

Foreword

Looking for a Little Inspiration

Dawn Abt-Perkins, *Lake Forest College*

Inspiration is difficult to find in schools that are underfunded, in communities that have been ravaged by deindustrialization, in families that face mounting economic and emotional pressures. We all need to be reading research that inspires us to think through the questions and issues that most influence our work in these communities, with these children and families, and within these classrooms. While there have been books written about culturally relevant pedagogy (see Ladson-Billings 1994; Irvine and Armento 2001), we have rarely been allowed inside the classrooms and the minds of teachers who are at work with this theory, molding it to fit their particular circumstances.

There are even fewer cases of teacher educators working within a self-reflexive framework on issues of cultural responsiveness. None has addressed the moral, ethical, and political dilemmas of this work while, at the same time, exploring the theoretical dimensions of culturally responsive pedagogical theory. By allowing the reader to enter into their critical reflections on their practice, the authors in this volume inspire us to engage in similar critical processes and theoretical exploration.

Culturally relevant instructional theory doesn't allow us many hiding or resting places. We are expected to be as fully conscious as possible about the choices we are making, the instructional mandates we reject, and the social and political consequences of the goals we uphold for the educational process. It requires a political diligence, an understanding that power relations and hierarchies exist within all social interactions and communities, including the classroom community.

Awareness of this dimension of practice is critical to the theory having a real impact on disenfranchised and unengaged students. Culturally responsive pedagogy calls on us to ask questions about instructional materials that extend beyond reading levels and standards-based instruction and examine the hidden curriculum supported by materials that present too limited a set of perspectives. We are called upon by culturally responsive pedagogy to engage in assessment practices that help us to know our students' full identity positions, subjectivities, and perspectives, not simply their achievement scores.

This theory calls on teachers to commit to dialogue as the center of instructional practice and to develop expectations that the results of instruction should lead to personal transformation of not only students, but of ourselves as well. In fact, it also calls on us to do as Malcolm X suggests, to "educate ourselves" about the cultural lives of others and the identity positions that our students have available to them for survival in their communities, our society, and their homes and families that might not fit with our expectations for them at school.

Context-specific inquiry processes are at the center of culturally responsive pedagogy. Culture is created within situations, among people, and through interaction. As such, it is always in motion and open to new interpretation and fresh responses. There is no such thing as a "stand still" approach that "works." Instead, this theory calls on a form of consciousness and openness to learning from teaching and from our students. Further, culturally responsive pedagogy challenges us to find valuable students' resources in home and community, instead of asking our students to leave this knowledge behind when they walk through our classroom doors.

Ladson-Billings and others call on teachers to reconstruct schooling, to make room for what students bring, and to create bridges between home and school. To work from this theory is not simply to accept, but also to value the fact that students—no matter their background or experience—bring knowledge to teaching and learning through just being themselves and living their lives inside and outside of the classroom.

To believe in this theory, one needs to look beyond the facades of student disengagement to see that students are indeed hungry for opportunities in school to share what they know, to engage with others in exploring and extending that knowledge, and to put that knowledge to work somehow for some greater good. To follow this theory requires a personal, not merely a professional, investment. The consequences of instructional action are not simply a test score.

Those of us who work from these principles know there is much more at stake. This is morally inscribed work; this is hopeful practice. Most of what has been written about culturally relevant pedagogy that has found its way into professional development workshops and school discourse since Gloria Ladson-Billings' (1994) popular rendition of the theory in *The Dreamkeepers* propagates certain assumptions: that there are universally definable features of a pedagogy called *culturally responsive instruction*, and that we can all engage in this pedagogy relatively easily if we are "culturally conscious" people.

In this volume, Lisa Scherff and Karen Spector and their colleagues usefully expose the issues, problems, and dilemmas of interpreting culturally responsive pedagogical theory in practice. They also demonstrate that there is no monolithic culturally responsive pedagogy.

Indeed, Ladson-Billings (1995) and James Cummins (1990) call for a paradigm shift—a change in a set of beliefs and assumptions about good teaching—along with some portraits based on their own research for what such practice could/should/might look like. Indeed, there are no data that show a cause and effect relationship or even a correlational relationship between any particular culturally relevant practice and student achievement, engagement, or school success. All we have is a powerful theory built on a set of principles based in other theories of sociocultural learning, culturally situated practice, and sociolinguistics.

These theories accept as givens the following premises: culture is situated in particular contexts; cultural practices are interpreted through interactions by particular people; people bring their own beliefs, stereotypes, and perspectives (carried from our own experience living in a larger American culture that has been marked by social prejudices) to all interactions—especially interactions that involve the negotiation of power, such as teacher-student interactions. Therefore, there can be no absolutes when discussing culturally responsive instruction.

Guided by a common theoretical framework and assumptions about the goals of teaching and learning, each teacher must invent his or her own rendition of culturally responsive pedagogy. It is crucial that we share these inventions with one another to build a community of practice that will support the development of the theory. Unfortunately, too few teachers and teacher educators are talking about culturally responsive practices.

Most discourse in teacher education is mired in the talk of accountability to ideas that are relatively insignificant when measured against the goals of culturally responsive pedagogy. Can students read at grade level? Are teacher education programs training teachers to meet the expectations of principals in their first year? Are schools meeting adequate yearly progress?

These questions seem relatively insignificant when measured against the questions addressed in culturally relevant pedagogy: Do all students feel accepted and valued in my classroom? Will my students find what we are doing together today relevant and worthwhile? Am I being as accepting and open to my students as I possibly can be? Are the experiences I am providing helping students find a useful, hopeful role within an unjust society?

These are not the types of questions being raised at faculty meetings or in most professional development experiences. Yet, these are the questions that will lead teachers to address the most important issues in schools today—how to engage the disenfranchised student, how to build relationships across racial, ethnic, and class boundaries that can support students who, at too young of an age, have been told they are failures, part of the "have nots" of our society.

Teachers who are interested in these critical questions and transformative outcomes feel isolated and out of touch in the professional cultures of schools today. We need more voices to further the conversation. In the chapters in this volume, we meet teachers who are fully engaged in this conversation and, by sharing their work, invite others to join in. The authors are careful to not contribute to the forces within educational research that call for "instructional models" and "research-based best practices."

This desire by the educational research community to use the guises of "scientifically based" methodologies to be deemed relevant to policy makers and curriculum marketers has led to too many administrative checklists and too many mandates forced upon teachers. Here are the signs of culturally responsive practice. This is how you will know it when you see it. This focus on defining the "it" of culturally responsive practice overly simplifies this theory. The potential of a good theory is in how teachers can make productive sense of it and have good, identifiable consequences come from the practices they invent when they are guided by it.

This volume—with its focus on dilemmas, situated practices, and ethical questions—provides teachers with the tools they need to investigate their own practices, uncover their own biases, and raise questions to guide revisions of practice. The research in this volume offers opportunities for intellectual engagement and productive discussion of practices, just the type of discourse teachers need most to sustain themselves in today's highly bureaucratized, under-resourced, and dehumanizing professional cultures (for an argument for why intellectual community is necessary for teacher sustenance, see Nieto 2003).

We need messy research, the kind of research that opens up the possibility of teachers sharing their own commitments, struggles, disappointments, and insights. The chapters in this volume are not easy reads. They should make all readers a bit uncomfortable, because they are filled with missteps and assumptions that lead to unintended consequences. We should cringe a little inside as we read.

At the same time, we should be grateful to these authors because they present opportunities for honest dialogue that can only lead to critical and cultural consciousness. As they seek ways to understand students who are very different than they are, as they reach for lofty goals of justice and personal transformation as the result of classroom work, as they theorize from their practice, we find ourselves and the teachers with whom we work. As we read, we find ways to strengthen our own research and practice.

I join Sonja Nieto (2003) in claiming that one of the main roles of teacher educators today is to provide opportunities and support for intellectual practice, the space for learning how to teach in culturally responsive ways. We need good research to guide our conversations with teachers, to inspire their own engagement in critical reflection, and to help them overcome the obstacles of standardized practices, materials, and administrative mandates.

As teachers fight their way through the concerns and issues that are inevitable when working in the messy instructional fields of culture, stereotypes, and prejudices, the authors in this volume are right beside them. It is our job to help teachers resist that which might tempt them to take the far easier instructional road and abandon the principles of cultural responsiveness in favor of "best" and standardized practices. Teacher educators who work outside of school systems and alongside teachers who share a commitment to making classrooms more engaging, personally meaningful, and just places need the work of researchers in this volume for support.

REFERENCES

Cummins, J. (1990). "Empowering Minority Students: A Framework for Intervention." In N. M. Hidalgo, C. L. McDowell, and E. V. Siddle (eds.), *Facing Racism in Education* (pp. 50–68). Reprint Series No. 21, Harvard Educational Review. Cambridge, MA: Harvard Educational Review.

Irvine, J. J., and B. J. Armento. (2001). *Culturally Responsive Teaching: Lesson Planning for Elementary and Middle Grades.* New York: McGraw Hill.

Ladson-Billings, G. (1994). *The Dreamkeepers: Successful Teachers of African-American Students.* San Francisco: Jossey-Bass.

———. (1995). "But That's Just Good Teaching! The Case for Culturally Relevant Pedagogy." *Theory into Practice, 34*(3), 159–65.

Nieto, S. (2003). *What Keeps Teachers Going?* New York: Teachers College Press.

Acknowledgments

We are deeply grateful for the support of family, friends, and colleagues during the research and editing of this book. As with all of our scholarly endeavors, our voices in this text have been shaped and reshaped by fleeting contacts with others and by the long-term relationships that have, throughout the years, left indelible marks on our thinking.

We also wish to gratefully acknowledge the work of the chapter and vignette authors who contributed to this volume: we know our readers will find your work useful and generative.

We reserve our deepest gratitude for the students at North End High School who have taught us so much about pedagogy during the brief time our pathways crossed. Without them, this book would never have come to be.

L.S. and K.S.
Tuscaloosa

Introduction

Clashes and Confrontations with Culturally Relevant Pedagogy

Lisa Scherff and Karen Spector,
University of Alabama

Teachers carry into the classroom their personal cultural background. They perceive students, all of whom are cultural agents, with inevitable prejudice and preconception. Students likewise come to school with personal cultural backgrounds that influence their perceptions of teachers, other students, and the school itself. Together students and teachers construct, mostly without being conscious of doing it, an environment of meanings enacted in individual and group behaviors, of conflict and accommodation, rejection and acceptance, alienation and withdrawal. (Spindler and Spindler 1994, as cited in Gay 2000, p. 9)

The idea for *Culturally Relevant Pedagogy: Clashes and Confrontations* emerged from our work with a class of all Black ninth-grade English students at a poorly performing school in the Deep South. Funded by a National Council of Teachers of English (NCTE) Research Foundation grant, our project was supposed to provide students with a culturally relevant experience, an experience that honored their funds of knowledge and utilized more progressive teaching methods than students were used to under the constraints of No Child Left Behind.

We asked students to write autobiographical accounts, poetry, and prose based on their interests and lived experiences. With backgrounds as secondary English teachers, college composition instructors, and education professors, with knowledge of culturally relevant pedagogies, we were fairly confident that the students would find this learning endeavor interesting, liberating, and perhaps even life-changing.

1

We soon realized that many of our pedagogical practices did not work so well with this *particular* set of Southern, Black students, most living in poverty. In fact, the students had trouble traversing the classroom landscape that we introduced, one that was much different than the English class they experienced on the days we were not there. Like Dutro, Kazemi, and Balf (chapter 2), we discovered that culturally relevant pedagogy is muddy and has the possibility of multiple snags.

We often left the school tired and frustrated. Things were not working out as we had envisioned and planned. We began to talk more and more about why some students did not seem engaged in what we thought was interesting and important work: we were letting them write about themselves using a range of "creative" prompts and genres (looking back, were we really "letting" students, or asking/demanding?); we provided them with cameras to take pictures of their lives to put in their final books; we read interesting texts with them. So, what was the problem?

We went back to the literature and read—then read some more. We talked and talked—on the most trying days over margaritas and chips and salsa. And we looked inward and reflected on our own positionalities, subjectivities, and motivations. Did the problem lie within us? Did we make a mistake assuming that poor students of color would want to write autobiographical accounts? Did our backgrounds and expectations clash with those of the students? Why did we suppose that this group of students would want to open up and write about their lives and would benefit from doing so?

We recalled Melanie Sperling's chapter in a volume by Greene and Abt-Perkins (2003). In studying two tenth-grade English classes, one comprised of working-class students of color and the other made up of middle- to upper-class white students, Sperling ultimately had to reflect on her own stance as a researcher and literacy educator. One question she asked herself also resonated with us: "Why should African-American students (and other racial and cultural 'minority' students) be expected to be self-aware in their literacy learning when students in the suburbs are expected to achieve in more conventional ways?" (p. 145)

Two years after our project we are left with haunting questions: Did we wrongly assume that all the students would relate to the "cultural" connections *we* wanted them to make and feel comfortable doing during the project? How did our culture(s) and background(s) influence the planning of and assumptions about the work? Were our attempts at being relevant really not that relevant at all? Did our pedagogical methods fit with competing cultures of the school, the existing English classroom, the teacher, the students? Did we, in doing this project, pathologize the students or the teacher (see Spector, chapter 5)?

CLASHES AND CONFRONTATIONS IN
CULTURALLY RELEVANT PEDAGOGY

Reflecting on our experience with the ninth-grade students, perhaps we simply made the mistake of looking at culturally relevant pedagogy (CRP) as one word rather than considering that the phrase actually contains three discrete terms—culture, relevance, and pedagogy—that concern several goals:

- Acknowledging the legitimacy of the cultural heritages of different ethnic groups, both as legacies that affect students' dispositions, attitudes, and approaches to learning and as worthy content to be taught in the formal curriculum.
- Building bridges of meaningfulness between home and school experiences as well as between academic abstractions and lived sociocultural realities.
- Using a wide variety of instructional strategies that are connected to different learning styles.
- Teaching students to know and praise their own and each others' cultural heritages.
- Incorporating multicultural information, resources, and materials in all the subjects and skills routinely taught in schools. (Gay 2000, p. 29)

Because the authors in this volume address CRP as it relates to their particular classroom and instructional circumstances, rather than present a lengthy discussion of it here, we instead briefly pause to consider culture, relevance, and pedagogy.

According to Ting-Toomey, "culture refers to a diverse pool of knowledge, shared realities, and clustered norms that constitute the learned systems of meanings in a particular society . . . [which] are shared and transmitted through daily interactions among members of the cultural group and from one generation to the next" (as cited in Ford and Moore, 2004, p. 35). Without fully considering students' cultural backgrounds, pedagogy that attempts to be culturally relevant will always be subject to failure.

Ford and Moore (2004) compare culture to an iceberg. We see just the tip, but most of the mass lies below the surface: culturally shared traditions (myths, legends, ceremonies, and rituals passed on); culturally shared beliefs (fundamental assumptions that people hold dearly and without question, which serve as the logic for behavior and desired goals); cultural values (sets of priorities that guide views of good/bad, fair/unfair, right/wrong); and cultural norms (shared explanations of what represents proper/improper behavior in a particular situation and guides the scripts we follow in certain situations, including discipline and classroom management) (pp. 35–36).

If acknowledging students' culture is foundational to any classroom, then relevance is essential for engaging and involving students in their learning, keeping them in school, and promoting academic achievement. Geneva Gay (2000) asserts that "curriculum content should be seen as a tool to help students assert and accentuate their present and future powers, capabilities, attitudes, and experiences [and that] 'relevant curriculum . . . includes information about the histories, cultures, contributions, experiences, perspectives, and issues of their [students'] respective ethnic groups" (pp. 111–12).

The impact of relevance on teaching and learning cannot be overstated. When Bridgeland, Dilulio, and Morison (2006), for example, asked high school dropouts what would prevent others from dropping out, over 80 percent said providing learning opportunities that made classroom topics more relevant to their lives.

Culture and relevance play individual and collective roles in teaching and learning, but what about pedagogy? In culturally relevant pedagogy, what does "pedagogy" look like? As Gay (2000) contends, "good will must be accompanied by pedagogical knowledge and skills as well as the courage to dismantle the status quo" (p. 13). Good technical skills may not always make up for a lack of relevance or attention to students' cultures; likewise, an awareness of culture and relevance cannot sweep away weak pedagogical skills or watered-down instruction.

Teachers don't need to be physically expressive and affectionate toward their students in order to practice culturally responsive instruction; they need to set high expectations and maintain a no-nonsense, no-excuses attitude. Students' love and admiration comes from being held to high expectations and attainable standards (Ford, Howard, Harris, and Tyson 2000).

Oser, Dick, and Patry (1992) emphasize the intellectual nature of all good teaching, including traits such as "reflection, imagination, self-criticism, knowledge of subject matter and the tools of best practice" (p. 834); in short, effective teaching is merged with the idea of being morally responsible. Ford et al. (2000) argue that culturally responsive teachers understand that a quality education is a fundamental civil right and suggest that becoming more culturally responsive involves a process of critical self-reflection about their pedagogy.

BOOK OVERVIEW

Much of what we both had read regarding CRP seemed to focus on what worked in classrooms, not what resonated with our experiences—which sometimes were frustrating and which quite often felt like failure. We feel it is important to share our missteps with others, and we wanted to invite others to do the same in order to open a space to talk about the intricacies of CRP.

Ladson-Billings writes that "Culturally relevant pedagogy urges *collective* action grounded in cultural understandings, experiences, and ways of knowing the world" (1992, p. 383). Each of the authors in this volume speaks to the complexity and difficulty in attempting to address students' culture(s), create learning experiences with relevance to their lives and experiences, and enact pedagogy(ies) that promote academic achievement while honoring students. At the same time, every author shows the clashes and confrontations that can arise between and among students, teachers, parents, administrators, and educational policies. It is our sincere hope that the honest set of writings in this volume will improve the quality of education for students.

Victoria Whitfield opens the volume with her vignette, "Recognizing Culturally Relevant Pedagogy: Then and Now," which narrates her experiences with CRP—from a high school student (where she was on the receiving end of insensitive, uninformed CRP), to teacher (where she had to question her own enactment of CRP), to doctoral student (where she now better understands CRP). She "now understand[s] the consequences of a culture-less curriculum and how it affects all students" (p. 13).

In chapter 1, "Unpacking the Critical in Culturally Relevant Pedagogy: An Illustration Involving African Americans and Asian Americans," Eileen Carlton Parsons and Steven Wall address questions regarding teachers' stereotypes and biases. They offer an illustration using African American and Asian American students, two minorities that are "diametrically positioned" in the American consciousness through negative and positive descriptions and discourse.

Next, Elizabeth Dutro, Elham Kazemi, and Ruth Balf (chapter 2, "Race, Identity, and the Shredding of a District Survey: Following Children into Relevance in an Urban Elementary Classroom") make the convincing argument that when teachers follow their students' lead into thinking about and exploring important ideas, teaching and learning are, by definition, relevant to students. They suggest that "if we begin instructional planning based on our own preconceptions about what will be meaningful for any given student or group of students, we may very well get it wrong" (p. 57).

Kysa Nygreen's (chapter 3) "The Central Paradox of Critical Pedagogy: Learning from Practice in an Urban "Last Chance" High School" complicates the notion of critical pedagogy and reports on the inescapable paternalism associated with all school curricula and teaching with the liberatory goals of critical pedagogy. Nygreen bravely and openly questions her motives and role in being a critical educator: "Did I *really* value the youth's local/subjugated knowledge? Or was acting like I did merely a better way to achieve my hidden agenda of replacing their perspectives on politics and schooling with mine?" (p. 83).

Teacher educator Melanie Shoffner and a former student and in-service teacher Matthew Brown (chapter 4) also question their purposes, aims, and beliefs regarding culturally relevant pedagogy. Engaging in a dialogue, they co-reflect on Matthew's struggle as a novice English teacher to live and teach in a school and community that are disconnected from his own background and values.

Jacqueline Deal, in her vignette, "Lotus: A Pedagogy of Listening," writes about her negative (irrelevant) school experiences and how later, as a teacher, she was forced to confront her own beliefs about what is relevant for her students—ultimately to discover that part of being relevant is simply being a compassionate audience for students. Of her students, she realizes that "all have the potential to become lotuses: to grow up and out of the muck, reach for the light, break through the surface, and bloom into something beautiful" (p. 117).

In chapter 5, "Reading *Romeo and Juliet* and Talking Sex: Critical Ideological Consciousness as Ethical Practice," Karen Spector explores how cultural ideologies converged and conflicted in a ninth-grade English classroom, and the teacher's assumptions about students' family and community cultures shut down various avenues of learning. She suggests that we can't always know what is behind what we witness, "but we can critically explore what ideological positions are taken up by teachers and students in classroom spaces and who is thereby empowered or disempowered by these positionalities" (p. 131).

Kimberly Adilia Helmer (chapter 6, "'Proper' Spanish Is a Waste of Time: Mexican-Origin Student Resistance to Learning Spanish as a Heritage Language") presents her two-year ethnographic study of Mexican students' resistance to speaking Spanish. She contends that understanding why Latino/a "youth were turned off to topics designed to empower and engage is crucial," especially "considering that they have the highest high school dropout rate in the United States" (p. 138).

In the powerful "Bodies before Me" (chapter 7) Stephanie Jones recounts a pedagogical moment that forced her to come to grips with her own guilt over enabling the status quo in teacher education classes. Jones poses questions for educators to consider: "Why must one perform such narrow constructions of middle-classness to be a teacher? Why must schools expect refined, rigid, discursive, and embodied practices from children and teachers rather than full-bodied curious beings living in the world in diverse, interesting ways?" (p. 177).

To close, teacher educator Aaron Kuntz relates his Southern students' (and others') resistance to calling him by his first name. In his vignette,

"The Distance of Formality: Working Within (and through) Propriety," he ultimately realizes that "through asking others to take on and share my value of informality I, at the same time, invoked the very power-laden relationships I was trying to disrupt, to value my culturally idiosyncratic experiences over their own" (p. 183).

REFERENCES

Bridgeland, J., J. DiIulio, and K. Morison. (2006). *The Silent Epidemic: Perspectives of High School Dropouts.* Washington, DC: Civic Enterprises.

Ford, D. Y., T. C. Howard, J. J. Harris, and C. A. Tyson. (2000). "Creating Culturally Responsive Classrooms for Gifted African American Students." *Journal for the Education of the Gifted, 23*, 397–427.

Ford, D. Y., and J. L. Moore. (2004). "Creating Culturally Responsive Gifted Classrooms: Understanding Culture is the First Step." *Gifted Child Today, 27*(4), 34–39.

Gay, G. (2000). *Culturally Responsive Teaching: Theory, Research, and Practice.* New York: Teachers College Press.

Ladson-Billings, G. (1992). "Liberatory Consequences of Literacy: A Case of Culturally Relevant Instruction for African American Students." *Journal of Negro Education, 61*, 378–91.

Morrison, K. A., H. H. Robbins, and D. G. Rose. (2008). "Operationalizing Culturally Relevant Pedagogy: A Synthesis of Classroom-Based Research." *Equity and Excellence in Education, 41*, 433–52.

Oser, F. K., A. Dick, and J. L. Patry (eds.). (1992). *Effective and Responsible Teaching: The New Synthesis.* San Francisco: Jossey-Bass.

Sperling, M. (2003). "Tenth-Grade Literacy and the Mediation of Culture, Race, and Class." In S. Greene and D. Abt-Perkins (eds.), *Making Race Visible: Literacy Research for Cultural Understanding* (pp. 131–48). New York: Teachers College Press.

Vignette

Recognizing Culturally Relevant Pedagogy

Then and Now

Victoria M. Whitfield, *The University of Alabama*

As a teenager, I attended high school at a low- to middle-income school with a small population. Half of the student body, most of them Black, resided in the same town as the school, while the other half (mostly White) lived in a neighboring town. Only 2 of the 35 faculty members lived within distance of either community. The others commuted from various neighborhoods surrounding the county, many of them economically and socially different from where their students lived.

There was much racial tension in the classroom due to our differing backgrounds. The Black students lived close to the school, while the White students commuted in. The Black students lived in a high-crime, but close-knit, community; the White students lived in a rural section of town primarily around other White students. At that time, culturally relevant pedagogy consisted exclusively of urban young adult novels and hip-hop rap assignments doled out to the poor and Black students. Many teachers truly believed that they were offering culturally relevant pedagogy by offering "minorities" and "low-income students" stereotypical cultural activities.

Reflecting upon my own experiences as a student and teacher, I recognize the intricacies and characteristics that make up culturally relevant pedagogy—or do I? Culturally relevant pedagogy may seem less intimidating to teachers than other educational jargon because many of us believe we are already knowledgeable of its practice. Viewing culture alternately as a student and then a teacher allows each perspective to speak to the other. Here are my stories.

BACK IN THE DAY: AS A HIGH SCHOOL STUDENT

I am sitting in my tenth-grade Advanced English class waiting for the music to begin. We were in the midst of our poetry unit, one of my most hated genres of all time. Although I loved English, I hated poetry. I had never fully been taught the patterns and structure of poetry or figurative language; therefore, thinking figuratively was very difficult for me to grasp. As the rap music began, I listened for the "poetry" and waited on further instructions from my teacher.

Ms. Jones was a middle-aged White woman, with a soft voice. She would always remind us of her drive from the "other" side of town. With the exception of my love for literature, there was nothing exciting about this class. Students never had a voice in the classroom, and often I would question the absence of relevant material. Our tenth-grade Advanced English class was predominately Black with a few White students sprinkled in.

When Tupac's "To Live and Die in L.A." played, we were instructed to analyze the meaning behind the poetry. I sat there for moments before I displayed the "this is stupid" look. I could not write an analysis as I didn't understand the relevance between this particular rap song and poetry. Ms. Jones boomed, "Class, I played this to show you all that not all music is poetry. You may think it is, but it is not." She continued her opinionated decree against rap music: "Rap is not poetry; it is an imitation of poetry. Poetry is something you can analyze. I don't know how anyone can analyze this nonsense." I sat at my desk with a flabbergasted look.

I raised my hand and said something like, "Ms. Jones, why did you choose rap music over country music or pop music? Those genres have songs also. Some of us happen to like rap music and just because it does not fit into your preference box, that doesn't classify it as nonsense."

Ms. Jones replied, "Victoria, I chose rap music because the majority of you listen to it. You all always complain that you are bored with the stuff I teach, so I was trying to make learning fun." I knew that I wanted my voice to be heard in the classroom, but I didn't understand the implications behind connecting and relating one's culture to the classroom; however, I did recognize that Ms. Jones's attempt to make the classroom culturally relevant failed. Instead of bridging the gap between the community and classroom, she had further created a divide.

And the Story Continues

It is two months later, and Ms. Jones has decided to do a novel study. We were to read our novels both independently and in class, focusing on discussion prompts and activities in small groups. Ms. Jones chose the students for each group study. I was placed in a group of all Black students. Our group was assigned a realistic young adult novel. The protagonist was a 15-year-old girl who was pregnant with her second child. She lived in an urban neighborhood and spoke heavy Ebonics. I resented Ms. Jones the entire semester as a result of assigning me a novel that stereotyped my culture and for using literature as a way to promote her socially and culturally biased views.

BLACK HISTORY: AS A TEACHER

It is eight years, two college degrees, and many cultural experiences later that I make my way to the front of my own high-school English classroom. I eagerly await the beginning of one of my favorite units in this eleventh-grade class: the Harlem Renaissance, where we study such famous poets as Langston Hughes, Countee Cullen, Alain Locke, Zora Neale Hurston, Claude McKay, and Jean Toomer. The class is fairly large; there are 25 students including 13 females and 12 males. The class is also racially mixed; many of the females are Black while the majority of males are White.

My unit on the Harlem Renaissance is usually taught during the month of March. However, due to a majority of students taking the graduation examination in March, I moved the unit to February. This would not be an unusual occurrence with the exception that February is Black History Month. Black History Month. What is it? Why is it celebrated? Is it significant? These questions never seemed to foster answers until my teaching of the Harlem Renaissance.

During day 3 of our Harlem Renaissance unit, Tyler questioned the cultural diversity of the Harlem Renaissance poets. "Ms. Whitfield, why didn't any White people write during the Harlem Renaissance. Why are all the people we're studying in this unit Black?" Tyler is a White male and is a proud wearer of everything Confederate.

Today, he sports his usual Confederate t-shirt, with a Confederate belt buckle; however, he has added a Confederate wristband to the wardrobe. Quite bewildered, I answered Tyler's question with information presented earlier in the unit. "Tyler, if you can recall from our introduction of this unit, we are studying Harlem poets and writers. These writers migrated from various places in the United States to Harlem, which was the Black Mecca at that time." Tyler wanted to continue, but decided against it. I could tell that my answer was not sufficient. He clearly wanted an explanation for this unit.

What made Tyler question the purpose of this unit? Although I clearly understood the connection between the Harlem Renaissance and today's students, and the unit's purpose, he did not see the relevance. Cultural relevance requires that one relates his or her culture to the issue at hand. If Tyler's culture, in part, consisted of big trucks and Confederate nostalgia, was I doing a proper job of incorporating his culture and relating it to our unit? Furthermore, was I seeing the relevance more clearly because I am Black and can relate to the culture of the Harlem Renaissance? Questions like these now cross my mind as an educator who is culturally relevant and aware.

Back to the scene at hand. After my attempt to inform Tyler of the purpose of this unit, one of my Black female students became very defensive. Shelia was very outspoken and one of my best readers and interpreters of literature in the class. She prided herself on being intellectual and was very protective of those in her inner circle, who consisted of her friends and me, her teacher. Sheila loudly retorted, "Tyler, what is your problem?"

Sheila continued, "The other 11 months are yours, why can't you let 'us' have one month?" This question was packed full of unanswered conundrums. Did Shelia or the rest of the students in the class think that we were only studying the Harlem Renaissance as a result of Black History Month? Why wouldn't they consider the Harlem Renaissance a viable topic throughout the year? Amongst other things, Shelia added, "I mean, we only study Black people during February anyways. He needs to let us have 'our' month!"

Had this become culturally relevant pedagogy? Sheila's boisterous attack, although borderline disrespectful, made me examine my own stance on culturally relevant pedagogy within my classroom. Although my intentions were to teach the Harlem Renaissance regardless of the time, some had interpreted the timing of this unit as simultaneous with Black History Month. I decided to end my unit that day and address the concerns within the classroom.

I stated, "Black History Month does not belong to a particular group. It is a month that is set aside to honor and recognize the achievements of African Americans." The class gazed at me with guilty expressions. I added, "Black history is important year-round as is any culture's history. We do not limit history to specific months." Sheila interrupted, "But Ms. Whitfield, this is the only time we usually ever hear about Black people and their accomplishments. We don't hear about it during other months."

The bell rang, and the students exited, ready for another class period. Then I reflected more on Shelia's statement. For many years, I harbored resentment towards Ms. Jones as a result of her insensitivity towards my culture; however, sitting in my classroom on this particular day, I realized that cultural relevance requires true dedication and takes much practice. It begins with a desire to involve all students in the curriculum. It also comes with awareness that students bring cultural value. This cultural value is essential to forming a relationship with students and impacting their learning. Ms. Jones saw a need; she just didn't realize how to fulfill it to benefit student learning.

TODAY'S REFLECTIONS

As an adult pursuing a doctoral degree, I have learned many new things about cultural relevance and awareness. I realize that being Black does not automatically mean I understand all Black culture and minority cultures. My graduate studies have shown me that there is a name to the type of instruction I received with Ms. Jones. I now understand the consequences of a culture-less curriculum and how it affects all students.

Having served as an instructor for a college methods course, I realize that culture is not primarily related to race, family, or ethnic backgrounds. There are many cultures that exist within racial groups, families, and educational groups. I realize now, as a result of my graduate studies, that culturally relevant pedagogy has many different viewpoints; however, when implemented successfully, it can positively affect the school, classroom, and community.

Chapter 1

Unpacking the Critical in Culturally Relevant Pedagogy

An Illustration Involving African Americans and Asian Americans

Eileen Carlton Parsons and Steven Wall,
University of North Carolina at Chapel Hill

As a consequence of its popularity in various educational venues, "culturally relevant pedagogy" is a commonplace phrase in the education canon. Its prominence extended beyond the conversations of academicians to the public arena after the publication of Gloria Ladson-Billings' (1994) *The Dreamkeepers: Successful Teachers of African-American Children*. In this text, Ladson-Billings described in rich detail the effective environments and successful practices of five elementary school teachers identified as excellent by both African American parents and school personnel.

Although the phrase "culturally relevant pedagogy" is frequently used, it is seldom couched in a manner that resonates with its original conception. In an article published in the *American Education Research Journal* (*AERJ*), Ladson-Billings (1995) discussed the theoretical premises of culturally relevant pedagogy, which are pertinent to but ignored in many practical enactments of culturally relevant pedagogy.

In this chapter, we view the tenets of culturally relevant pedagogy in relation to two United States (U.S.) ethnic groups: African Americans and Asian Americans. We offer examples specific to science education. We also highlight the kinds of considerations that are necessary in implementing culturally relevant pedagogy as espoused by Ladson-Billings (1995) and how these considerations are often absent in pedagogical practices in general.

15

CULTURALLY RELEVANT PEDAGOGY AND CRITICALITY

In the United States, numerous educational disparities exist among groups, with notable attention given to differences in achievement; these disparities are often referred to as the achievement gap. The achievement gap, bracketed by Asian Americans at the upper end and African Americans at the lower end, has been viewed, discussed, and approached from various perspectives. Irvine (2003) grouped these various vantage points into four general categories—socioeconomic, sociopathological, genetic, and cultural. The cultural domain is pertinent in this chapter; the challenge of characterizing the work in this domain relates to the competing and sometimes contradicting views on culture.

Numerous conceptualizations of culture exist. Cole (1995) notes that contending definitions of culture are more akin to theories in that they seek to form substantive propositions about an aspect of the world. The definitions one proposes depend upon what kinds of propositions about what aspects of the world one is interested in. Because of the diverse ways in which culture is defined, cultural perspectives vary greatly in their emphases.

For example, cultural congruency (Au and Mason 1983) stresses the compatibility or incompatibility between operating cultural systems (e.g., values of student's community and those of school) within a context, whereas cultural synchronization (Irvine 1990) focuses on the interpersonal dimension of settings. Even though the areas highlighted in cultural perspectives differ, Ladson-Billings (1995) argued that they are similar in two fundamental ways: they only target the contexts in which the individuals of interest are directly involved, and they work within the mainstream status quo.

Culturally relevant pedagogy deviates from other cultural perspectives in its criticality, a critical and intentional deconstruction of the status quo. In many encapsulations of culturally relevant pedagogy, three elements are emphasized: (1) academic excellence for all students, (2) the fostering of cultural competence, and (3) the development of a critical social consciousness. More often than not, descriptions and interpretations of subject-area specific practices within classrooms accompany the discussion of these elements.

In discussions of practice within the classroom (e.g., instructional practice) to the public at large (e.g., debates, educational policy) academic excellence for all students becomes the catch phrase "all students can learn." The fostering of cultural competence is reduced to connections with everyday life, and the development of critical social consciousness is delimited to concerns of the general populace.

In the aforementioned, criticality that underlies culturally relevant pedagogy as posited by Gloria Ladson-Billings is not present. The central role of criticality in culturally relevant pedagogy is featured in the following statement: "a culturally relevant pedagogy is designed to problematize teaching and encourage teachers to ask about the nature of student-teacher relationships, the curriculum, schooling, and society" (Ladson-Billings 1995, p. 483). In the 1995 *AERJ* article and in other publications (Ladson-Billings 1996, 1998, 2000; Ladson-Billings and Tate 1995), Ladson-Billings articulates the aim and nature of this criticality.

The criticality in Ladson-Billing's culturally relevant pedagogy seeks to interrogate and disrupt the status quo. Specifically, it attempts to change the symbiotic relationship that exists among structures, resources, and the status quo. That is, the social structures and conscious and unconscious procedures and protocols (Sewell 1992) involved in the reproduction of the status quo—the substantiation and fortification of it through the distribution of human, material, and symbolic capital (assets that only accumulate value)—are exposed, examined, and altered.

For example, consider education in the United States where European Americans are the dominant group in numerous aspects of social life (e.g., representation in decision-making capacities, ownership of physical and symbolic goods). Of the U.S. public schools that are identified as high poverty, enrolling 75 percent or more of students from economically impoverished backgrounds, 4 percent of European Americans versus 32 percent of Black Americans and 34 percent of Hispanic Americans attended these schools in 2002–03 (National Center for Educational Statistics 2009).

These high-poverty schools receive fewer resources, as evident in per-pupil expenditures and fewer qualified science teachers, a content area in which many states experience shortages at crisis levels. Specifically, across the country, the discrepancy in spending per pupil in the most affluent and highest poverty schools is $908.00 (i.e., $27,240.00 for a class of 30 students); the percentages of teachers who do not have adequate credentials in science are 5 percent in affluent public schools and 16 percent in high-poverty schools (National Center for Educational Statistics 2009).

This status quo, the distribution of resources that ultimately reinforces one's station in U.S. society, is also evident in classroom teaching that is described later in the chapter—teaching for low-level memorization and skill development for some groups and high-level, problem-solving for others (Mickelson 2001; Oakes 2005). The culturally relevant pedagogy espoused by Ladson-Billings requires teachers and other educationalists to examine what they do or do not do in relation to a social order replete with inequities that includes but extends beyond their own classrooms.

Criticality and Academic Excellence

As previously stated, in practice "all students can learn" is exhaustive of the culturally relevant pedagogical tenet "academic excellence for all students." A belief in students' capabilities to succeed is fundamental to culturally relevant pedagogy, but it is not enough. Culturally relevant pedagogy does not end with high expectations for students. With regard to academic excellence, the teachers in Ladson-Billings' (1994, 1995) study held conceptions of themselves and others that enabled the successful enactment of the fundamental belief that students are capable of success. These conceptions of self as teacher and teachers' conceptions of others receive very little attention in efforts to implement culturally relevant pedagogy.

These teachers of African American children saw themselves as integral members of the students' communities and viewed their teaching as an art—a craft designed to help students construct knowledge, comprehend existent canonical knowledge, and develop a critical understanding of their relationships to knowledge as individuals separate from and a part of different collectivities (e.g., U.S. citizens, members of U.S. marginalized groups). The teachers viewed their responsibilities of helping students succeed as giving back not only to the society at large but also to the students' communities. They continually examined themselves and their practices for limitations and shortcomings and made changes to engender student success.

In facilitating student success, they acknowledged, celebrated, and *used* the cultural and social capital of their African American students *as* the curriculum and employed them as vehicles to assist students in learning the accepted canon. These teachers did not view their African American students and their communities as entities that needed to be fixed. Instead, they viewed and treated both as sites of value situated within various societal structures that often ignore, dismiss, marginalize, or negate their worth.

The teachers in Ladson-Billings' (1994, 1995) study critically examined the status of African Americans with respect to academic success and asked questions to reveal underlying assumptions of that status. They questioned the existing status quo and their role as teachers in perpetuating or disrupting it. Teachers who wish to enact criticality in relation to the culturally relevant pedagogical tenet of academic excellence might begin by posing and answering questions similar to the following:

- Who experiences academic excellence in my classroom, and why?
- How does the curriculum I teach align with the experiences of students who excel and those who do not?

- How and for whom does the environment of my classroom facilitate or hinder development?
- What characterizes my interactions with students, and how do those interactions vary by student or student groups?
- What structures within the classroom and school act as obstacles to students realizing academic excellence?
- Who defines academic excellence, and how?
- What knowledge and whose knowledge are included in and represented by this definition?

To adequately address the aforementioned questions and others similar in nature, the remaining two aspects of culturally relevant pedagogy are essential.

Criticality and Cultural Competence

As previously stated, numerous conceptualizations of culture exist and the emphases vary according to the phenomena of interest. In discussing the culturally relevant pedagogy element of cultural competence, we employ three distinct but complementary conceptions of culture. First, culture is considered the primary medium through which individuals mediate their interactions with each other and the physical world (Cole 1998).

Second, these mediations consist of and occur through repertoires of practices acquired from an individual's prolonged immersion in a cultural community (Gutierrez and Rogoff 2003), a coordinated group of people who share common understandings across generations (Rogoff 2003). As implied by Gutierrez and Rogoff (2003), some of these practices are dynamic and receptive to alterations, but others are founded upon deep structures that are resistant or slow to change (Boykin 1994; Lee 2002), the third view of culture employed in this chapter.

In attempts to enact culturally relevant pedagogy, interpretations of culture are not intentionally considered; hence, the enactment of cultural competence defined by Ladson-Billings (1994) as the acceptance and affirmation of students' cultural identities conforms to dominant norms. Many equate cultural competence with demonstrating a connection of phenomena to students' lives. The phenomena and aspects of students' lives selected as pertinent in culturally relevant pedagogy in practice most frequently represent, couch, and treat these aspects of students' lives from a dominant perspective founded upon mainstream U.S. culture (see Parsons 2003).

The individual is at the center of U.S. mainstream culture, with the individual and individual rights paramount. Within the context of education, individual achievement, individual success, and individualization of instruction to address the needs of the individual are examples of the centrality of individualism. Competition to be the best in lieu of cooperation to help all achieve is promoted; material outcomes for individuals rather than the substance of the interactions or benefits for the group are highly esteemed. This worldview values the rational over the emotional and reduces reality to the observable.

Fostering cultural competence as conceived by Ladson-Billings (1994) is not problematic if mainstream U.S. culture reflects and resonates with students' cultural identities. In the instances in which students' cultural identities and mainstream U.S. culture are not in sync and students' cultural identities are marginalized, this cultural competence "uses student culture in order to maintain it [student culture] and to transcend the negative effects of the dominant culture" (Ladson-Billings 1994, p. 17).

Criticality and Critical Social Consciousness

The default conformance to what is dominant in a society in addressing the cultural competence element of culturally relevant pedagogy is also a concern for the last element: critical social consciousness. Critical social consciousness is the ability to recognize, understand, and critique assumptions underlying a phenomenon, the phenomenon itself, and the effects or influences of a phenomenon. In the enactment of the critical social consciousness component of culturally relevant pedagogy, efforts often identify issues of concern to the general populace.

For example, it is common for science projects that connect students to their communities to feature studies of water quality, composting, or recycling. The treatment of these important issues falls short of the criticality threshold posed by Ladson-Billings (1995): "Not only must teachers encourage academic success and cultural competence they must help students to recognize, understand, and critique current social inequities" (p. 476).

To meet the benchmark of critical social consciousness promoted in culturally relevant pedagogy, the studies of water quality, composting, or recycling might examine the quality and resources (e.g., space, material) across communities within a geographical locale with respect to community demographics (e.g., class and race of occupants). That is, the science projects would interrogate the distribution of human, material, and symbolic resources across demographics like wealth or race and ethnicity (e.g., predominantly European American versus predominantly Mexican American).

The dearth of criticality within enactments of culturally relevant pedagogy is understandable. The interrogation of the current system that the aforementioned criticality necessitates is difficult and is met with widespread resistance. There are numerous obstacles and costs for individuals who wish to develop this criticality and act upon it.

OBSTACLES IN IMPLEMENTING
CULTURALLY RELEVANT PEDAGOGY

The United States, like many societies worldwide, is stratified. On a large scale, as a consequence of history, public life in the United States is stratified by wealth, education, and race, and these strata do not exist in isolation but often overlap. For example, wealth and race intersect; the percentage of European Americans, the dominant U.S. group, living in poverty is 8 percent in comparison with 10 percent for Asian Americans, 20 percent for Hispanic Americans, and 24 percent for African Americans (U.S. Bureau of the Census 2007).

Individuals as separate entities and individuals as collectives are socially identified by and positioned within these strata in many facets of life; hence, an individual's as well as a group's collective experiences and views of being a U.S. citizen differ across strata. In other words, groups and the individuals that comprise different strata in the United States perceive and live substantially different realities although each is branded an "American" or "U.S. citizen." These stratification-induced differentiations underlie the obstacles in implementing culturally relevant pedagogy as posited by Gloria Ladson-Billings.

Like the proverb of the blind man who interprets experience according to the part of the elephant he is able to perceive, the realities of the groups and individuals living in a stratified society are influenced by the positions they occupy in the stratification. A majority of individuals who play important roles in the implementation of culturally relevant pedagogy occupy strata of privilege (e.g., middle class, college educated) and enjoy the benefits and advantages associated with these strata. Consistent with the U.S. mainstream cultural value of individualism, many attribute their privileged positioning to individual factors like hard work, ingenuity, and perseverance.

Research shows that individual-level factors are insufficient in explaining attainment (Feliciano 2006). These individual-level factors are heralded to the *exclusion* of group-level factors and facilitative structures—the operation of conscious and unconscious procedures and protocols influencing the distribution of human, physical, and symbolic resources—that enabled progressions into and maintenance in privileged strata.

Consequently, it is a formidable task for people and groups to acknowledge the existence of inherent inequities in a stratified society that privileges them—a herculean obstacle to surmount in order to interrogate and disrupt social inequity, a call of culturally relevant pedagogy. If privileged individuals and the groups to which these individuals belong are able to perceive inequities that are evident to those who occupy less privileged strata in the United States, then the implementation of culturally relevant pedagogy is less daunting.

As in the case of the first obstacle to the implementation of culturally relevant pedagogy, individualism plays a role in the second challenge. In discussions of social inequities, a primary emphasis of culturally relevant pedagogy, the mainstream U.S. cultural value of individualism, most often operates, and the individual is given center stage in equity (or inequity) considerations. This focus on the individual is often myopic, and this narrow employment of individualism limits the implementation of culturally relevant pedagogy.

Similar to doctors' attempts to meet the needs of their individual patients, teachers strive to meet the individual needs of their students. In the case of physicians, they open themselves to malpractice accusations if, at a minimum, they do not possess some understanding of their patients' needs, both group (e.g., higher incidence of a condition in certain populations) and individual (includes family) histories of those needs. Physicians utilize but do not *restrict* their considerations to individual idiosyncrasies when determining how to assist patients; they use historical and contextual information to determine the most appropriate measures.

Unlike physicians, the attempts of many teachers to meet the individual needs of their students are made in a vacuum; the focus of these attempts commences and concludes with students positioned within the immediate here and now. In well-intentioned efforts to address the individual needs of students, many teachers do not consider pertinent historical and contextual information surrounding individuals, especially as those surroundings pertain to societal stratification in the United States.

As previously stated, a culturally relevant pedagogy that addresses social inequities requires criticality. A criticality pertaining to social inequities and stratification, though implicit, with respect to individuals situated in U.S. historical and contemporary contexts distinguishes Ladson-Billings' (1995) culturally relevant pedagogy from what is often labeled culturally relevant pedagogy in K–12 classrooms. In the following illustration, we make explicit the historical and contemporary contexts that are implicit in culturally relevant pedagogy.

AN ILLUSTRATION

By way of an illustration, we demonstrate why it is important to consider stratification in the implementation of culturally relevant pedagogy. The illustration involves African Americans and Asian Americans, two nondominant

groups in the United States that are diametrically positioned in the A[...]
psyche via negative and positive imagery and discourse surroundin[...]
group.

The Imagined Context

Imagine a traditional public school with enrollments that include a sign[...]
cant percentage of African American and Asian American students but w[...]
the largest absolute number of students classified as European American[...]
East Asians (Chinese, Filipino, Japanese, and Koreans) and South Asian[...]
(Bangladeshi, Burmese, Asian Indian, Nepali, Pakistani, and Sri Lankan)[...]
comprise the Asian American student population of this school. This imagined school is rare in its student composition.

A racially and ethnically balanced public school in the United States is an
anomaly. With respect to the criteria of 75 percent or greater enrollment used
by U.S. bureaus of statistics, public schools are populated by either predominantly European American students or predominantly students of color. From
the data repository that extends several decades, it is reasonable to assume
for illustrative purposes several characteristics of the imagined school and its
student enrollees as members of racially and ethnically classified collectives.
Even though the characterizations cross subject areas, science is featured in
this illustration.

Considering general population, educational and economic statistics, and
research on subgroups, it is likely that the African American students are classified in the low socioeconomic strata of society (e.g., poor, working class) while
their Asian American and European American peers are situated in higher
socioeconomic strata (e.g., middle, upper-middle class). Asian American and
European American students are more likely to have two college-educated parents with at least one parent employed as a white-collar professional earning a
salary that sustains a middle-class to upper–middle-class lifestyle (e.g., ownership of property, healthcare, educational supplements).

Although these students from diverse backgrounds attend a "desegregated"
school in line with the existing statistics and research, the students are segregated by curricula within the school building. In science, African Americans
populate the standard classes, courses most often taught by teachers who do
not meet the quality standards established by many states. They have less
than an undergraduate minor in the subject they are assigned to teach, are not
fully certified, and have fewer than five years of teaching experience (Young
2005). Instruction in standard science classes is back-to-the-basics, with
drill and memorization both the means and ends of learning (Barton, Koch,
Contento, and Hagiwara 2005).

23

neric̦an
g each

.id advanced placement science courses are almost
Asian American and European American students.
.es of high-quality science experiences (e.g., problem-
juiry, use of technology) and are usually instructed
with advanced degrees or advanced preparation in the
.gersoll 2002; Soloranzo and Ornelas 2004).

'fi-
th
).

description of the imagined school are elements that teach-
onalists must critically entertain in order to implement cultur-
.edagogy as proposed by Ladson-Billings (1995). The elements
.lly interrogated in a vacuum, the approach usually employed in
.e needs of individual students. The elements must be considered
.f stratification, its historical origins, and its contemporary remnants
plications.

onsidering Stratification in the United States

With respect to social inequities in regard to opportunity, discussions frequently situate nondominant groups as the same and compare and contrast them to European Americans. Ogbu (1978) challenged this equalizing of U.S. minorities with respect to social inequities and opportunity in his classification of minority groups: autonomous minorities, immigrant minorities, and caste-like minorities. Encapsulated in Ogbu's (1978) classification are the ideas that U.S. minority groups differ in their historical origins; in how they are perceived and treated by others; in how they perceive themselves; and in their actual statuses in the United States (Perry 2003).

Autonomous minorities (e.g., Amish, Jews) are minorities in a numerical sense. Their minority status is not socially defined through biological attributes and is often self-ascribed; consequently, they are not broadly subjected as a collective to fulfill specialized and denigrated roles like other U.S. minorities. *Immigrant minorities* groups are those who have come to the United States voluntarily to improve their economic, political, or social status. Shibutani and Kwan (1965) contended:

These minorities may hold menial jobs, lack political power, and have little or no prestige initially. But, this objective socioeconomic position does not reflect their true status in the social hierarchy, because it does not include how the immigrants themselves think of their position, which is not the same way the dominant group members evaluate it. Contrary to the perception of dominant group members, the immigrants may consider their menial position better than what they had before they emigrated, or they may consider the menial job a temporary situation. Also, the immigrants tend to compare themselves, not with the elite members of the dominant group of their host society, but with their peers back home, the people they left behind. When they compare themselves with their peers back home—their reference group—they often find much evidence of self-improvement for themselves and good prospects for their children because of better opportunities. (as cited in Ogbu 1978, p. 27)

In essence, immigrant minorities have a different perspective than the last group, caste-like minorities. Immigrant minorities have a vision of possibilities that is substantiated by evidence. They believe that these possibilities can be realized. This realization is buttressed by evidence abundant enough to warrant it as normal, a common occurrence, rather than as an exception, a rare incident.

The third group, *caste-like minorities*, contrasts immigrant minorities.

Caste-like minorities are incorporated into the country more or less involuntarily and permanently and then relegated to menial positions through legal and extralegal devices. . . . Membership in a caste-like minority group is often acquired at birth and retained permanently. Its members are regarded and treated by the dominant . . . group as inferior and are ranked lower. . . . Caste-like minorities lack political power, and this powerlessness is reinforced by economic subordination. . . . Moreover, the structural subordination of caste-like minorities—economic, political, and social—is reinforced by overarching ideology of the dominant group, which rationalizes the menial status of minorities . . . caste-like minorities do not accept their ascribed menial position. They reject the ideology and beliefs of the dominant group that rationalize their position. . . . As a result, caste-like minorities often develop what may be called a collective institutional discrimination perspective. That is, they appear to believe that it is difficult for them to advance into the mainstream . . . through individual efforts. . . . They believe that their chances are better through collective efforts . . . (Ogbu 1978, p. 28)

Caste-like minorities are negatively regarded in society, and positive images of the group are rare relative to the barrage of negative portrayals. Caste-like minorities do not share the optimism of immigrant minorities. Progress and evidence of it are exceptions rather than the norm. In the literature, Asian Americans are positioned as immigrant minorities and African Americans as caste-like minorities. As illustrated later, the positioning and status of non-dominant groups in the United States are important in the contemplation and implementation of culturally relevant pedagogy.

Asian Americans as Immigrant Minorities

According to O. Lee (1997), the historical immigration of Asian Americans can be viewed in three waves. The first wave occurred in the mid-nineteenth century with immigrants from China followed by immigrants from Japan. Because of various laws prohibiting emigration, these immigrants often came from the upper echelon of society (Ichihashi 1932; Ichioka 2006). The second wave, beginning in the mid-1960s, included Asian immigrants from the Philippines, Korea, Hong Kong, and Taiwan. The last wave started in the mid-1970s with groups emigrating from Vietnam, Cambodia, and Laos.

The label "model minority," which emerged in the characterizations of the first wave of Asian immigrants, is frequently used in the literature to refer to Asian Americans. The model minority stereotype was constructed in the 1960s (Kawai 2005), approximately a century after the first wave of Asian immigration. Specifically, the model minority stereotype originated with two articles published in 1966; one focused on the success of Chinese Americans and another featured Japanese Americans (Kawai 2005).

As discussed in Kawai (2005), the model minority stereotype did not emerge as happenstance but was developed to counteract various social movements in the 1960s, particularly the Black Power and civil rights Movements. Contrasting Chinese and Japanese Americans to African Americans, the model minority stereotype positioned African Americans as the opposite—the problem minority (Kim 2000).

Additionally, the stereotype was employed to promote an image of America as a land of opportunity devoid of institutional racism at a time when social movements highlighted its existence (Osajima 2000); to substantiate the view that upward social mobility was available to all (Kim 1999); and to cast the existence of racial inequities and inequalities as the shortcomings of individuals and individual groups (Kim 2000). The model minority label has been and continues to be a double-edged sword for Asian Americans. Both positive and negative implications emanate from it.

On one hand, the stereotype influences expectations. For example, teachers and other educationalists have high expectations for Asian American students (Chang and Sue 2003), which affect the quality of the educational services and the experiences they enjoy. On the other hand, because of the pervasiveness of the stereotype, Asian Americans often do not receive the individual assistance they need (O. Lee 1997; Zhou, Siu, and Xin 2009). In addition, their access to opportunity (e.g., college admission, scholarships) is sometimes restricted because of their overrepresentation (O. Lee 1997).

Asian American and non–Asian American scholars address the positive and negative implications of the model minority stereotype by calling into question its premises and political purposes. The model minority stereotype highlights the educational successes of Asian Americans. In comparison to other racial and ethnic groups, including European Americans, they tend to score higher on standardized tests, have higher grade point averages, attend four-year educational institutions at higher rates, and are represented in percentages greater than their representation in the general population in science, technology, engineering, and mathematics (STEM) and other fields.

Several scholars disaggregated this success by subgroups within the Asian American collective and found that the groups experiencing success implicated in the model minority stereotype were distinguished by certain characteristics. Among them, the high-performing groups occupied higher strata (e.g., more education, greater financial wealth) in their pre- and post-migration societies and enjoyed the benefits therein (Feliciano 2006; Goyette and Xie 1999).

It is also argued that values and orientations of these groups complement structures in U.S. society such that the likelihood of the groups' successes is enhanced.

For example, the belief that shortcomings can be overcome with diligence and duty (Mau 1997) aligns with the idea of meritocracy; the idea that hard work translates into advancement is prominent in the American worldview; and the acceptance of life situations as they are and willingness to adjust to them (Zhou et al. 2009) corresponds with a common perspective in the United States that minorities should assimilate into U.S. society.

The Asian American collective is not comprised by only high-performing groups. Low-performing groups (e.g., Hmong) exist within the Asian American collective. These subgroups were positioned as caste-like minorities in their home countries and are not situated in the higher strata of U.S. society; their performance resembles the performance of caste-like minorities in the United States (Feliciano 1999; Goyette and Xie 1999; Norman, Ault, Bentz, and Meskimen 2001).

African Americans as Caste-like Minorities

The history of Africans in America, beginning with the captivity of the first Africans in 1619, is well documented. Africans in America initially served in the capacity of indentured servants. With the increasing need for labor in the mid-1600s and an escalation in England's disapproval and condemnation of the coerced servitude of fellow Europeans, racial segregation was mandated across social classes. Chattel slavery for Africans (a small percentage were also Native American and European American) was instituted, and Europeans of low wealth and social status were separated from other groups through the conferral of material possessions (e.g., land) and privileges (Smedley 2001).

Africans were dehumanized, marketed as a distinct species with a depraved culture in need of salvation (Banks 1995), and reconstituted in the American psyche as property of no value beyond servitude. Even though slavery was largely delimited to the southern states, the racial ideology of Black inferiority and Black depravity, supported and promulgated by science (Gould 1981; Manning 1993; Smedley 2001), was prevalent in the practices and policies across America.

After the constitutional abolition of chattel slavery, African Americans were subjected to second-class citizenship (e.g., limited rights to own property, restricted mobility). What was attributed to Blackness encompassed what was devalued and dejected in society (Prager 1982). In order to prevent the cultural and social contamination of American society, all things "Black" were sectioned off, a segregation legitimized by laws and informal structures, and relegated to the margins of society. These efforts to subjugate and subordinate were met with continuous overt and covert resistance and are chronicled in the centuries-long history of Black captivity, Black enslavement, and Black freedom.

Ogbu (1992) contended that the culture of African Americans as a collective was and continues to be one means of resistance. For example, in contrast to the centrality of the individual and individualism in mainstream U.S. culture, the group and cooperation are highly valued in the African American worldview. Human interactions in concert with the material outcomes of those human interactions are esteemed and the intuitive and affective are regarded as integral to rationality. These cultural practices, among others, counter practices dominant and characteristic of mainstream United States.

Even after the dismantling of legalized segregation that began in 1954, racial ideologies persisted into the 1960s and 1970s with the seminal IQ work of Arthur Jensen (1968). Jensen's (1968) research heralded the racial ideology that African Americans were genetically inferior to European Americans (Hilliard 2003). In the 1980s, certain work in sociobiology attempted to link heredity to behaviors like criminality (Manning 1993).

In the 1990s, Herrnstein and Murray's (1994) *The Bell Curve: Intelligence and Class Structure in American Life* repackaged the racial ideologies espoused during past centuries so that they appeared different on the surface, but the premises remained unchanged: intelligence was genetically determined, and African Americans were inferior to European Americans. (The data briefly introduced in the imagined school context indicate the same racial ideology.) The inequitable distribution of human, material, and symbolic resources positions African Americans as inferior and signifies African Americans as of less worth in comparison to their racial and ethnic counterparts.

Stratification and Social Equity: Implications for Culturally Relevant Pedagogy

The complexities of culturally relevant pedagogy surface in juxtaposing the historical and contemporary positioning of the Asian American collective as an immigrant minority and the African American collective as a caste-like minority. One group's origin in the United States was voluntary; the other's was coerced. The culture of one group's country of origin was untouched by the United States and served to facilitate the group members' entry into and subsequent progress in life; the culture of the second group was systematically vilified, subjected to extirpation attempts, and situated as an impediment over centuries. One group was perceived as a model; the other was viewed as a problem.

Considering the contrast in how Asian Americans as a collective and African Americans as a collective are positioned, historically and contemporarily in the United States, is the same culturally relevant pedagogy appropriate for both? The elements of culturally relevant pedagogy are pertinent to both groups, but the enactment of them with respect to mainstream United States may differ.

For the culturally relevant pedagogical tenet of academic excellence, both groups face challenges. Asian Americans are expected to achieve; hence, their needs are overlooked, and their access to opportunities is restricted in reaction to their overrepresentation. African Americans' achievement is seen as a rarity and a shortcoming of the group; therefore, they are treated as inferior, and their access to opportunities is restricted as a result. In both instances, culturally relevant pedagogues would examine how expectations translate into practice and if these practices perpetuate restricted access to opportunity, but from different vantage points and with different results.

The perception of Asian Americans as successful is not inherently detrimental. It often gives them access to high-quality experiences. Culturally relevant pedagogues supplement this access with receptiveness to students' needs, needs that are overlooked when acting from the standpoint of the model minority stereotype. In addition, culturally relevant pedagogues work to eliminate Asian Americans' restricted access to opportunities by educating them, educating their students and the students' significant others, and taking action to challenge and change the inhibiting structures.

Prior to implementing the aforementioned on behalf of African Americans, culturally relevant pedagogues undergo the very difficult process of revealing and confronting the deeply engrained perceptions of African Americans as inferior. After these often unconsciously enacted perceptions are exposed, culturally relevant pedagogues work to interrogate and change them in recognizable ways (e.g., equitable distribution of human, material, and symbolic resources).

With regard to the cultural competence element of culturally relevant pedagogy, culturally relevant pedagogues foster the development of students' cultural identities as members of their racial and ethnic group, if the students identify as such, and as Americans, members of the larger U.S. milieu. As culturally relevant pedagogues, they also help all students to develop an appreciation and respect for different cultures. In doing so, culturally relevant pedagogues are aware of and respect the various repertoires of practice that constitute cultures and the nature of the relationship among those cultures.

Many aspects of Asian Americans' culture as a collective complement or align with mainstream U.S. culture; consequently, culturally relevant pedagogues assist in the articulation, comprehension, and critique of the two cultural systems. Because mainstream U.S. culture and African Americans' culture as a collective are at odds, and the culture of African Americans is demeaned in mainstream United States, culturally relevant pedagogues not only assist in the articulation, comprehension, and critique of the two cultural systems but also facilitate African American students' negotiation of them and African American students' affirmation of their own culture.

With respect to the last aspect of culturally relevant pedagogy, critical social consciousness, the nature of the criticality that culturally relevant pedagogues foster among their Asian American and African Americans students is the same, but the aim and outcomes of the criticality may be different. Some scholars contended that Asian Americans accept the system as it is and work within it. In line with this orientation, a critical social consciousness emphasizes understanding the system and how it works.

Other scholars advocate that Asian Americans work to change the status quo; in light of this orientation, a critical social consciousness not only fosters an understanding of the system and how it works, but also identifies, investigates, and initiates efforts that address issues of concern to Asian Americans (e.g., restricted access to scholarships in higher education).

Because of the historical and contemporary positioning of African Americans in the low strata of U.S. society and the partial attribution of this positioning to inhibitive structures, the latter criticality in the case of Asian Americans, critical social consciousness to change the status quo, is promoted in the literature on African Americans. Consequently, culturally relevant pedagogues teach social action—for African Americans to identify, investigate, interrogate, and initiate efforts with the conscious intent to change their current conditions in the United States.

CONCLUDING REMARKS

Teachers and educationalists encounter numerous challenges on a day-to-day basis. One result of this bombardment is the implementation of initiatives counter to their intents. This is often the case with culturally relevant pedagogy. It is enacted to fit the norm, which is antithetical to the very notion of culturally relevant pedagogy. To implement culturally relevant pedagogy as it was intended, teachers and educationalists must be involved in a criticality about the status quo that is neither easy nor comfortable. This criticality raises issues about social equity, privilege, race, and the like, topics around which silence is not only preferred but sometimes mandated.

We have the ability to implement culturally relevant pedagogy as it was intended, but do we have the courage? Are we willing to step outside our stratified position of privilege to ask and answer difficult questions that challenge the very structures that enabled and facilitated our progression into and maintenance of privilege? Are we willing to participate in the unsettling process of interrogating and claiming ownership of our practices—the learning environments we create and the knowledge we teach and perpetuate—and their results with regard to those individuals who do not succeed under our watch? Are we willing to speak truth to power and pay the costs that accrue?

REFERENCES

Au, K., and J. Mason. (1983). "Cultural Congruence in Classroom Participation Structures: Achieving a Balance of Rights." *Discourse Processes, 6*(2), 145–67.

Banks, J. (1995). "The Historical Reconstruction of Knowledge about Race: Implications for Transformative Teaching." *Educational Researcher, 24*(2), 15–24.

Barton, A. C., P. D. Koch, I. R. Contento, and S. Hagiwara. (2005). "From Global Sustainability to Inclusion Education: Understanding Urban Children's Ideas about the Food System." *International Journal of Science Education, 27*, 1163–86.

Boykin, A. (1994). "Harvesting Talent and Culture: African American Children and Educational Reform." In R. J. Rossi (ed.), *Schools and Students at Risk: Context and Framework for Positive Change* (pp. 116–38). New York: Teachers College Press.

Chang, D. F., and S. Sue. (2003). "The Effects of Race and Problem Type on Teachers' Assessments of Student Behavior." *Journal of Consulting and Clinical Psychology, 71*(2), 235–42.

Cole, M. (1995). "Culture and Cognitive Development: From Cross-Cultural Research to Creating Systems of Cultural Mediation." *Culture & Psychology, 1*, 25–54.

———. (1998). "Can Cultural Psychology Help Us Think about Diversity?" *Mind, Culture, and Activity, 5*, 291–304.

Feliciano, C. (2006). "Beyond the Family: The Influence of Pre-Migration Group Status on the Educational Expectations of Immigrants' Children." *Sociology of Education, 79*, 281–303.

Gould, S. J. (1981). *The Mismeasure of Man.* New York: Norton.

Goyette, K., and Y. Xie. (1999). "Educational Expectations of Asian American Youths: Determinants and Ethnic Differences." *Sociology of Education, 72*(1), 22–36.

Gutierrez, K., and B. Rogoff. (2003). "Cultural Ways of Learning: Individual Traits or Repertoires of Practice." *Educational Researcher, 32*(5), 19–25.

Herrnstein, R. J., and C. Murray. (1994). *The Bell Curve: Intelligence and Class Structure in American Life.* New York: The Free Press.

Hilliard III, A. G. (2003). "No Mystery: Closing the Achievement Gap between Africans and Excellence." In T. Perry, C. Steele, and A. G. Hilliard III (eds.), *Young, Gifted, and Black: Promoting High Achievement among African-American Students* (pp. 131–65). Boston: Beacon Press.

Ichihashi, Y. (1932). *Japanese in the United States.* Stanford: Stanford University Press.

Ichioka, Y. (ed.). (2006). *Before Internment: Essays in Prewar Japanese American History.* Stanford: Stanford University Press.

Ingersoll, R. M. (2002). *Out-of-field Teaching, Educational Inequality, and the Organization of Schools: An Exploratory Analysis.* Seattle, WA: University of Washington, Center for the Study of Teaching and Policy.

Irvine, J. J. (1990). *Black Students and School Failure.* Westport, CT: Greenwood.

———. (2003). *Educating Teachers for Diversity: Seeing with a Cultural Eye.* New York: Teachers College Press.

Jensen, A. (1968). "Social Class, Race, and Genetics: Implications for Education." *American Educational Research Journal, 5*(1), 1–42.

Kawai, Y. (2005). "Stereotyping Asian Americans: The Dialectic of the Model Minority and the Yellow Peril." *Howard Journal of Communication, 16*(2), 109–30.

Kim, C. J. (1999). "The Racial Triangulation of Asian Americans". *Politics & Society, 27*(1), 105–38.

———. (2000). *Bitter Fruit: The Politics of Black-Korean Conflict in New York City.* New Haven: Yale University Press.

Ladson-Billings, G. (1994). *The Dreamkeepers: Successful Teachers of African American Children.* San Francisco: Jossey-Bass.

———. (1995). "Toward a Theory of Culturally Relevant Pedagogy." *American Educational Research Journal, 32*(3), 465–91.

———. (1996). ""Your Blues Ain't Like Mine": Keeping Issues of Race and Racism on the Multicultural Agenda." *Theory into Practice, 35*, 248–55.

———. (1998). "Just What is Critical Race Theory and What's it Doing in a *Nice* Field like Education?" *International Journal of Qualitative Studies in Education, 11*, 7–24.

———. (2000). "Fighting for Our Lives: Preparing Teachers to Teach African American Students." *Journal of Teacher Education, 51*, 206–15.

Ladson-Billings, G., and W. F. Tate. (1995). "Toward a Critical Race Theory of Education." *Teachers College Record, 97*, 47–68.

Lee, C. (2002). "Interrogating Race and Ethnicity as Constructs in the Examination of Cultural Processes in Development Research." *Human Development, 45*, 282–90.

Lee, O. (1997). "Diversity and Equity for Asian American Students in Science Education." *Science Education, 80*(1), 107–22.

Manning, K. (1993). "Race, Science, and Identity." In G. Early (ed.), *Lure and Loathing: Essays on Race, Identity, and the Ambivalence of Assimilation* (pp. 317–36). New York: Allen Lane/The Penguin Press.

Mau, W. C. (1997). "Parental Influences on the High School Students' Academic Achievement: A Comparison of Asian Immigrants, Asian Americans, and White Americans." *Psychology in the Schools, 34*(3), 267–77.

Mickelson, R. A. (2001). "Subverting Swann: First- and Second-Generation Segregation in the Charlotte-Mecklenburg Schools." *American Educational Research Journal, 38*, 215–52.

National Center for Educational Statistics. (2009). *Contexts of Elementary and Secondary Education: School Characteristics and Climate.* Retrieved from nces. edu.gov.

Norman, O., C. Ault, B. Bentz, and L. Meskimen. (2001). "The Black-White "Achievement Gap" as a Perennial Challenge of Urban Science Education: A Sociocultural and Historical Overview with Implications for Research and Practice." *Journal of Research in Science Teaching, 38*, 1011–14.

Oakes, J. (2005). *Keeping Track: How Schools Structure Inequality* (2nd ed.). New Haven: Yale University Press.

Ogbu, J. U. (1978). *Minority Education and Caste: The American System in Cross-Cultural Perspective.* New York: Academic Press.

———. (1992). "Understanding Cultural Diversity and Learning." *Educational Researcher, 21*(8), 5–14.

Osajima, K. (2000). "Asian American as the Model Minority." In M. Zhou and J. V. Gatewood (eds.), *Contemporary Asian America: A Multidisciplinary Reader* (pp. 419–58). New York: New York University Press.

Parsons, E. C. (2003). "Culturalizing Instruction: Creating a More Inclusive Learning Context for African American Students." *High School Journal, 86*(4), 23–30.

Perry, T. (2003). "Competing Theories of Group Achievement." In T. Perry, C. Steele, and A. G. Hilliard III (eds.), *Young, Gifted, and Black: Promoting High Achievement among African American Students,* (pp. 52–86). Boston: Beacon Press.

Prager, J. (1982). "American Racial Ideology as Collective Representation." *Ethnic and Minority Racial Studies, 5*, 99–119.

Rogoff, B. (2003). *Cultural Nature of Human Development.* New York: Oxford University Press.

Sewell, W., Jr. (1992). "A Theory of Structure: Duality, Agency, and Transformation." *American Journal of Sociology, 98*, 1–29.

Smedley, A. (2001). "Social Origins of the Idea of Race." In C. Stokes, T. Melendez, and G. Rhodes-Reed (eds.), *Race in 21st Century America* (pp. 1–24). East Lansing: Michigan State University Press.

Solorzano, D. G., and A. Ornelas. (2004). "A Critical Race Analysis of Latina/o and African American Advanced Placement Enrollment in Public High Schools." *High School Journal, 87*(3), 15–26.

United States Bureau of the Census. (2007). *Current Population Survey, Annual Social and Economic Supplements.* Poverty and Health Statistics Branch, HHES Division [electronic database]. Retrieved from www.census.gov//hhes/www/poverty/histpov/hstpov2.html.

Young, H. (2005). "Secondary Education Systemic Issues: Addressing Possible Contributors to a Leak in the Science Education Pipeline and Potential Solutions." *Journal of Science Education and Technology, 14*(2), 205–16.

Zhou, Z., C. Siu, and T. Xin. (2009). "Promoting Cultural Competence in Counseling Asian American Children and Adolescents." *Psychology in Schools, 46,* 290–98.

Chapter 2

Race, Identity, and the Shredding of a District Survey

Following Children into Relevance in an Urban Elementary Classroom

Elizabeth Dutro, *University of Colorado at Boulder*;
Elham Kazemi, Ruth Balf, *University of Washington*

When officials in a large, urban school district distributed surveys that were designed to assess social issues in the schools, they surely did not expect that the children in one fourth- and fifth-grade classroom would, both literally and figuratively, tear the survey to shreds. In this chapter, we discuss how one class of elementary students directly engaged a district agenda in ways that revealed how students brought their own ideas and identities to bear on a goal that many districts share: to learn about the racial climate in schools. The survey and the children's response reveal some of the complexities around the issue of relevance.

As we will discuss, the survey, a document that the children targeted as lacking connection to their lives, became a context for conversations that were highly relevant to their experiences. In this case, the classroom teacher (Ruth, one of the authors of this chapter) harnessed the children's responses to the survey as an opportunity to foster conversations about race and identity and to provide a context for social action.

As we argue, when a teacher follows children's lead into important ideas, the resulting curricular events and activities are almost by definition relevant to children and signal to them that their ideas matter. Before proceeding further, however, it is important that we begin with the story of how the children encountered the survey.

THE STORY OF THE SURVEY

The children's experiences with the survey began on a Wednesday morning in April when Ruth passed the required district survey to each of her students. She read the script that she was given to introduce the survey, and the children began to fill it out with sharpened number-two pencils in hand. Almost immediately, children began to grumble and raise their hands. Questions of "Why do they want to know that?" and "What do they mean?" erupted throughout the classroom.

Several minutes later, as they passed the surveys back to Ruth, many students said that they didn't like taking the survey and that it made them uncomfortable. A few students immediately suggested that the class should let the district know how they felt about the survey. Ruth promised to give them time the next day to discuss the survey and possible responses.

The next morning, Ruth called a class meeting to debrief the survey and to follow up on students' suggestions that the class should communicate their concerns to the district. As we will discuss, children raised issues of racial categorization, racism, and the district's right to access experiences and opinions that the children considered private. Ultimately, with Ruth's support, the class decided to send a videotaped statement of protest to the district along with their completed surveys. They also met with their principal to express their concerns, and the principal conveyed the students' issues and her own concerns about the survey to the district leadership.

A few days after the surveys had been distributed, the district announced that it was canceling the survey due to strong protest from students, teachers, and the teachers' union. Ruth announced the district's decision to her class and asked, "What do you think? Would you like me to tear them up? Would you like to tear up your own? What's your preference?" Stephanie raised her hand and enthusiastically responded, "I'd like to tear up my own."

It was a unanimous decision. As soon as the students received their surveys, the sound of ripping paper filled the room. Some students shouted, "Yea!" as they tore. A few said, "Let's do it together!" and shredded them in unison. Others covered the survey in dark blue, green, or black marker before shredding it. A few students stomped on the pieces that had fallen on the floor. The surveys were obliterated.

RACE, IDENTITY, AND THE "RELEVANT" CLASSROOM

The children's complicated response to the district's agenda provoked questions for us about the contexts through which children can and will engage important ideas surrounding race and racism in elementary classrooms. As we will discuss in more detail, issues surrounding race and identity had been central in our analysis of children's interactions with other curricular events in this classroom (Dutro, Kazemi, and Balf 2005; Dutro, Kazemi, Balf, and Lin 2008), and the discussions surrounding the district survey became a context through which students extended some of the understandings and arguments about race and their own racial identities that had begun in those other contexts.

With this context in mind, we now turn in this section to some of the scholarship and perspectives that have informed our thinking about the children's and Ruth's responses to the survey, including issues of identity and research on children engaging race and racism in classrooms.

Considering Relevance and Identity in Classrooms

As we have discussed previously (Dutro et al. 2008), the term "culturally relevant pedagogy" can be murky and is rife with potential pitfalls, particularly in highly diverse classrooms like Ruth's. Although the emphasis on changing pedagogy and content to centrally engage the knowledge and resources that students bring to school has been crucial to the field, tensions have been raised by the focus of some scholarship that has attempted to identify the culturally preferred learning styles of particular groups of students (e.g., Dunn, Griggs, and Price 1993; Irvine and York 1995; Hickson, Land, and Aikman 1994).

One concern is that an emphasis on learning styles could result in some children being confronted with stereotyped ideas about how and what they should learn. Gutierrez and Rogoff (2003) argue that a focus on cultural styles of learning risks viewing groups of people in "ways that are overly static and categorical" (p. 19). As Scherff and Spector emphasize in the introduction to this volume, even the most well-informed and well-intentioned expectations about what will resonate with students can be way off base. Although we hope that those misdirections become clear and lead to revised plans, too often students may be left with irrelevant activities or instruction that masquerades as relevant.

Given our stance that a priori assumptions about what constitutes any given child's or group of children's culture can lead just as quickly to irrelevant as to relevant curriculum and instruction, we bring a particular view of identity to our analysis of the survey and its aftermath. When we use the term "identity" in our discussion, we refer to individuals' ways of being in particular contexts, including how they view themselves and are viewed by others in any given social space.

How we define ourselves is, of course, complex and includes, for instance, how our perceptions of others' views of us influence our views of ourselves and vice versa and how our sense of who we want to be—or need or are

allowed to be—shifts according to where and with whom we are located.
Such ways of thinking of identity are rooted in particular theories that view
identity as fluid and shifting rather than stable and fixed (e.g., Davies and
Harré 1990; Hall and DuGay 1996). Thus, we find the plural "identities"
more useful than the singular when considering how Ruth's students took
up important, complex topics that were highly relevant to their lives and
learning.

The theorists to whom we turn also argue that since identity cannot be
pinned down, we must turn to language if we are to understand how individuals position themselves in particular places and times. In this view, language
is the medium through which we and those around us may explicitly provide
clues through words about how we see ourselves and are viewed by others. In
turn, language is also our only tool for understanding and interpreting our own
and others' positions. Further, language is never neutral but always reveals
something, whether implicitly or overtly, about power (e.g., Fairclough 1995;
Gee 1999; Luke 1995).

Who defines what gets talked about? How do those involved in a discussion use language to create, sustain, or resist hierarchies of power? In the
case of the children's responses to the district survey, the survey itself is an
example of language that not only implied certain assumptions about race and
racism but also wielded power through the very fact that the children were
required to complete it and submit it to the district.

Encountering that language, however, provided a context in which children
enacted their own power, actively resisting, in some cases, the assumptions
they perceived in the survey's language about their own and their peers'
racial identities and experiences with racism. So, just as institutions can
employ language that may, whether inadvertently or purposefully, work to
silence, exclude, or control the voices of certain people or groups of people,
those with seemingly less institutional power can use language to resist those
attempts at control (Bonfil Batalla 1990).

Indeed, in this case, the children's resistance to the survey led to a discussion in which children *did* engage the very issues of race, racism, and the
social climate of their classroom and school that were the district's central
concerns. It is not that those issues were not relevant to the students' school
experiences; rather, it is that the children needed to, even insisted on, engaging those issues on their own terms.

Race and Classrooms

Although research continues to offer insights into the social, academic, and
pedagogical role of race in K–12 classrooms (e.g., Comber and Simpson 2001;

Delpit 1996; Enciso 1997, 2003; Ferguson 2001; Greene and Abt-Perkins 2003), we know too little about how issues of race arise in elementary classrooms and are taken up by children and teachers and about the process and consequences of critically engaging race with students. There is particularly scant research on how students make sense of race in highly racially diverse elementary classrooms.

As Orellana and Bowman (2003) emphasize, social categories such as those used to mark race and ethnicity are too often treated as they were in the district's survey, as "fixed and often essentialized categories rather than as multifaceted, situated, and socially constructed processes" (p. 26). In Ruth's classroom, the very presence of the multiple racial identities contradicted many of the assumptions about race and racial categories that the children encountered in the survey (Dutro et al. 2005; Dutro et al. 2008). And, because Ruth allowed space for their questions and concerns, the children were able to make that very critique about the mismatch between the survey's language and their own and peers' claimed identities.

Although our own research and that of others shows that elementary children are very capable of discussing race in complex and thoughtful ways (e.g., Dutro et al. 2005; Enciso 1997, 2003), research also suggests that discussions of race in elementary classrooms are rare and, when they do occur, are most likely to emphasize racism as a historical issue that has largely been eliminated (Banks 1997). Certainly, race and racism are viewed as fraught topics, and engaging in discussions of those issues can feel risky at all educational levels (e.g., Cochran-Smith 2000; Ellsworth 1993).

However, our experience suggests that there are costs in containing or curtailing discussions of race and that relevance is chief among those. For instance, one consequence of discussing racism only as a historical artifact is that it denies children the opportunity to engage those issues as highly relevant to their own lives and the society in which they currently live. Instead, connecting the threads of the history of race and racism in the United States to children's lived knowledge and experiences can allow them to make deep connections to, say, a unit on the Civil Rights Movement, because the relevance of that era to their own and peers' current lives will be more tangible.

In addition, our experience with the survey and other classroom events that engaged issues of race suggest that relevance is not something for which a teacher can necessarily plan in advance. Indeed, the children in Ruth's classroom demonstrated that some of the moments in teaching that we would characterize as highly "relevant" occur when a teacher follows children down a curricular path that she or he could not have anticipated.

LEARNING FROM THE CHILDREN IN RUTH'S CLASSROOM

The event we discuss in this chapter occurred in the second year of a two-year, collaborative study of children's experiences across literacy and mathematics in Ruth's fourth- and fifth-grade urban classroom. Twenty-five children, mostly boys, were in Ruth's class during the year in which the district survey was administered. Their school is located in a large northwestern city and reflects the city's shifting demographics.

In addition to Native American, African American, white, and Asian American families who have lived in the United States for two or more generations, Ruth's class included many families who had more recently emigrated from Africa (primarily Ethiopia, Eritrea, and Somalia), Southeast Asia, Pakistan, and Mexico. Students spoke a total of 12 languages other than English, although only one student (Sylvia) was not fluent in English.

From the start of the school year, Elizabeth (a literacy educator) and Elham (a mathematics educator) visited Ruth's classroom frequently, and it was not long before our laptop-toting, note-taking presences were integrated into the classroom routine. We also hung out with the kids at recesses and attended field trips, including the fifth-grade overnight camp experience in the spring. The children knew that our goal was to learn from them and that our audio and video recordings, notes, and copies of their work would help us in that learning.

We were in the classroom during the children's interactions with the district climate survey, and we read their written reflections and spoke with some of them after the experience in order to build deeper understandings of their perspectives on what occurred. We also analyzed the survey itself and, although the details of that analysis are beyond the focus of this chapter, we describe some of the content of the survey in a later section.

Our primary focus in this chapter is on the children's discussions that occurred after they completed the survey. In order to carefully consider how the children and Ruth engaged the issues of race and privacy that were raised during the experience of filling out the survey, we typed up detailed transcripts of their conversations based on our audio and video recordings. We then read and analyzed those transcripts based on questions suggested by linguists who focus their work on issues of power and identity in language. For instance, we followed Norman Fairclough's (1995) suggestion that language should be analyzed on three levels.

First is the level of production: How did the interaction arise? What contexts surrounded the specific instance of language being analyzed? The interaction itself is the focus of the second level of analysis: What is the focus of talk? What ideas or themes arise consistently, if any? Who is present? Who is actively participating, and how are they participating? What can we learn about the participants in the interaction through a close analysis of their language and how a discussion unfolds?

Third, Fairclough (1989) emphasizes the importance of considering the social and cultural meanings of any particular instance of language. For instance, in this classroom, it was crucial to consider the children's and Ruth's discussions about the survey in light of the high level of racial, cultural, and language diversity present in the room as well as Ruth's goals and stance as the teacher. In the sections below, we discuss what we discovered in that analysis and what we see as the implications of the children's experience with the survey for fostering more relevant classrooms.

CONTEXTS FOR THE SURVEY AND
THE CHILDREN'S RESPONSE

Of course, the children's strong response to the district's efforts to learn about the racial climate in schools did not arise out of nowhere. Their reaction built from both the survey itself and the language it employed around racial issues and the history of experiences and discussions surrounding race in Ruth's classroom.

The Survey Meets a Fierce Response

The large urban district that was the site of this research had anonymously surveyed students in third through eleventh grades on school climate for several years prior to the experience we describe here. In 2002, however, the district made significant revisions to the survey, including adding new questions about race and racism and revising the survey form to include students' names, grade levels, and race/ethnicity.

As reported by the city's newspaper, the district's director of research and evaluation explained that the questions were added to explore issues of bullying, safety, and racial climate within and across district schools. Students' names and identification numbers were used so that the district could correlate answers to demographic information.

After distributing the survey, the district administration almost immediately began receiving messages of concern from principals and teachers. Most of the students filled out the survey on May 18, and the city's teachers' union called an emergency meeting on May 22, during which they voted to boycott the survey and filed an official protest with the district. The ACLU also sent a letter to the district outlining their criticisms of the "intrusive" and "coercive" nature of the survey.

In response to the union's actions, the district informed principals that the survey would be voluntary that year and schools could opt to destroy the completed surveys. The principal of Ruth's school sent the district a letter confirming that her school had opted to destroy the survey and expressing her hope that the district would employ experts in survey research to construct an effective survey for the following year.

In their school, Ruth's fourth- and fifth-grade students were the most vocal in their protests about the district survey. They began to voice their concerns almost immediately after its distribution, and Ruth's own concerns about the survey grew in tandem with and response to those of the children. In addition to planning a letter and video of protest to the district, the children asked to speak with their principal about their concerns. The principal subsequently used quotes from the children in Ruth's class in her correspondence about the survey with the district administration.

The Roots of the Response in Ruth's Classroom

The children's response was impressive in both its passion and sophistication, and we clearly saw its roots in an experience the children had shared two months before they encountered the survey. In a curricular experience that we have analyzed in detail elsewhere (Dutro et al. 2005; Dutro et al. 2008), Ruth's students were required to research and share an aspect of their cultural background.

The children had interviewed their parents, consulted books and the Internet, written reports, gathered artifacts, created art projects, and, finally, synthesized their research in a poster presentation for peers from other class-rooms. For the public presentations of their projects, Ruth's students stood beside their posters and answered questions as children visiting from other classrooms walked around the room.

After the visitors left, two of the biracial children in her class lingered after school to tell Ruth that some children from other classrooms had questioned their claim to their self-identified cultural backgrounds, saying things such as, "He can't be from Africa. He's only half." In ways that Ruth had not antici-pated, the public presentations of the project resulted in feelings of hurt and frustration for her three biracial students.

Ruth offered to call a class meeting the next day if the children wanted to discuss their experiences with their classmates, and they enthusiastically agreed. The following morning, the biracial children led their classmates in a lengthy discussion that raised complex issues of racial categorization, including how people are placed and misplaced into categories, the tension between the desire to identify oneself and the inevitability of being identified by others, the social construction of racial categories, and the meaning of whiteness.

The experience with that project was relevant to the children's encounter with the district survey in at least two important ways. First, it illustrated Ruth's student-centered approach to addressing critical issues and concerns expressed by children. The children were provided a forum for addressing important issues with one another. As with the class meeting called following the biracial children's experiences, Ruth adjusted her lesson plans to create an immediate opportunity for students to discuss the survey.

The morning after the survey had been completed, she said to her students,

> Little change in plans. We're not doing math. I think you'll be okay with this. I'm going to hand you guys back these surveys, so you'll have them to look at while we're talking about them. That way you won't have to depend on your memory. [passes back papers] Alrighty. So, yesterday we did this survey, and you weren't pleased. And so we said that we'd talk about it today and let you vent, say everything that is bothering you, and then figure out how we can send a letter to the district, whoever the district is, to tell them what we think and why we think it. So, the floor's open.

A second important connection to that previous experience was related to content. The issues surrounding race and racism and the questioning of racial categorization that had occurred in the earlier discussion appeared to set the stage for children to question and critique the issues of race and racial categorization that arose in response to the survey.

The Language of the Survey

In order to understand the children's response, it is important to have a sense of both the kinds of questions that appeared on the survey and the language employed to address issues specific to race. The survey's questions addressed several areas related to school climate, including academic expectations, bullying, weapons, smoking, and racism. The following are examples of the range of items included:

- Teachers in my school expect me to do my best. (always, sometimes, never)
- I feel safe at my school. (always, sometimes, never)
- Students at this school make fun of, bother, or hurt me. (always, sometimes, never)
- My teachers listen to my ideas. (very true, sometimes true, not true)

- I think it is okay to cheat at school. (yes, no)
- How wrong do you think it is for someone your age to: take a handgun to school? (very wrong, sometimes wrong, not at all wrong)
- How wrong do you think it is for someone your age to: smoke cigarettes? (very wrong, sometimes wrong, not at all wrong)

The items specific to race and racism were at the end of the survey and included all of the following (each with response options of very true, sometimes true, not true):

1. At my school, I play with students who are a different color than I am.
2. I get along with or feel comfortable with teachers who are a different color than I am.
3. I feel comfortable talking to teachers who are a different color than I am about my problems.
4. I can ask for help with schoolwork without my color working against me.
5. In my school, there are posters, books, and magazines with pictures of people of my color.
6. I can do well in school without being called a credit to my race.
7. In school, we learn about how people of my race helped make history.

As we will discuss further in the analysis of the classroom discussion, the students in Ruth's class consistently spoke of feeling as though the survey was implicating them in the negative behaviors it addressed in questions. In addition, the children understood immediately that the survey was trying to determine if they or their teachers were racist and, in response, many adopted a defensive stance. The language of the survey also raises questions of developmental appropriateness.

Two of the questions (4, 6) explore race using language that would arguably be very difficult for elementary students to understand. In item 34, "My color working against me" implies an understanding that sometimes a person's race might impact how a teacher or other staff member would respond to a student asking for help with schoolwork. Likewise, understanding the phrase "being called a credit to my race" (item 6) requires not only background knowledge about racial discrimination (which many of the children did have), but a particular kind of racial bigotry (i.e., the belief that individuals who are high achievers are an exception in certain racial groups) and a very specific way of speaking about that discrimination.

Also, whereas those writing the survey opted to use "color" as a stand-in for "race" in each of the other questions, question 6 not only uses "race" but employs it in a complex way. Although the intent of the racial climate items must surely have been to try to locate and address racism in the city's schools, the survey's language makes it unlikely to effectively serve that purpose. However, even if inadvertently, the survey *did* accomplish something very important in Ruth's classroom.

RACE, RACISM, AND PRIVACY: THE CHILDREN'S RESPONSE TO THE SURVEY

We now turn to our analysis of two excerpts from the classroom discussion that followed the survey. We chose these excerpts because they include talk about issues that children consistently raised about their experiences with the survey in this discussion and in their subsequent interviews and written reflections. One of the key issues illustrated in these excerpts is that the idea of privacy was tightly woven into the children's explorations of race and identities.

Thus, in the first excerpt, we discuss the convergence of race and privacy in how the survey was initially taken up in the classroom discussion. We then turn to the second excerpt, which illustrates how the issue of racial categorization arose as a central issue as the discussion unfolded.

Issues of Privacy and Race Converge

The overarching goal of this discussion was for children to express their concerns about the survey and for the class to arrive at consensus about the action they wished to take (voicing their concerns by writing a letter or making a video were options that children posed). In our analysis, we closely examined the language used by children and Ruth to critique the survey and district and to voice their desire to make an active response (see Figure 2.1).

For instance, we noticed that through shifts in pronoun usage, the children and Ruth align themselves with or distance themselves from the district (and the "powers that be" within it) or ideas encountered in the survey. Some telling pronoun shifts occur early in the discussion, beginning in line one when Zack uses "it" to refer to the survey. Very soon (by line 11), Laura has shifted to "they" when discussing the survey, signaling a change from talking about the survey as a passive document to focusing on the human beings behind the survey.

The other children and Ruth consistently used "they" from that point in the conversation, situating themselves in relation to the survey in at least two ways. First, the children seemed to not only recognize that there are human actors

Figure 2.1   Students raise issues of race and privacy

1 Zack:	Yeah, I didn't like it because it was asking about like can you work with people who are like a different color than you. I didn't think that was right because it's like kinda personal.
RB:	Ah, okay, so questions (writing on board). OK, other comments. Laura.
5 Laura:	I didn't like the questions either and it was all, if you think a kid your age would take a cigarette or like skip school. That was really like stupid.
RB:	OK, can you explain why you think that was really stupid.
Laura:	Because what kids would say, like I don't think most kids would say that. I don't know, it just kinda bothered me.
10 RB:	Could you explain a little bit more what bothered you about it?
Laura:	Well, it's just like they're asking me about, it's kind of like have you ever done it. It kinda made me feel like—
RB:	OK, so it feels like they're asking do you do these kinds of things. OK. Grace.
15 Grace:	So, like all the questions about the color. They could have just shortened it down to one question. I mean, they don't need to have like five questions down here. They could have just wrote, "do you mind people who are a different color than you."
RB:	OK. Other comments? Tavor.
20 Tavor:	You know on the question that Laura was talking about. [referring to the question about smoking] I think that's a good question because a lot of kids in our age group, I know kids who do that.
RB:	So, you're kind of disagreeing with Laura. You think there are kids your age who do this.
25 Tavor:	Yes.
RB:	OK. Other thoughts. Tavor.
Tavor:	On that one, I disagree with Laura and agree with Laura. Because if they're asking you. I know some kids do that, but they don't need to ask you. I don't want to be asked that, because I'm thinking that they're
30	thinking that I did it too.
RB:	So, you're also having this feeling [referring to board] that they're asking are you doing that and you don't like that. Jeff. Jeff, actually I did want to hear from you because one of the first things you said to me this morning was that you don't like this survey—
35 Jeff:	I didn't like it because of what Zack said. About your color, that's personal. They shouldn't just. . . . It's your own life.
Zack:	They shouldn't be able to just go and ask you those questions.
RB:	The interesting thing about this is that this survey is not anonymous. It has your name on it, doesn't it. So, they can just go and find out what Zack
40	thinks about these things, so it is not an anonymous survey. Messing with your privacy. Yep.
Laura:	Well, some of these questions are a bit too personal. Like have people made fun of you and have you made fun of people. Or like have people hurt you and stuff like. It's just too personal.
45 RB:	So, we're having issues of privacy. So it's not necessarily their business to know about your personal experiences.

responsible for constructing and distributing the survey but also felt that they could speak back to those people. Second, Ruth's use of "they" instead of "we" when speaking of the survey actively resisted the alignment between teachers and the district that was signaled through the pronouns used in the directions to teachers (the script directed teachers to use "we" and "us"). Ruth employed pronouns that aligned her with her students and positioned her, like them, as someone who can question and critique the actions of those in power.

In the first part of the discussion, three children—Zack, Jeff, and Grace—raised the issue of race. Zack and Jeff are biracial (African American/White and Filipino/White respectively), and both were prominently involved in the class's previous discussions of race. Grace is White and a consistently vocal participant in classroom discussions.

Zack's opening comments interlink the issues of race and privacy that are subsequently picked up by many of his classmates. He connects his dislike of the survey to a question about whether students can "work" with peers of other races, deeming such a question "kinda personal" (the actual item includes "play" instead of work). As one of the biracial children who called for and led the class's discussion of race several weeks earlier, Zack had demonstrated his comfort with speaking about race and his desire to engage in such discussions with his peers.

Therefore, it did not seem to be the topic of race, per se, that made Zack uncomfortable. The survey item he quoted is one with particularly strong connotations of personal racism on the part of the student taking the survey (they must answer if this is very, sometimes, or not true of them) and he deemed this not "right" *because* it is too personal.

Following Zack's initial introduction of the topic, Grace raises race again (line 15). Her suggestion that the survey could have asked only one question on race, rather than "like five," points to the quantity of items on race as the source of student discomfort. Her language also suggests her sense that racial climate is something that can be determined quite straightforwardly by simply asking, "Do you mind people who are a different color than you?"

Her suggested question avoids the subtleties of racism, instead focusing on identifying only overt and explicit racism (only an overt racist would admit to "minding" the presence of other races). As we will discuss in our later discussion of the implications of this discussion, Grace's comment is one moment, and foreshadows others, that we now see as a teachable moment that went unheeded in this conversation.

Jeff was the next student to speak explicitly about race and, as Ruth acknowledged Jeff, she prefaced his comment (line 32), recalling that he was someone who had expressed strong feelings about the survey. Jeff was not a student who often voluntarily contributed to discussions that occurred in the context of instruction. Indeed, throughout a typical school day, Ruth often had to remind him to focus, and he rarely raised his hand.

However, during and following the experience in which he and the other biracial children had drawn on their own experiences to spearhead a discussion of race, Jeff had been very vocal about his own experiences as a biracial person. Here, he raised the issue of race as a privacy issue. His comment, "about your color, that's personal," very explicitly articulated the link between race and privacy and suggests that one's race is no one else's business.

This is a particularly interesting argument coming from Jeff, who identified as biracial (Filipino/White) but looks White. For him, being identified as "of color" is in his control (he is only identified as biracial if he identifies himself) in a way that it is not for the other biracial and children of color in the classroom. Although that issue was not specifically pointed out to Jeff in this discussion, his comments point to the complex ways that children position themselves and are positioned by others around race.

Zack's, Grace's, and Jeff's comments about race-specific questions within the survey, as well as the connections they made between privacy and race, introduced a convergence of race and privacy that became more prominent as the discussion continued. The convergence of those issues was also influenced by Ruth's move to raise more complex issues related to privacy and the children's experiences of the survey.

Toward the end of this part of the discussion (line 38), Ruth raised the issue of anonymity that, up to that point, had been only implicitly present. She validated the children's sense of the survey "messing with" their privacy by reminding them that their names were on the survey. She even more explicitly used an example that "they" can "find out" what an individual thinks about any of the items on the survey. Ruth's comments raised the stakes in the discussion. The children's sense that the items addressing race were too "personal" and intrusive was linked to the survey as a tool by which those in power could access children's personal responses.

The next excerpt we examine arose from this shift of focus to the issue of lack of anonymity and reflected the concerns about race raised both in the above excerpt and in the class's previous discussions of race and racial categories.

The Complexities of Racial Categories

As their discussion of the survey unfolded, the children and Ruth delved more deeply into issues of race (see Figure 2.2). It is important to recall that the discussion that had occurred several weeks prior to the survey had centered on racial categorization—the tension between being identified by others and identifying oneself and the meaning and consequences of arbitrary racial categories.

Figure 2.2   Children delve deeper into race and racial categories

1 Stephanie:	I agree with Laura about the privacy thing. Why does it matter if you play with kids of different color. It shouldn't really matter if you play with a person that's the same color or if you play with someone who's a different color. It makes it sound like they want to know if you're racist or not.
5	That's what it seems like.
RB:	[writing Stephanie's idea on the board] Grace.
Grace:	Well, when it has your identification on here. I don't think it should have your ethnicity on here, because I don't think that should matter.
RB:	Is your ethnicity on here? Under the—
10 Grace:	Yeah—
RB:	By gosh it is. So on the front it labels what your ethnicity is. So, they can sort through this and they can go, "ah, all the black kids who answered this or the majority, or most of the black kids who answered this said this and most of the white kids said this," so they're collecting a whole lot of
15	information about you. OK.
Stephanie:	The ethnic stuff. It says that I'm white.
RB:	[laugh] And sometimes the ethnic stuff is not true. OK. OK.
Tavor:	Well, she really is. . .
RB:	Well, it's partially true, it's partially true. Right. Laura.
20 Laura:	There's a question that says something about teachers, about if they give you credit, about teachers, and that's kind of like being really rude to your teachers. Yeah, something like does my teacher judge me by my color and you don't really do that, so. . .
RB:	Right. Where is that one?
25 Laura:	37. 36.
RB:	Right. [reading the question] I can do well in school without being called a credit to my race. How many of you understood that question when you first heard it. How many of you didn't know what the heck they're asking? [kids raise hands to answer RB; most hands are raised]
30	So, how reasonable do you think the answers are that they're going to get if you don't understand the question? So, you're being asked to say things about your teachers. So, that's another privacy issue. It's a privacy issue about the kids and the teacher [writing on board].
Zack:	You don't want to hurt the teacher's feelings.
35 RB:	I appreciate that. I'm just a lovely, wonderful teacher. A little irritating sometimes, but not so bad. Luke.
Luke:	You know, under ethnicity, what does AI stand for?
RB:	AI? American Indian. That's the label they put on you. Anybody else want to check out their ethnicity if they're not sure what it means on there.
40	What do you have?
Laura:	VI?
RB:	VI. Vietnamese.
Asma:	EI?
RB:	EI? EI? East Indian! They're saying you're from India.

(Continued)

Figure 2.2   (*Continued*)

45 Asma:	I'm not from India!
RB:	Geez, I thought you were from Pakistan.
Asma:	I am!
RB:	OK. Now, you're labeled as East Indian. OK—K. Yes?
Kofi:	BL?
50 RB:	Black.
Kofi:	OK.
RB:	Anybody else have an ethnicity that they want to check out? Zack, what did they give you?
Zack:	BL.
55 RB:	They say you're black, they find Stephanie's white. OK—K. [laughter]
Student:	They should say BH or something. Black and white.
RB:	Don't talk out. Yes?
Tavor:	They're saying the BL if you're black, right? But I'm not black, black. I'm not *only* black, I'm Ethiopian.
60 RB:	They don't have a category for Ethiopian. So, anybody who has a black skin, who comes originally from Africa, whether you came from Africa four years ago or four hundred years ago you get a BL. You are black. And, if you have a white skin and you originally came from Europe whether it was two years ago or four hundred years ago, you get a WH for white.

The children constructed several arguments in this excerpt that were conflicting, at times, about race. Stephanie, a biracial African American/White girl who had also been central to the class's previous discussion of race and racial categories, initially argued that race "shouldn't really matter" in one's choice of playmates. She also articulated what is surely one of the district's central goals in distributing the survey—"to know if you're racist or not"— but raised it as a critique of the survey. Her critiques imply an assumption that the district would view playing only with kids who are the same color as one is as "racist" behavior, an assumption with which she appears to disagree.

Her argument resonates with ideas about the socially very important reasons (including safety, shared language, and, in racially segregated towns and cities, shared neighborhoods) why students of color sometimes opt to self-segregate by race in school (e.g., O'Connor 2001; Tatum 2003). Stephanie's critique suggests that the survey's implicit goal of identifying individual acts of racism based on a question related to choice of playmates was misplaced and inappropriate.

Grace raised a different argument about race: that it "shouldn't matter" at all. Hers is different from both Stephanie's and the "race as personal or private" argument raised by some of the students of color. Grace, who is White, makes a more general argument, insisting that knowing someone else's race or ethnicity is not important because it "shouldn't matter," period. This argument, which is often called a "colorblind" stance, is commonly adopted in relation to race in the United States.

Although it has been powerfully critiqued by scholars of color who argue for the importance of paying attention to the role that race inevitably plays in sustaining inequities in American society, the colorblind stance is still prevalent and is often apparent in schools where well-meaning White teachers claim that they do not see color, only children. Grace's argument that race doesn't matter is not explicitly challenged in this excerpt, but as the children begin to talk about racial categories, their arguments clearly undermine the argument that race and ethnicity should be irrelevant.

About a third of the way into this part of the discussion, Laura raised another issue related to race and privacy: the children's desire to protect and not be "rude" to their teacher (lines 20–23). In her comment, she referred to a survey item we discussed in our section on the survey's language: "I can do well in school without being called a credit to my race." Her description of the item, "about teachers, if they give you credit," demonstrates both her misunderstanding of the meaning of the item and her concerns about its potential consequences. She read the item through a very personal lens.

Rather than as a question about teachers in general, Laura read it as implicating her teacher, saying to Ruth, "You don't really do that." Because the language of the survey conveys that teachers might be racist, answering such an item seemed "like being really rude to your teachers." Zack echoed Laura's concern (line 34): "You don't want to hurt the teacher's feelings," although his worry about hurt feelings brought the issue even closer to his personal relationship with teachers. Indeed, Ruth clearly interpreted his statement as directed at her, not at teachers in general, replying (in her humorous way), "I appreciate that. I'm just a lovely, wonderful teacher. A little irritating sometimes, but not so bad."

The children's response to this item emphasizes our earlier point that the language of some of the items about race were likely to prompt children to provide answers they believed to be the most innocuous for themselves and their teachers. Whether out of affection (which appeared to be the case here) or fear, children are not likely to respond in ways that would imply that their teachers discriminate against them.

In addition, the complexity of children's relationship to this particular survey item is compounded by the fact that they are likely to misunderstand it. Further, children's responses to any of the survey items are inextricably linked to the fact that it was not anonymous, making very real indeed their concerns with either personally hurting the feelings of a teacher about whom they cared and, thus, jeopardizing that important relationship, or facing retribution from a teacher they feared.

Ruth's response to Laura (lines 26–33) emphasized her assumption that the question about being "a credit to my race" is one the children were not likely to have understood. The grammatical construction of her query, "How many of you didn't know what the heck they're asking?" suggests both a critique of the survey and that their misunderstanding of this item was understandable, a rhetorical move that served to raise further questions about the validity of the survey.

Her response also confirmed that the children are right to be concerned about questions that probe their teachers' actions and linked this apprehension to children's other worries about privacy: "You're being asked to say things about your teachers. So, that's another privacy issue." Indeed, this exchange links privacy to race and racism in complicated ways.

Ruth's validation of the children's points about the teacher-focused items is understandable, for it is issues of privacy, identification, and accountability that were of most concern for teachers, and that prompted the swift response by the teachers' union and the ACLU. On the other hand, the personal nature of the children's response to the survey items that addressed race and racism coupled with Ruth's response to the issues of teachers and racism included in the survey does not allow the class to fully engage with the role that racism *could* potentially play in some children's interactions with teachers.

We now turn our focus to the issue of racial categorization, a topic of discussion that is raised early but gains traction as children begin to notice the racial and ethnic designations that were printed on each individual's copy of the survey. The issue of racial/ethnic categories is first introduced by Grace (line 7) who points to the printed categories to support her argument that race/ethnicity should not matter.

In response to Grace, Ruth appeared to realize for the first time that the survey includes a racial or ethnic category, and she provided a reason why the district might want that information, saying, "They can sort through this, and they can go, 'Ah, all the black kids who answered this, or most of the black kids who answered this said this, and most of the white kids said this.'" She then linked her explanation to the issue of personal privacy, signaling that the inclusion of a racial/ethnic category provided the district "with a whole lot of information about you," suggesting that such information is a violation of privacy.

Stephanie's announcement that the district identified her as white and Ruth's response of laughter and: "Sometimes the ethnic stuff is not true. Okay. Okay," worked to further call into question the validity of the survey (lines 16–19). Ruth's words in this exchange were expressed in a skeptical tone that, along with pronoun usage (again, the use of "they" to refer to the district), worked to position her in opposition to the survey and those who constructed it.

The theme of racial categorization that Grace and Stephanie raised early in this part of the discussion returned when Luke asked Ruth what "AI" means (line 37). These children's past conversations about racial categories made this a particularly salient issue for them. For instance, when Ruth responded to Stephanie by agreeing that the survey was wrong when it designated her "white," Tavor responded by insisting that "she really is" (line 18).

Given their recent experiences, it makes sense that these children would be invested in "getting it right" and being very mindful of whether these printed "official" racial and ethnic designations matched their peers' self-inscribed identities (Dutro et al. 2005; Dutro et al. 2008). Stephanie, Zack, and Jeff had made strong arguments for why their identities as biracial people were important, and Tavor's comment signaled his sensitivity to that issue—if it was "wrong" to designate her White, it also would be wrong, he seemed to indicate, to deny that part of her biracial identity.

As children shared their racial/ethnic labels and the class determined the validity of those categories, the language they used placed positive value on individuals' rights to identify themselves and negative value on an authority's right to make arbitrary designations about racial and ethnic identities. Ruth makes this explicit when she tells Luke, "That's the label they put on you."

Luke is, in fact, American Indian (although he referred to himself as Native American, and such a difference in identifying terms is not necessarily benign), but her words critiqued the "they" who were imposing identities on the students. Her invitation to "check out" the racial/ethnic labels and her sardonic tone throughout this section of the discussion invited and supported the children's critical stance toward issues of race in the survey.

Ruth's proactive role in shaping a particular conversation about racial categories in the context of the survey was further apparent when she asked Zack to share the category he was assigned (line 52). By asking Zack, one of the biracial children who had been central to the class's previous discussion of racial categories, she invoked that earlier discussion and provided the class with another example of the arbitrary nature of the survey's designations.

In this case, it turned out that Zack provided a contrast to Stephanie—both were biracial African American/White but were placed in different categories—a part of the discussion that several children pointed to in post-interviews as an example of the importance of allowing people to describe their own racial identities. Asma's misidentification as East Indian, rather than Pakistani, also made a significant impression on many of the children (lines 43–47). In interviews and written reflections following the survey experience, children often raised Asma's experience as an example of the survey's flaws.

Although her classmates most likely did not understand the complex political context that lay behind Asma's response to her ethnic designation, the emotional, adamant nature of her reaction certainly signaled that a significant mistake had been made. She exclaimed, "I'm not from India!" Then when Ruth supported her indignation by replying, "Geez, I thought you were from Pakistan," Asma said loudly, "I am!" Asma's response worked to make the already highly contested issue of racial categories and who assigns them even more significant for the children.

Kofi and Tavor, both of whom had emigrated from Ethiopia as young children, raised another issue around race within the survey that was particularly salient to several immigrant children in the class. After Kofi confirmed that "BL" designated Black, Tavor returned to the issue, expressing resistance to being designated "Black" by the district (lines 58–59). He said, "They're saying the BL if you're black, right? But I'm not black, black. I'm not *only* black; I'm Ethiopian."

Ruth replied, "They don't have a category for Ethiopian. So, anybody who has black skin, who comes originally from Africa, whether you came from Africa four years ago or four hundred years ago, you get a BL. You are black. And, if you have white skin and you originally came from Europe, whether it was two years ago or four hundred years ago, you get a WH for white."

As Ruth pointed out, the district had only one category for students with roots in Africa, even though that identity was not salient for Tavor, and included no nuances for strong ethnic identifications such as his self-identification as Ethiopian or, in his words, "not *only* black." Ruth's response also implied that those ethnic identities are likely to be stronger for more recent immigrants of all races than those whose families had been in the United States for multiple generations, which connected her comment directly to Tavor, a first-generation immigrant. Unlike Asma, Tavor's category was not wrong; instead, his experience pointed to a more subtle issue of racial categorization that allowed Ruth to emphasize the nuances of identity that could be lost when arbitrary racial categories are assigned.

RACE AND RELEVANCE: LEARNING FROM RUTH'S STUDENTS

The district survey was striking in the directness with which it raised issues of race and racism. If the intent had been to raise points of discussion for students and teachers, it may have been a very fruitful endeavor. However, the intent was not discussion; rather, the district wanted the surveys completed quickly and efficiently and returned promptly. Absent a larger agenda to raise issues of race and racism in critical ways, students and teachers were left to navigate their own way through a very provocative text.

In Ruth's classroom, her stance and the class' previous engagements with issues of race as an explicit topic for conversation resulted in opportunities to delve into important and provocative ideas related to race and identity. The issues of race, racism, and privacy that arose in the discussion demonstrate the complex theories and ideas that children bring to conversations of topics that matter to them and connect to their individual and collective experiences and concerns. Such discussions allow children both to voice their own theories and lived knowledge on crucial social issues and to hear their peers' ideas, which may or may not coincide with their own.

Indeed, the children's engagement of complex issues resonates with recent arguments by literacy researchers that children function as social theorists in classrooms in ways that too often go unrecognized (Campano 2007; Jones 2006). As Jones argues, viewing children as theorists of the social world "positions children as intellectual beings who practice the complex processes of reading a world that pushes them and their families to the side and attempting to reclaim a space in that world by making sense of what one does when she is marginalized" (p. 24).

If children's social theorizing is to have an impact on the ideas examined in classrooms, teachers need to provide space for children to share theories and students need to feel that their ideas are valued. In this case, because Ruth, as the teacher, had actively supported the students' previous engagement with issues of race and identity, they could raise questions, even outrage, about an official document with the expectation that their response would be taken seriously.

We certainly do not claim that the discussion following the survey experience illustrates only exemplary practice. To the contrary, in our analysis we saw not only the powerful moments when important ideas were raised and connections made but also some of the constraints imposed by how topics unfolded as well as examples of lost opportunities to push even more deeply and critically into some issues. For instance, the coupling of race and privacy that occurred throughout the classroom discussion had at least three potential effects.

First, it framed race and racism as issues about which the district had no right to inquire. Second, it contradicted experiences that these children had shared and talked about in previous discussions—that is, that as much as they might argue that racial identity *should* be a personal matter, individuals are often misread and misplaced by others who make assumptions about race and racial identities. Third, it functioned to close off opportunities to use the language of the survey to talk about the realities of racism and that schools as institutions are not immune from racism.

The survey's form and language, however, particularly the identifying information that was so prominently displayed, makes the linking of privacy to all issues addressed in the survey understandable. When all responses can potentially be traced directly to the responder, it is simply too risky to decouple an issue such as racism from the issue of privacy.

Our analysis also shows some opportunities to discuss the realities of racism in schools that were not pursued in the discussion. Those moments certainly emphasize the difficulties inherent in tackling ideologically contested topics, particularly in a context in which power differentials had been subtly and not so subtly emphasized by the document being critiqued, fostering a defensive stance in both students and teacher.

Ruth, who was very open to discussing both race and racism, seemed constrained by her personal reaction and the district teachers' collective response to the survey. Indeed, the issues most prevalent in her language were privacy and the threat of personal accountability. Given that those issues were also key concerns of the students, they became the primary focus of discussion. In addition, delving into the topic of racism in schools would require conceding that the survey was addressing important issues. Aside from a few instances in which Ruth and Tavor took rather tepid devil's advocate stances, this was not a concession made in this discussion.

Although Ruth now sees opportunities in the transcripts for moving the conversation to more critical territory, it was arguably the hierarchical, power-laden language of the survey and its accompanying directions that served to block those paths. The value of the kind of close analysis we present here is that it points to those paths in ways that make it more likely to see and anticipate those important conversations in subsequent discussions with students. Such analysis also allows for the recognition and critique of the contextual factors that may have made those opportunities difficult to see.

CONCLUDING THOUGHTS

By the end of the discussion about the survey, the majority of the students voted to make a video expressing their critiques of the survey to the district. Their decision to create a visual response seemed connected to race. As Tavor said, "When you tell them, they see *how you are* and they see how you feel" (emphasis added). Ruth followed, saying, "They will see how you are, and I think it would be, in some ways, pretty powerful with this class because this is a very diverse class."

Grace then made a comment that spoke to the importance as well as the complexity of visual representations of identity, saying, "We should have Asma stand there, because she's not East Indian, okay? Even I know that." In Grace's mind, Asma's ethnic misidentification on the survey could not help but be a powerful statement to the district. Of course, although this was not raised at the time, it would be difficult for anyone to visually distinguish Asma from an East Indian girl, which points to the complexity of the issues of identity and categorization in which the children were engaged.

What is clear is that the children were building understandings that those issues were important and that they played out differently for their peers, depending on a range of factors. In the end, despite arguments periodically raised by a few students that race "doesn't matter," the conversation about racial categorization and the children's decision to videotape their protest confirmed that race, and the racial and ethnic identities claimed in that classroom, mattered very much.

Discussions of race and the complexity of racial identities certainly can and should be planned for in connection with curriculum. However, children will identify paths for discussion and action that teachers cannot anticipate, and those paths are by definition germane to students' interests. Our research suggests that if we begin instructional planning based on our own preconceptions about what will be meaningful for any given student or group of students, we may very well get it wrong. Rather, we can start by watching closely for opportunities to follow students' lead into important topics that connect to their experiences, needs, and interests and provide the space, support, and companionship for such student-initiated journeys.

REFERENCES

Banks, J. (1997). *Multicultural Education: Issues and Perspectives* (3rd ed.). Boston: Allyn and Bacon.

Bonfil Batalla, G. (1990). "Aculturación e Indigenismo: La Respuesta India. [Acculturation and Indigenism: The Indian response]." In J. A. French (ed.), *Indianismo e Indigenismo en América Latina* [*Indianism and Indigenism in Latin America*] (pp. 189–209). Madrid: Alianza Editorial.

Campano, G. (2007). *Immigrant Students and Literacy: Reading, Writing, and Remembering.* New York: Teachers College Press.

Cochran-Smith, M. (2000). "Blind Vision: Unlearning Racism in Teacher Education." *Teachers College Record, 70,* 157–90.

Comber, B., and A. Simpson. (2001). *Negotiating Critical Literacies in Classrooms.* New York: Lawrence Erlbaum.

Davies, B., and R. Harré. (1990). "Positioning: The Discursive Production of Selves." *Journal for the Theory of Social Behavior, 20*(1), 43–63.

Delpit, L. (1996). *Other People's Children: Cultural Conflict in the Classroom.* New York: New Press.

Dunn, R., S. Griggs, and G. Price. (1993). "Learning Styles of Mexican-American and Anglo-American Elementary School Students." *Journal of Multicultural Counseling and Development, 21*, 237–47.

Dutro, E., E. Kazemi, and R. Balf. (2005). "The Aftermath of "You're Only Half": Multiracial Identities in the Literacy Classroom." *Language Arts, 83*, 96–106.

Dutro, E., E. Kazemi, R. Balf, and Y. Lin. (2008). "What Are You and Where Are You From? Race, Identity, and the Vicissitudes of Cultural Relevance in Diverse Classrooms." *Urban Education, 43*, 269–300.

Ellsworth, E. (1993). ""Why Doesn't This Feel Empowering?" Working Through the Repressive Myths of Critical Pedagogy." In L. Stone (ed.), *The Education Feminism Reader* (pp. 300–27). New York: Routledge.

Enciso, P. (1997). "Negotiating the Meaning of Difference: Talking Back to Multicultural Literature." In T. Rogers and A. Soter (eds.), *Reading Across Cultures* (pp. 13–41). New York: Teachers College Press.

———. (2003). "Reading Discrimination." In S. Greene and D. Abt-Perkins (eds.), *Making Race Visible: Literacy Research for Cultural Understanding* (pp. 149–77). New York: Teachers College Press.

Fairclough, N. (1989). *Language and Power.* New York: Longman.

———. (1995). *Critical Discourse Analysis: The Critical Study of Language.* New York: Longman.

Ferguson, A. (2001). *Bad Boys: Public Schools and the Making of Black Masculinity.* Ann Arbor: University of Michigan Press.

Gee, J. (1999). *An Introduction to Discourse Analysis: Theory and Method.* New York: Routledge.

Greene, S., and D. Abt-Perkins. (2003). *Making Race Visible: Literacy Research for Cultural Understanding.* New York: Teachers College Press.

Gutierrez, K. D., and B. Rogoff. (2003). "Cultural Ways of Learning: Individual Traits or Repertoires of Practice." *Educational Researcher, 32*, 19–25.

Hall, S., and P. DuGay. (1996). *Questions of Cultural Identity.* Thousand Oaks, CA: Sage.

Hickson, J., A. J. Land, and G. Aikman. (1994). "Learning Style Differences in Middle School Pupils from Four Ethnic Backgrounds." *School Psychology International, 15*, 349–59.

Irvine, J. J., and D. E. York. (1995). "Learning Styles and Culturally Diverse Students: A Literature Review." In J. A. Banks and C. A. M. Banks (eds.), *Handbook of Research on Cultural Education* (pp. 484–97). New York: Macmillan.

Jones, S. (2006). "Language with an Attitude: White Girls Performing Class." *Language Arts, 84*, 114–24.

Luke, A. (1995). "Text and Discourse in Education: An Introduction to Critical Discourse Analysis." *Review of Research in Education, 21,* 3–48.

O'Connor, C. (2001). "Making Sense of the Complexity of Social Identity in Relation to Achievement: A Sociological Challenge in the New Millennium." *Sociology of Education, 74,* 159–68.

Orellana, M. F., and P. Bowman. (2003). "Cultural Diversity Research on Learning and Development." *Educational Researcher, 32*(5), 26–32.

Tatum, B. (2003). *"Why are All the Black Kids Sitting Together in the Cafeteria?" A Psychologist Explains the Development of Racial Identity.* New York: Basic Books.

Chapter 3

The Central Paradox of Critical Pedagogy

Learning from Practice in an Urban "Last Chance" High School

Kysa Nygreen, *UC Santa Cruz*

In this chapter, I examine the core principles, foundations, and theoretical limitations of critical pedagogy, an educational theory/practice aimed at empowering historically oppressed groups to engage in social action for a more just society. Second, I examine one attempt to implement critical pedagogy in a youth-led social justice class at an urban "last chance" high school.

Drawing from ethnographic research conducted in the class, I explore some key limitations and contradictions of critical pedagogy that emerged in practice, ultimately constraining the liberatory potential of the class. By exploring what went wrong in the youth-led social justice class, this chapter seeks to inform a more practical theory of critical pedagogy—one that is grounded in and informed by practice in urban schools.

The context of this chapter is a youth-driven participatory action research (YPAR) project conducted at Jackson High, a high-poverty, urban continuation high school in California where I worked as a classroom teacher, substitute, volunteer, and researcher. In California, a continuation high school is a public alternative school to which students are involuntarily transferred due to poor academic performance. As such, Jackson High is a "last chance" school serving youth who have been labeled as academic failures (Kelly 1993, p. 222). Located in a large urban district, Jackson served approximately 130 students, 80 percent of whom were African American and 97 percent of whom were students of color.

After working at Jackson High for five years in various capacities, I initiated a small YPAR project there. My goal was to engage current and former Jackson students in collaborative research aimed at understanding and addressing the social inequalities affecting their lives and education. With a total of eight youth participating over two years, the project came to be known as the participatory action research team for youth (PARTY), and it culminated in the youths' choice to design and teach a social justice class at their school. Working together with me, PARTY members taught the class once a week for one semester as part of the U.S. government course. The design of the class was both explicitly and implicitly informed by critical pedagogy.

This chapter draws on two years of ethnographic data collection and participant-observation in the PARTY group to illustrate how PARTY members (including myself as group facilitator and co-teacher) conceptualized and attempted to implement a school-based critical pedagogy in the context of a youth-led social justice class. It argues that our experience in the classroom exposed a core theoretical contradiction of critical pedagogy—what I call the *central paradox of critical pedagogy.*

This term refers to critical pedagogy's paradoxical aims of, on the one hand, valuing the popular or subjugated knowledge of participants while, on the other hand, seeking to impose particular forms of specialized knowledge on those very participants. I show how the central paradox of critical pedagogy emerged within the PARTY group and the social justice class, and I argue that our failure to confront this paradox limited the project's liberatory potential.

WHAT IS CRITICAL PEDAGOGY?

Critical pedagogy is a theory and practice of education aimed at stimulating social critique and political engagement among historically oppressed groups for the purpose of progressive social change. First coined by Henry Giroux in *Theory and Resistance in Education* (1983), critical pedagogy has evolved as a field of study that employs critical social theory to deconstruct the oppressive nature of schooling and to promote an alternative vision of education for social change.[1]

A wide variety of scholars, educators, and activists employ the core principles and practices of critical pedagogy in their work—often without giving it a name or writing about it—and often under the rubric of other pedagogical traditions such as popular education (Adams 1975; Hall 1978; Horton and Freire 1990), decolonizing pedagogy (Tejeda, Espinoza, and Gutierrez 2003), feminist pedagogy (hooks 1994), critical literacy (Freire and Macedo 1987; Gee, Hull, and Lankshear 1996), empowerment education (Shor 1992), or critical multiculturalism (Nieto 1999; Sleeter 1996).

These different labels reflect slightly distinct emphases, but all of these pedagogical traditions share five basic principles. I refer to these as the core principles of critical pedagogy: (1) The assertion that all education is political; (2) the goal of eliminating interlocking oppressions of race, class, gender, sexuality, nation, and ability; (3) the value of popular, community-based, and subjugated knowledge; (4) the pedagogical practices of problem posing and dialogue; and (5) the concepts of critical consciousness and action for social change, or *praxis*. These principles are widely associated with the writings of Paulo Freire (especially 1970/1999), but their application in education predates Freire, and they are not unique to his work.[2]

In the PARTY project, youth researchers chose to design and teach a social justice class at their school. Teaching this class was the *action* they chose after one school year spent in collaborative research about educational inequality. As the PARTY members prepared to teach, they explicitly connected the *educational* goals of the class to larger goals of social change and racial or economic justice. Their vision of education for social change closely mirrored the five core principles of critical pedagogy. I outline each of the five principles, illustrating how PARTY members employed them to construct a vision of critical education for social change.

Principle #1: All Education Is Political

Critical pedagogy begins with the assumption that all education is political. Educators who claim to be neutral by avoiding controversial topics or simply transmitting objective information do, in fact, support the status quo and legitimize the tacit assumptions of dominant society (Freire 1970/1999; Horton and Freire 1990; Shor 1992). Teaching students to succeed within the present social and educational systems without challenging or questioning them offers a tacit endorsement of those systems.

Since all knowledge is socially constructed and tied to relations of power, the practice of transmitting official knowledge without challenging or questioning it also serves to legitimize the system (Apple 1990; Shor 1992). As such, all education either *upholds* or *challenges* existing social structures and their prevailing assumptions (Freire 1970/1999; hooks 1994).

Critical pedagogy also emphasizes the inherently political nature of schooling as an institution. Schools are political in terms of funding, regulation, certification, goals and objectives, the manner in which these goals and objectives are evaluated, the nature of the textbooks, what is taught and what is left out, what knowledge is valued, and who has the power to make these and other decisions (Apple 1990; Kincheloe 2004; Shor 1992; Spring 1991). The cumulative result of these processes is a school system that serves to perpetuate oppressive social structures and relations of power.

In other words, schools reproduce existing social inequalities and then legitimize these outcomes by propagating the myth of a meritocratic system (Apple 1990; Bowles and Gintis 1976; Giroux 1983). Although critical pedagogy begins with the assertion that schools are oppressive and reproductive institutions, it also frames the classroom as a potential site of consciousness raising and social change. Critical pedagogy calls on students and teachers to critically analyze and deconstruct patterns of social inequality as a path toward taking action to change them. This view of the school as a site of "domination and contestation" (Giroux 1983, pp. 62–63) is central within critical pedagogy.

The notion of schooling as a site of reproduction and liberation also emerged within the PARTY project and powerfully shaped the ways in which PARTY members conceptualized the social justice class. One of the PARTY members, named "D," advanced this critique of traditional/mainstream schooling:

> D: This country is ran off of followers. They never go in deep, and have their own opinion. They follow somebody else. You know, but schools, schools, it's all about schools though. What schools teach today is they teach you how to be followers, instead of teaching you how to have your own opinion.

This quote—which is representative of many of D's comments about schools—illustrates D's belief that schools create a passive populace that follows orders rather than voicing opinions. In this way, D suggests that schools help perpetuate existing structures of power because students are not encouraged to voice opposition and critique. Other PARTY members regularly expressed similar views about the role of schools in producing "followers," as when Suli claimed that "education molds you into the oppressive society" and identified the major problem of schooling as the fact that students are prohibited from voicing their opinions.

The stated beliefs of PARTY members about the role of schooling echo Freire's (1970/1999) statement that: "the more completely [students] accept the passive role imposed on them, the more they tend simply to adapt to the world as it is and to the fragmented view of reality deposited in them" (p. 54). In contrast, PARTY members conceptualized their social justice class as a space in which students would question, challenge, critique, and "voice their opinions."

Principle #2: The Goal Is to Eliminate
Interlocking Structures of Oppression

Should schools teach students how to succeed within existing social and economic structures? Or should schools teach students to *change* these structures and make them more equitable? This tension between *social mobility* and *social change* is central in American educational history and politics. U.S. society is characterized by a strong belief in education as a means of individual social mobility (Brint and Karabel 1989; Labaree 1997), and as a result, many reform movements for educational justice focus on realizing this goal more effectively—in other words, they focus on improving the ability of schools to help individual students succeed within present socioeconomic structures.

When this focus is geared toward students from historically oppressed groups, it is often framed as a path toward a larger goal of equity and social justice because it reflects equality of opportunity and increases racial diversity in positions of power and privilege (Tejeda et al. 2003). In contrast, critical pedagogy rejects the goals of assimilation and mobility within existing structures of power (ibid.), and seeks instead to empower students to *transform* those structures to make them more socially just and equitable.

Rather than hold to *individual social mobility*, critical pedagogy frames education as a path to *collective social change*, toward the goal of a more equitable and democratic society (Giroux 1983, p. 201). Unlike many models of civic or citizenship education, which promote civic engagement as a politically neutral exercise, critical pedagogy explicitly seeks to "contribute to the transformation of the social relations and formations that produce social inequalities and injustices" (Tejeda et al. 2003, p. 32). Specifically, critical pedagogy seeks to dismantle interlocking oppressions based on race, class, gender, sexuality, nation, and ability.

The PARTY group youth also considered the tensions between *individual social mobility* and *collective social change* as they sought to more broadly articulate the purpose of the social justice class and of social justice education. The first time I posed this question to the group, they generally agreed that education should do both: help students succeed within existing social structures *and* work to change those structures. However, when asked to speak in concrete terms about their goals for the social justice class, PARTY members rarely, if ever, mentioned traditional measures of academic achievement (i.e., good grades, going to college), except for the modest goal of encouraging students to graduate from high school.

In contrast, they regularly and elaborately discussed social change-oriented goals such as empowering students to voice their opinions, knowing how to vote, joining protests, and seeing that "people have the power." Moreover, as the project advanced, the group moved toward a vision of social change and racial or economic justice as the ultimate goal of the social justice class, often describing the class within the context of a larger social movement for racial or economic justice. This connection between their work in the school and the larger goals of social justice reflects the core principle of critical pedagogy that aims to eliminate structures of oppression.

Principle #3: The Value of Popular, Community-based, and Subjugated Knowledge

Critical pedagogy assumes that historically oppressed communities possess valuable local knowledge that contains not only deep wisdom but also a critique of dominant power structures. This critique is developed as a result of persistent exclusion and marginalization, experiences that facilitate the creation of a "double consciousness" (DuBois 1903/1953; Ladson-Billings 2000), or subversive forms of knowledge (see also Ferguson 2000 and hooks 1990).

Critical pedagogy is not unique in the attention paid to popular, indigenous, and community-based knowledge within historically oppressed groups. The subversive potential of subjugated knowledge has long been theorized within anticolonialist, feminist, critical race, and critical social theories; writers from oppressed positionalities have often emphasized this point in their work.[3] These writers argue that the construction of official or expert knowledge systematically excludes or devalues the experiences of women, the poor, and people of color. Recognizing the subversive potential of subjugated knowledge, critical pedagogy aims to access and build upon it to promote critique and political engagement for social change.

Critical pedagogy calls on teachers and students to scrutinize "the formal corpus of school knowledge" (Apple 1990, p. 9) and examine its role in sustaining oppression. By engaging in critical analysis and deconstruction of official knowledge, students and teachers will come to understand the multiple ways that structures of oppression are legitimized and sustained through the production of official knowledge (Apple 1990; Tejeda et al. 2003).

Within the PARTY group, youth researchers routinely and emphatically asserted the value of Jackson students' local, subjugated knowledge and ways of knowing *in contrast to* the expert, official knowledge and ways of knowing that my own presence in the group represented. This occurred both in the planning process for the class and in the reflection and debriefing meetings over the semester of teaching.

In planning for the class, PARTY members rejected my attempts to predetermine curricular themes and learning goals for students. Instead, they assumed that Jackson students already possessed deep knowledge and deep questions; our role as educators was not to impose official knowledge *on* students, but rather to engage them in a dialogue rooted in their existing subjugated knowledge. In reflecting on the class midway through the semester, two PARTY members had the following exchange:

Leila: [Students] know that the government's not looking out for them. I mean it's pretty obvious.

Suli: [*rolling his eyes*] You don't have to be a rocket scientist to understand *that*!

Leila: It seems like the facts on the pages kind of prove what [students] already kind of knew about the government and how their lives work.

Here, Leila suggests that the official curriculum of the social justice class merely confirms what students already know from life experience, or "how their lives work." Suli's response, "You don't have to be a rocket scientist to understand *that*," underscores the obviousness of Leila's observation, suggesting that *of course* the lived experience of oppression provides valid knowledge and a certain kind of expertise about oppression. PARTY members took it for granted that students possessed valuable knowledge and deep insights about inequality and social justice. The goal of the class, therefore, was to access and build on their knowledge as a resource, not to supplant or ignore it.

Principle #4: The Use of Dialogue and Problem Posing as Pedagogical Strategies

Critical pedagogy rejects traditional models of teaching in which a teacher-as-expert transmits an unquestioned body of knowledge to students in a one-way fashion. This banking model of education, according to Freire (1970/1999), reproduces and reinforces authoritarian power relations inside the classroom while also presenting the teacher's official knowledge as immutable and absolute.

In contrast, critical pedagogy employs egalitarian, dialogue-based teaching practices that push students to problematize, challenge, and deconstruct prevailing societal assumptions and taken-for-granted beliefs (Apple 1979). Through this process, students and teachers gain a critical awareness of oppression in their own lives and learn to decode dominant discourses that sustain oppressive power relations (Adams 1975; Freire 1970/1999; Hall 1978; Shor 1992).

This critical reflection process is achieved through problem posing, a strategy that "offers all subject matter as historical products to be questioned rather than as universal wisdom to be accepted" (Shor 1992, p. 32). Problem posing continually emphasizes the constructed nature of knowledge and expertise, and it engages students and teachers in a "critical dialogue" (ibid., p. 31) that facilitates learning.

As the youth in PARTY designed their social justice class, they consistently emphasized the importance of engaging students in dialogue and remaining flexible enough to let students determine the direction of the class. When examining formal lesson plans as part of the participatory research process, PARTY members consistently responded that they were "too contrived" or "too structured," and "students wouldn't do it." Instead of structured classroom activities, PARTY members opted for open-ended discussions starting from students' lived experiences and student-generated questions.

Rejecting *my* attempts to predetermine at least a few curricular themes and goals, D insisted that his only curricular plan was to "ask [students] what they want to learn, and then teach it to them." This statement aptly summarizes the pedagogy that PARTY members ultimately implemented in their social justice class. "Voicing your opinion" became the primary goal, teaching method, and measure of success for the class, and PARTY members often asked questions that pushed students to critically reflect on the social issues affecting their lives. This emphasis on critical dialogue as a teaching tool reflects a key principle of critical pedagogy.

Principle #5: The Cycle of Critical Consciousness and Praxis

Critical pedagogy aims to initiate and sustain a cycle of critical consciousness and *praxis* for the purpose of social change. These concepts of critical consciousness and praxis are central to critical pedagogy. Freire (1970/1999) describes critical consciousness as the realization that structures of oppression are social constructions that are built and potentially changed through collective action. This consciousness brings a sense of empowerment and agency because the possibility of change becomes visible (ibid.). With critical consciousness, people "perceive oppression not as a closed world from which there is no exit, but as a limiting situation which they can transform" (ibid., p. 31).

Yet consciousness, by itself, does not lead to social change. Critical pedagogy strives to effect social change through *praxis:* "reflection and action upon the world in order to transform it" (ibid., p. 33). The concept of praxis implies the *unity* of consciousness and action: the relationship between them is dialectical rather than linear. Said another way, praxis can be defined as "guided action aimed at transforming individuals and their world that is reflected upon and leads to further action" (Tejeda et al. 2003, p. 16). To facilitate praxis, critical pedagogy considers the classroom as a space for reflecting on social action (through critical dialogue) in order to inspire and guide further action.

In the PARTY group, the youth defined critical consciousness in similar terms—as a recognition that structures of oppression are socially constructed and, therefore, capable of change through collective social action—and they identified the role of critical consciousness as a precipitator of action for social change. They designed the social justice class with this goal of critical consciousness in mind, as suggested in the four official goals that we articulated in the following written statement:

"Students will learn:
1. Why things are the way they are.
2. How all of this affects their life.
3. To question why it is the way it is.
4. What they can do about it: People have the power."

The first goal suggests that PARTY members wanted Jackson students to understand the root causes of social problems, or "why things are the way they are." Secondly, they wanted students to see connections between structural and individual problems: "how all of this affects their life." The third goal emphasizes the practice of questioning dominant assumptions, or as Freire (1970/1999) has written, to "permit the oppressed to begin to question: why?" (p. 67). The fourth goal speaks to the role of collective social action to effect social change: that "people have the power."

The four goals suggest that PARTY members prioritized critical consciousness as a central goal of the social justice class and viewed this as a necessary precondition for engaging in social change action. Although PARTY members did not articulate a strong understanding of *praxis,* the class goals clearly exhibit a focus on critical consciousness as a first step toward social change.

Critical pedagogy offers a compelling vision of education for social change, one that inspired us as we undertook our work together. Yet, critical pedagogy did not insulate us from the risk of reproducing the very same power inequalities that we sought to challenge. We found that translating critical pedagogy from theory to practice was hard work and fraught with contradictions. However, PARTY was not the first group to experience such tensions; in fact, many scholars and practitioners before us had produced insightful critiques of critical pedagogy that foreshadowed our experience in PARTY. I review some of these in the next section.

THE CENTRAL PARADOX OF CRITICAL PEDAGOGY

Critical pedagogy has been the target of many critiques and sometimes vicious attacks. Three major criticisms of critical pedagogy are worthy of discussion here: (1) it is not informed by practice; (2) it has ambiguous political aims; and (3) it has ambiguous academic aims. In this section, I review these criticisms and then synthesize them to advance my own theoretical critique: the *central paradox of critical pedagogy*. This refers to the contradictory aims of empowering students to be their own agents and authors of social change while simultaneously influencing—perhaps even determining—the *direction* of social change action.

Criticism #1: Theory Not Informed by Practice

Much of the scholarly literature on critical pedagogy relies on abstract theoretical constructs that are rarely located in practice. Knight and Pearl (2000) point out that the central theorists on which critical pedagogy is based— Gramsci, Adorno, Horkheimer, Marcuse, Althusser—were never teachers and are not relevant to North American classrooms today. Despite the merits of critical theory, Knight and Pearl question critical pedagogy's reliance on theorists from a different social context and historical era. They do so without also incorporating insights gained through practice or through working with students and teachers in the contemporary North American context.

An example of this reliance on theory is Giroux's (1983) *Theory and Resistance in Education*. While Giroux outlines the need for critical pedagogy and its key theoretical principles, the reader is left with little idea about what this pedagogy might actually look like in practice. There are no examples from practice and no hint about how one might try to teach this way. Ironically, Giroux claims that critical pedagogy "must provide the conditions that give students the opportunity to speak with their own voices, to authenticate their own experiences" (p. 203), yet his book offers no voice of students or teachers.

Moreover, much of the literature on critical pedagogy uses arcane language and theoretical jargon that renders these texts inaccessible, especially to audiences that critical pedagogy should wish to reach (e.g., teachers and historically oppressed groups). Such language can serve to exclude rather than include, thereby contradicting the inclusive aims of critical pedagogy. Here again, Giroux's (1983) *Theory and Resistance in Education* offers a telling example.

Despite its important theoretical insights, Giroux's book may turn people away from critical pedagogy and contribute to the field's reputation as an elitist, detached, irrelevant form of "antiseptic politics" (Knight and Pearl 2000, p. 222). In response to frequent criticisms that critical pedagogy is purely theoretical and detached from practice, scholars of critical pedagogy reject attempts to reduce critical pedagogy to a teaching method (Kincheloe 2004; McLaren 2000; Tejeda et al. 2003). They defend the necessity for theoretical rigor and tacitly suggest that inaccessible language is necessary for achieving such "rigor."[4]

Criticism #2: Ambiguous Political Aims

The long-term political goal of critical pedagogy is to eliminate interlocking structures of oppression, yet the shorter-term political objectives remain ambiguous in the scholarly literature. This ambiguity exists at the microlevel of student outcomes as well as at the macrolevel of steps toward social change. On the microlevel, critical pedagogy does not specify the precise skills that students need to become active agents of social change (Knight and Pearl 2000). On the macrolevel, the literature contains ample references to abstract concepts like "praxis" and "action for social change" without specifying the precise activities that these concepts imply.

For example, do these concepts suggest voting and writing congressional representatives? Do they include community organizing, protesting, boycotts, civil disobedience, or armed revolution? Do they include other forms of social responsibility like recycling or bicycling instead of driving? I would argue that action for social change may include all of these activities and more. But without exploring what political engagement would look like in practice, especially for students, the literature on critical pedagogy mystifies the process of social change and leaves critical educators with few concrete ideas about what to teach or how to measure success.

The tendency to mystify the outcomes of critical pedagogy occurs on the macrolevel as well. Larger questions about the purpose of critical pedagogy are obscured by theoretical abstractions or by palatable language like "democracy" and "equitable society." These euphemisms mask a much more specific political agenda, which becomes apparent when one digs into the more dense theoretical texts.

As Ellsworth (1989) points out, the word "critical" is a code word for "antiracism, antisexism, antielitism, antiheterosexism, antiableism, anticlassism, and antineoconservatism" (p. 302). She points out that advocates of critical pedagogy seek to "appropriate public resources (classrooms, school supplies, teacher/professor salaries, academic requirements and degrees) to further various "progressive" political agendas that they believe to be for the public good—and therefore deserving of public resources" (p. 303). The literature on critical pedagogy often glosses over this point, using theoretical jargon to mystify its true political aims.

Criticism #3: Ambiguous Academic Aims

Critical pedagogy strives for a two-tiered curriculum (Kincheloe 2004) that pushes students to master traditional academic content while challenging, questioning, and deconstructing official forms of knowledge. The two-tiered approach to teaching echoes Lisa Delpit's (1988) widely cited argument that educators have a responsibility to teach students of color the rules and codes of the culture of power and to simultaneously teach them to critique the role of this culture in sustaining oppression.

The literature on critical pedagogy provides few insights about how to translate this two-tiered curriculum into practice. Much of the literature tacitly assumes that students naturally come to see the importance of traditional academic achievement and skills as they develop a critical consciousness. For example, Kincheloe's *Primer on Critical Pedagogy* (2004) describes this two-tiered curriculum with an example from Paolo Freire's teaching:

> [Freire's] students were motivated to gain literacy in order to take part in chang-
> ing both their own lives and the society. The process of learning was inseparable
> from individual empowerment and social change. They could not achieve the
> goals they sought without knowing how to read and write. Because the domi-
> nant classes did not want students from the peasant class to succeed with their
> academic studies, Freire's students knew that they had to excel in their studies
> in order to overcome the oppressors. (p. 71)

Accounts like this of students growing "motivated to gain literacy" through critical pedagogy are plentiful in the literature. These accounts gloss over the difficult work of how this motivation was achieved. Moreover, they often draw on educational projects like Freire's as an example, even though Freire worked primarily with voluntary adult students in South America—a very different social and historical context than a North American high school classroom.

Those working in high school settings know that critique of the power structure does not automatically translate into aspirations for academic achievement. Students often voice extremely sophisticated criticisms of schooling and society that demonstrate deep insights about the nature of oppression and injustice. Yet this critical understanding does not appear to correlate with academic achievement or a commitment to acquisition of traditional academic skills. In fact, the experiences of countless high school educators and school-based ethnographies[5] suggest the opposite may be true: for high school students, critical consciousness sometimes appears to *discourage* academic achievement.

MAKING SENSE OF THE CRITICS:
THE CENTRAL PARADOX OF CRITICAL PEDAGOGY

When we consider the five principles of critical pedagogy outlined above, it becomes clear that critical pedagogy is not simply a method of teaching; it is more accurately conceptualized as a *theory of social change*. Like all theories of change, critical pedagogy begins with a theory of society. It asserts that existing social structures are unjust and unequal: some groups are systematically privileged while others are systematically oppressed.

Second, it asserts that this situation is not inevitable or immutable because social structures are created and changed through collective human action. Third, it asserts that a certain *type* of collective human action is capable of changing social structures to be more equitable and democratic. Historically oppressed groups can exercise action reflection, or *praxis,* on the social world in order to change it. Finally, it frames broad-based *praxis* as both the means *and* the goal of social change. These principles constitute a theory of social change that tells us how existing social structures are perpetuated, how they *should* be changed, and how they *can* be changed.

This theory of social change relies on a strong belief in human beings and the powerful role of education. It might reasonably be considered a leap of faith to assume that broad-based social critique and political engagement by historically oppressed groups can bring about a more just, equitable, and democratic society. After all, what is to prevent these groups from reproducing the same structures of oppression that exist now? Critical pedagogy responds to this question by highlighting the transformative power of education: with critical consciousness, students will pursue social change to eliminate oppressive social structures, not reproduce them.

Given the pre-existing *political* goals of critical pedagogy as well as the implicit *academic* goals in the two-tiered curriculum, a paradox emerges: How can critical pedagogy empower students to construct their own knowledge and vision of social change while simultaneously seeking to *direct* social change and academic achievement in a particular direction? What if, in the course of dialogue and problem posing, students express views and political agendas that are inconsistent with the antiracist, antisexist, and anticapitalist aims of critical pedagogy? What if, in the course of increased critical consciousness, students do not become motivated to gain literacy but instead reject school-based forms of knowledge even more forcefully?

These questions are glossed in much of the critical pedagogy literature. There is an implicit assumption that students from historically oppressed groups will almost naturally perceive society, justice, and injustice in ways that are consistent with an antiracist, antisexist, and anticapitalist political agenda. Critical pedagogy assumes that students who develop critical consciousness will adopt an antioppressive and prodemocratic position on all social and political issues while also strengthening their academic skills and motivation to succeed. But in practice, dissent is inevitable, even within groups of historically oppressed students, and academic achievement rarely follows automatically from increased critical consciousness.

This inevitable diversity of opinion leads Ellsworth (1989) to argue that the assumed "unity of values" among historically oppressed groups of students is incorrect, at best, and "potentially repressive" at worst (p. 308). Although critical pedagogy values local and popular knowledge, it also holds that there is a correct social and political analysis to which all students will eventually arrive. This commitment to a correct political analysis seems inconsistent with the value placed on local and popular knowledge, egalitarian classroom relationships, and the shared production of knowledge.

Ellsworth suggests that critical pedagogy's embrace of democratic teaching practices (such as dialogue, problem posing, and "teacher-as-learner") is less an expression of valuing popular knowledge and more a strategy for effectively bringing students to the "correct" political analysis. To enforce this correct analysis, critical educators may be tempted to silence or discredit dissenting voices. This dilemma leads Ellsworth to ask: "What diversity do we silence in the name of "liberatory" pedagogy?" (ibid., p. 308).

This dilemma is what I refer to as the *central paradox of critical pedagogy:* the simultaneous attempt to value local, popular, and subjugated knowledge while at the same time directing or leading that knowledge in a particular direction. I borrow this term from Gee, Hull, and Lankshear (1996), who defined "the central paradox of the new capitalism" as the contradictory attempts of businesses to "empower" workers through various worker-empowerment or workplace-democracy schemes while also asserting a set of "core values" to which workers were expected to adhere despite having had no input in creating them.

The authors criticize new-capitalist corporate projects like "worker empowerment" as a thinly veiled form of "soft-touch hegemony" (p. 23). Can the same criticism be leveled at critical pedagogy? In the next section, I reflect on this question as I share the experiences of PARTY members who attempted to implement critical pedagogy in a youth-led social justice class. I show how the central paradox of critical pedagogy emerged in practice, constraining the liberatory potential of the class and the PARTY project overall.

INSIDE THE SOCIAL JUSTICE CLASS: NEGOTIATING THE CENTRAL PARADOX OF CRITICAL PEDAGOGY

Three members of PARTY taught the social justice class at Jackson every Tuesday for one semester, as part of Ms. Barry's third period U.S. government class. The class met for 80 minutes right after lunch, from 12:20–1:40 p.m. The youth teachers were: D, a 20-year-old African American man and Jackson graduate; Suli, a 20-year-old mixed race (African American and

Latino) man and Jackson graduate; and Leila, a 17-year-old White woman who had attended Jackson for two years but had recently transferred to an independent studies program.

I also participated in the planning and teaching of the course; I am a White woman and was a doctoral student in my late twenties at the time of the social justice class. D, Suli, and Leila had all been involved in PARTY since the inception of the project, having participated in the collaborative research and design of the social justice class. (Other PARTY members had discontinued their participation for various reasons.) Below, I describe a typical day in the social justice class, which occurred in our third week of teaching. The purpose of this scene is to illustrate what the class was like and to serve as the basis for a discussion of the central paradox of critical pedagogy.

The Social Justice Class: A Typical Day

When the second bell rang at 12:20 p.m. signaling the beginning of class, there were exactly zero students in the classroom. The PARTY members—D, Suli, Leila, and I—all sat at desks in a front corner of the room as we waited for students to arrive. As usual, about 20 desks were arranged in a semicircle, facing the whiteboard at the front of the room. Windows along one wall opened up to an interior courtyard at the center of the school and were open today to let the warm breeze circulate into the classroom.

The U.S. government teacher, Ms. Barry, announced, "I'm going to round up the kids," as she walked toward the classroom door and disappeared into the courtyard. Shortly thereafter, students began to trickle into the classroom, one or two at a time. They took seats as they talked with each other in pairs or small groups, often consuming the rest of their lunches from the brief lunch period before. A full 10 minutes after the official start of class, I told Suli that I thought we should get the class started. There were 12 students in the room: 6 boys and 6 girls.

Suli walked to the front of the class and stood facing the students. He inhaled deeply as if to begin speaking but stopped short, hesitating perhaps because students were still talking among themselves; none showed any sign of noticing his approach to the front of the room. Even Ms. Barry was talking to a student at her desk. When a few moments had passed, Suli inhaled again and this time spoke in a loud and commanding voice that caught most students' attention: "Alright, everybody, we're gonna get started." Ms. Barry was still talking to a student. In the rest of the class, a continuous soft buzz of side conversations never completely died down, although most students gave some evidence of looking up toward Suli's direction.

Suli continued to speak: "I'm gonna read you this fact of the day." He gestured to the whiteboard where a fact was written across the top: "One in three African American men will serve time in prison during their lifetime." Suli turned back to the students and asked, "Do you think this is true?"

Several answers came out at once: "It's higher than that!" said one; "I think it's *two* out of three!" said another; "No, it's two-and-a-*half* out of three!" came the next. Then Frank, a student who often played the class clown, called out, "No, it's *three* out of three! 'Cuz if they're not in jail now, they've *been* there!"

Suli attempted to engage the class in a discussion of the fact: its root causes; its effects on students' lives, families, and communities; and its relation to other social issues and to social structures of power. As a group, we had prepared problem-posing questions in the previous PARTY meeting, but Suli did not use them because the discussion focused on other things. "Do you smoke?" "Do you drink?" "Have you been in jail?" students called out to Suli.

To each of these questions, Suli offered responses: "If I'm not old [enough] to buy it, then I'm not old enough to drink it!" he said, and, "No, I haven't been to jail." Frank (class clown) called out to Suli: "Maybe that's because you're light skinned." Another student corrected him: "No, Suli is *mixed*."

The class discussion quickly dissolved into several cross-conversations, with Suli in one corner of the room explaining to Frank and others that although he was mixed race, "To the cops, I'm just as Black as you are." More than five minutes passed as the class relaxed into separate group conversations—some, but not all of which were loosely related to the issue of criminalization and incarceration. The other PARTY members observed the action but made no attempt to restart the class discussion or move onto the next item of the lesson plan.

This discussion of the fact of the day was typical of how the social justice class began each week. PARTY members always selected an alarming social statistic that they believed students could relate to and used it as an opening prompt for class discussion. In weekly meetings, we developed problem-posing questions to focus discussion on the fact (e.g., "What do you know about this issue?" "How does this issue affect you?" "Who or what causes this issue?"). Each class opened with the fact written on the whiteboard, and it was Suli who always volunteered to lead the opening class discussion. Suli commanded students' attention and always led the class with charisma and charm.

However, the fact-of-the-day discussion rarely if ever progressed beyond exclamations of disbelief or surface-level reactions to the fact. Frequently, it broke up into multiple competing group conversations or was dominated by students' playful taunting of Suli as in the above example. In addition, the fact-of-the-day discussion routinely started at least a full 10 minutes after the official start of class due to students' late arrival to class after lunch.

An almost-identical sequence ensued immediately after the fact-of-the-day discussion. Each week, the second item on the lesson plan was called "the news." In this segment, PARTY members selected a news story from local, state, or national news to share with the class. They prepared problem-posing questions to engage students in a discussion of the story and its significance. News stories focused on issues ranging from the war in Iraq, to the impasse over the state budget, to the passage of a local ordinance.

In the typical day described above, Leila shared a news story about an antiloitering law passed in a neighboring city, which civil rights groups had criticized on the grounds that it would lead to more racial profiling. Again, students called out comments: "This is a stupid law!" and "This ain't gonna stop drug dealing!" Leila told the class that the city council would review the law in one year to assess its impact on racial profiling and encouraged students to register formal complaints with the city for this purpose.

"Nobody's gonna make a formal complaint!" called out Frank (class clown), adding, "Real talk; tell me *who* is gonna make a formal complaint?" Then he added, as if it just occurred to him, "Hey, why don't we know about this law anyway?" Frank's questions were potentially provocative entry points for a critical discussion of local legislative procedures, available pathways to political voice (and their limits), and information flow. However, they never led to any such discussion; instead, the chorus of student comments branched off into simultaneous side conversations, despite Leila's call for students to talk "one at a time."

After the fact-of-the-day and the news discussions, the remainder of class time was dedicated to the main lesson plan—usually an activity, debate, or project carried out in small groups. On this day, we broke students into four groups to engage in a discussion of the prison-industrial complex, and each PARTY member led a group. By this time, 3 additional students had arrived to class, bringing the total attendance for the day to 15 students (there were 28 students on the roll sheet).

To anchor the small-group discussions, we used a lesson plan with discussion questions developed by a local advocacy organization that fights prison expansion. During this activity, many students appeared to be engaged, and rich discussions occurred in the groups. Toward the end of class, groups were asked to present what they talked about to their classmates. Each group selected a spokesperson who shared back to the class, and students watched intently as their classmates presented. The small-group activity and presentations were the one time during this class period in which most students appeared to be seriously engaged in critical discussion of a key social issue.

As soon as the last student had presented about her group's discussion, we announced that students should write their reactions to the class in their journals. Students were familiar with the journal by now, as this was our third class session. Every class ended with a journal assignment in which students were asked to freewrite their ideas about the topic of the day's class and were encouraged to give their opinions, questions, and feedback to the PARTY teachers.

No sooner had the announcement of journals been made than a student called out: "We don't have time! Class is already over!" I corrected the student, saying that 15 minutes remained and that this was plenty of time to write a thoughtful journal response. Frank (class clown) stood up from his seat and announced in his loudest possible voice: "Class ends at one thirty-five! It's a new schedule!" The room quickly filled with sound and motion as students rose to their feet, joined their friends in conversation, whipped out makeup and mirrors, or repositioned themselves closer to the classroom door.

Suli and D disappeared from the room, which prompted Frank to insist, "If the *teachers* are leaving early, I think *we* should leave early too!" Ms. Barry—the classroom teacher, who had been at her desk the whole class period—called out to students: "This is not chill time. You should be working on your journal assignments." Nobody acknowledged her directive.

As the sound and movement in the classroom escalated, Frank's voice rose noticeably above the rest: "I'm done for the day!" he announced confidently. I approached him and said quietly, "In that case, could you at least lower your voice so that others can write in peace?" He answered me in high volume, "No one is working! Look around!" He was right. Few students were even seated anymore; no journals were open, and certainly no one was writing.

A few moments later, Suli was outside the classroom popping his head through the open window and ruffling the plastic blinds. This made Frank start laughing uncontrollably, which propelled him from his seat. He walked in circles around the room, punctuating his laughter with exaggerated, over-dramatic body movements. When I (instinctively) asked Frank to quiet down, he replied: "Kick me out so that I can leave early! I'm ready to go!" I ignored his request.

Somehow, in the midst of all the activity, 4 students managed to scribble a few sentences into their journals and hand them in. When the bell finally rang at 1:40, only 8 of the 15 students were still in the classroom; the others had quietly slipped away in the last 15 minutes of class—a common phenomenon at Jackson High.

Interpreting the Typical Day

This typical day in the social justice class illustrates how school schedules, classroom rules, and writing assignments created points of tension in the class and between the youth PARTY members and myself. As shown, students' participation in organized class activities or discussions could not be taken for granted; it constantly had to be negotiated. When participation in an organized class activity or discussion was achieved, it was temporary and fragile, ready to disintegrate at any moment. When it disintegrated, widespread noncompliance and a feeling of disorder prevailed. The room erupted into exhilarating noise, movement, and play.

The class also illustrated how Jackson students routinely arrived late and left early, rendering the first and last 15 minutes of every class session as "chill time." As a result, the 80-minute class period was regularly reduced to 45 or 50 minutes of instructional time, and those remaining minutes were frequently interrupted.

In addition to school assemblies, standardized testing, fire alarms, and other schoolwide interruptions, students participated in a range of classroom interruptions through "active not-learning" (Kohl 1991), or "the conscious effort of obviously intelligent students to expend their time and energy in the classroom actively distancing themselves from schoolwork, thereby short-circuiting the trajectory of school failure altogether" (Ferguson 2000, p. 99).

What is perhaps most notable about the typical day described above is how students creatively avoided doing an assignment they did not want to do: the journal. Even though many students had been engaged in previous parts of the class—especially during the small-group discussion—they vehemently avoided the journal assignment, and their avoidance was tacitly supported by PARTY members. The emphatic nature of student resistance to the journal seemed out of proportion to the demands of the assignment itself.

The journal was a freewrite assignment in which students could write about *anything* they chose, and for which they would receive full credit simply for writing a paragraph, regardless of the quality of their responses. No doubt students expended more energy *avoiding* the journal than they would have spent writing something—anything—to receive credit for the assignment. Yet every week, without fail, the announcement of journals spurred an identical reaction from students: collective, determined noncompliance that seemed to be both spontaneous and expertly coordinated.

Over the course of the semester, a debate grew within the PARTY group about whether to continue assigning the journal at all. In our weekly meetings, D and Suli began to voice opposition to the journal, and they devalued the journal during class time. According to D and Suli, the social justice class was supposed to engage students in meaningful discussions and learning for the purpose of social change. For it to be successful, the class could not reproduce traditional forms of schoolwork or assignments that depended on coercion for compliance.

The two young men argued repeatedly that if students did not want to write the journal assignment, we had no business requiring it of them. Suli explained:

Suli: I don't feel like we should necessarily even be forcing them to *do* the journal. That's just my opinion. I wasn't, I mean, I understand where *you're* coming from where it's like, you want to see if they're getting something out of the class on a day-to-day basis so, it's cool for you to give the journal, you know, to see what they really think, and how they respond to what we do. [pause] I don't like the journal. I never did.

Kysa: So, why . . . explain more why you don't like it.

Suli: I just don't think, personally I just don't think anybody wants to do it. And that's before we actually went in there and assigned it though. I mean I didn't feel like they would want to do it anyway. It's like, it basically just makes it kinda like, after they enjoy like, I guess, say enjoy the class, the last 15–20 minutes then it's just like, "Aawh, they're givin' us *work*." 'Cuz I know if I went there, I wouldn't do the journal.

Here, Suli describes assigning the journal as "forcing them" [students] to do something against their will, portraying the assignment as an unjust act of coercion. He identifies with students' reaction of "*aawh, they're givin' us work*" and in this way casts the journal assignment as decontextualized work, devoid of intrinsic value. In one of many heated discussions to occur in our weekly PARTY meetings, D argued that "if [students] don't want to do it, they won't do it. So we shouldn't make them." In all of these discussions, the question focused on whether students should be "forced" to do a writing assignment against their will.

The debate over journals reflected and reinforced a growing chasm within the PARTY group, with Leila and me (White women in a teacher-like role) on one side and Suli and D (men of color siding with students) on the other. In supporting the journal, Leila and I drew on the intrinsic and instrumental value of writing both as a tool for reflection and deeper understanding and as a necessary skill for mobility and school success.

Yet D and Suli were not convinced that writing assignments were needed to advance the four goals of the social justice class. Moreover, they were unwilling to "force" students to do assignments that looked and felt like "schoolwork" in a class that was supposed to be liberatory and egalitarian. Their opposition raised important questions about the role of the teacher, of coercion, and of schoolwork in critical pedagogy.

Despite the call for a two-tiered curriculum in critical pedagogy, the PARTY group struggled week after week to entice students to write even a simple, nongraded paragraph in a journal. This prevented us from using writing as a tool for reflection and deepening consciousness—an outcome that I believe limited the liberatory potential of the class. In addition, it created a deep divide within the PARTY group that eerily resembled a stereotypical conflict between teacher and students over questions of classroom authority.

My initial reaction was to interpret D's and Suli's opposition to the journal assignment as a combined result of false consciousness and youthful immaturity. Like the lads in Willis's (1974/1982) *Learning to Labour,* I reasoned, perhaps the young men were acting on a reproductive critique of society: although they saw through the myths of dominant society, including the myth of meritocracy, their critical consciousness led them to reject schooling and thereby reproduce their existing subordinate class positions.

Later, I reinterpreted the young men's position as the result of their desire to be liked by students in the class. D and Suli achieved popularity by siding with students in an ongoing contest with teachers over classroom authority and schoolwork. Indeed, the young men tried hard to gain acceptance and popularity, even breaking school rules on one occasion by taking their small groups off campus to play basketball during class time. While all of these factors surely played a role in encouraging their opposition to the journal, a more significant factor was also at play: the central paradox of critical pedagogy.

THE CENTRAL PARADOX OF CRITICAL PEDAGOGY

The central paradox of critical pedagogy refers to the problem of how to value students' local, subordinated knowledge and empower them to be their own authors and agents of social change, while at the same time *directing* their knowledge and agency in a particular and predetermined direction. Critical pedagogy is ostensibly committed to valuing student agency, student knowledge, and student-teacher democracy in all circumstances.

In reality, however, critical pedagogy seeks to lead students toward a particular political perspective *and* to accept and master school-based knowledge and traditional academic skills. It is not theoretically possible to pursue both goals at the same time: to value local knowledge unconditionally while also seeking to shape that knowledge in predetermined ways.

The central paradox of critical pedagogy applies in all contexts, whether formal or informal, voluntary or involuntary educational settings. In the *formal* and *involuntary* setting of the school, however, the critical educator's role is marked by an additional layer of contradiction. Public schooling is compulsory, and students do not attend by choice. Critical pedagogy strives to promote student agency, but in the context of a school, student agency is always confined by a set of non-negotiable parameters, including the imperatives to build academic skills and promote school success.

In the youth-led social justice class at Jackson, PARTY members encountered students who refused (or were not able) to attempt assignments requiring even minimal levels of writing. When confronted with student opposition to these assignments, PARTY members abandoned their attempts to promote writing as a reflective practice and instead took the path of least resistance— opting to give up the assignment altogether. D and Suli, the two young men in the PARTY group, sided unconditionally with students in their opposition to the journal assignment, even when this put them at odds with teachers and the academic aims of schooling.

Rather than dismiss the men's actions as immature or misguided, I contend that they were consistent with the core principles of critical pedagogy discussed earlier. In many heated PARTY meetings, I argued that journal writing (and academic literacy skills generally) should be a non-negotiable aspect of the social justice class. D and Suli, on the other hand, took seriously the notion that critical pedagogy should be egalitarian and dialogical, supporting student knowledge and student agency in all circumstances. They did not accept that a teacher could impose a non-negotiable expectation on students in an undemocratic fashion— not while remaining true to the principles of critical pedagogy.

I realized then that my own role within the PARTY group also reflected the central paradox of critical pedagogy. I chose participatory action research and critical pedagogy as the guiding approach of PARTY, as a way of engaging youth in a democratic, egalitarian project for social change. I imagined the PARTY project would be transformative and liberatory for all participants and hoped that our work together would lead to meaningful change at the school or community level. I was committed to the principles of egalitarian decision making and critical pedagogy, sharing these explicitly with PARTY members and making a concerted attempt to implement them in our work together.

But in creating and facilitating PARTY, I also brought my own hidden agenda that mirrored the hidden agenda of critical pedagogy: I wanted the youth PARTY members to develop a critical consciousness similar to mine, *and* I wanted them to develop a commitment to academic achievement and skills that would enable them to access college and, ultimately, to achieve social mobility. When, despite our deepening collegial relationships, collaborative research, problem posing, and critical conversations, the PARTY members did not come to share my agenda in full, I was confused and disappointed, believing that I and the project had failed.

Yet the PARTY members never saw the project as a failure; they evaluated it highly and spoke of its transformative impact on their lives. It had not failed in their eyes because they had not brought a hidden agenda of convincing others to adopt their particular political and academic goals. They were satisfied to experiment with democratic decision making and democratic pedagogy, seeing what happened without being attached to a particular outcome.

Their actions and approaches more closely embodied the core principles of critical pedagogy than mine did, despite my status as a doctoral student specializing in critical pedagogy. I realized then that my intentions in starting the PARTY project were as deeply contradictory as were those of critical pedagogy. Did I *really* value the youth's local, subjugated knowledge? Or was acting like I did merely a better way to achieve my hidden agenda of replacing their perspectives on politics and schooling with mine? The answer to the first question was a resounding yes. But the answer to the second question was—and it troubled me to admit this—also a yes.

CONCLUSION

In reflecting on the outcomes of the PARTY project and the social justice class, I remain confident in my belief that school-based critical pedagogy should incorporate academic writing and skills building as a non-negotiable expectation, while at the same time pushing students to critique the narrow definition of those skills and the ways they are used to exclude and marginalize alternative ways of knowing or communicating (Delpit 1988; Tejeda et al. 2003). This is the two-tiered curriculum discussed earlier.

But rather than gloss over the challenges of realizing this two-tiered curriculum—or worse, pretending there is no deep theoretical contradiction embedded within it—I believe that theories of critical pedagogy must deal more substantively with the challenges of practice and engage seriously with the internal theoretical contradictions that they expose. Specifically, I believe that confronting the central paradox of critical pedagogy means confronting the essentially paternalistic nature of all education (Ellsworth 1989).

All education reflects the view that "I know what's good for you." The assertion that "writing in your journal is good for you" is no exception. It is difficult to reconcile this inevitable paternalism with the liberatory goals of critical pedagogy. But the experience of PARTY in the social justice class convinces me that it is important to do so in order to move toward a more practical theory of critical pedagogy that is rooted in practice and attuned to the realities of the compulsory classroom context.

In focusing on the limitations and contradictions of critical pedagogy, this chapter does not seek to discredit but rather to engage with and add to the literature on critical pedagogy. The purpose is to take one small step toward the development of a more practical theory of critical pedagogy, one that is informed by practice and takes into account the specific context of a high-poverty, urban "last chance" high school. Such a theory will inform future attempts to implement critical pedagogy in similar contexts and provide a more accurate understanding of the real, imagined, and potential role of public schooling in advancing the goals of social justice.

NOTES

1. The Frankfurt School of critical theory builds on Marxist social theory and Gramsci's theory of hegemony (1971) to illuminate how power operates in advanced capitalist societies, focusing on the realm of cultural institutions including schools. Giroux (1983) has been acknowledged as the first major work to connect the Frankfurt School of critical theory to the study of education and pedagogy in the United States (Kincheloe 2004; Morrow and Torres 1995). Giroux integrated critical theory, social reproduction theory (Bowles and Gintis 1976), and the pedagogy of the oppressed (1970/1999) to construct the notion of critical pedagogy. For a review of the Frankfurt School of critical theory and its implications for critical pedagogy, see Giroux (1983) and Kincheloe (2004).

2. The use of education as a tool for consciousness raising and political change is timeless. Many of these core principles of critical pedagogy overlap with principles in social movement theory (Morris and Mueller 1992), critical race theory (Ladson-Billings 2000), anticolonialist theory (Tejeda et al. 2003), Marxist and critical theory (Gramsci 1971), community organizing theory (Alinsky 1946), double-consciousness theory (DuBois 1903/1953), the popular education of the Highlander Center (Adams 1975), and the Danish folk schools movement (Hall 1978).

3. For an example outside the field of education see Dubois (1903/1953), Fanon (1963), Gaventa (1993), Collins (1990), and Delgado-Bernal (2002).

4. hooks (1989) writes about a similar tendency within feminist theory (pp. 35–41). In equating convoluted language and inaccessible texts with theoretical rigor, feminist scholars reproduce racist and colonialist assumptions about scholarship; they contribute to academic elitism within feminist studies departments and anti-intellectualism within the feminist movement. I believe this same bifur-cation (between academic elitism and anti-intellectualism) can be said of critical

pedagogy, distancing those who "theorize" from those who work primarily as educators, teachers, and activists. hooks writes: "Feminist theory is rapidly becoming another sphere of academic elitism, wherein work that is linguistically convoluted, which draws on other such works, is deemed more intellectually sophisticated, in fact is deemed more theoretical (since the stereotype of theory is that it is synonymous with that which is difficult to comprehend, linguistically convoluted) than work which is more accessible. Each time this happens, the radical, subversive potential of feminist scholarship and feminist theory in particular is undermined" (p. 36). Reflecting on the value of theory that is inaccessible, hooks concludes, "There is a place for theory that uses convoluted language, metalanguage, yet such theory cannot become the groundwork for feminist movement unless it is more accessible" (p. 39).

5. Such as: Bettie 2003; Eckert 1989; Fine 1991; MacLeod 1995; Ogbu 1987; Sefa Dei, Massuca, McIsaac, and Zine 1998; Willis 1977.

REFERENCES

Adams, F. (1975). *Unearthing Seeds of Fire: The Idea of Highlander*. Winston-Salem: John F. Blair.

Alinsky, S. (1946). *Reveille for Radicals*. Chicago: University of Chicago Press.

Apple, M. (1990). *Ideology and Curriculum*. New York: Routledge.

Bowles, S., and H. Gintis. (1976). *Schooling in Capitalist America*. New York: Basic Books.

Brint, S., and J. Karabel. (1989). *The Diverted Dream: Community Colleges and the Promise of Educational Opportunity, 1900–1985*. New York: Oxford University Press.

Collins, P. H. (1990). *Black Feminist Thought: Knowledge, Consciousness, and the Politics of Empowerment*. London: Harper Collins.

Delgado-Bernal, D. (2002). "Critical Race Theory, LatCrit Theory, and Critical Race-Gendered Epistemologies: Recognizing Students of Color as Holders and Creators of Knowledge." *Qualitative Inquiry, 8*(1), 105–26.

Delpit, L. (1988). "The Silenced Dialogue: Power and Pedagogy in Educating Other People's Children." *Harvard Educational Review, 58*(3), 280–98.

DuBois, W. E. B. (1903/1953). *The Souls of Black Folk*. New York: Fawcett.

Ellsworth, E. (1989). "Why Doesn't This Feel Empowering? Working Through the Repressive Myths of Critical Pedagogy." *Harvard Educational Review, 59*(3), 297–324.

Fanon, F. (1963). *The Wretched of the Earth*. New York: Grove Press.

Ferguson, A. A. (2000). *Bad Boys: Public School in the Making of Black Masculinity*. Ann Arbor: University of Michigan Press.

Freire, P. (1970/1999). *Pedagogy of the Oppressed*. New York: Continuum.

Freire, P., and D. Macedo. (1987). *Literacy: Reading the Word and the World*. Westport, CT: Bergin & Garvey.

Gaventa, J. (1993). "The Powerful, the Powerless, and the Experts: Knowledge Struggles in an Information Age." In P. Park, M. Brydon-Miller, B. Hall, and T. Jackson (eds.), *Voices of Change: Participatory Research in the United States and Canada* (pp. 21–40). Westport, CT: Bergin & Garvey.

Gee, J., G. Hull, and C. Lankshear. (1996). *The New Work Order: Behind the Language of the New Capitalism.* Boulder: Westview Press.

Giroux, H. (1983). *Theory and Resistance in Education: A Pedagogy for the Opposition.* South Hadley, MA: Bergin & Garvey.

Gramsci, A. (1971). *Selections from the Prison Notebooks.* London: Lawrence and Wishart.

Hall, B. (1978). "Continuity in Adult Education and Political Struggle." *Convergence, XI*(1).

hooks, b. (1989). *Talking Back: Thinking Feminist, Thinking Black.* Boston: South End Press.

———. (1990). *Yearning: Race, Gender, and Cultural Politics.* Boston: South End Press.

———. (1994). *Teaching to Transgress: Education as the Practice of Freedom.* New York: Routledge.

Horton, M., and P. Freire. (1990). *We Make the Road by Walking: Conversations on Education and Social Change.* Philadelphia: Temple University Press.

Kelly, D. M. (1993). *Last Chance High: How Girls and Boys Drop In and Out of Alternative Schools.* New Haven: Yale University Press.

Kincheloe, J. (2004). *Critical Pedagogy.* New York: Peter Lang.

Knight, T., and A. Pearl. (2000). "Democratic Education and Critical Pedagogy." *The Urban Review, 32*(3), 197–226.

Kohl, H. (1991). *I Won't Learn from You: The Role of Assent in Learning.* Minneapolis: Milkweed Editions.

Labaree, D. (1997). "Public Goods, Private Goods: The American Struggle over Educational Goals." *American Educational Research Journal, 34*(1), 39–81.

Ladson-Billings, G. (2000). "Racialized Discourses and Ethnic Epistemologies." In N. Denzin and Y. Lincoln (eds.), *Handbook of Qualitative Research* (2nd ed., pp. 257–77). Thousand Oaks: Sage Press.

McLaren, P. (2000). "Paulo Freire's Pedagogy of Possibility." In S. F. Steiner, M. Krank, P. McLaren, and R. Bahruth (eds.), *Freirean Pedagogy, Praxis, and Possibilities* (pp. 1–22). New York: Falmer Press.

Morris, A. D., and C. M. Mueller. (1992). *Frontiers in Social Movement Theory.* New Haven: Yale University Press.

Morrow, R. A., and C. A. Torres. (1995). *Social Theory and Education: A Critique of Theories of Social and Cultural Reproduction.* Albany: State University of New York Press.

Nieto, S. (1999). "Critical Multicultural Education and Students' Perspectives." In S. May (ed.), *Rethinking Multicultural and Antiracist Education: Towards Critical Multiculturalism.* London: Falmer Press.

Shor, I. (1992). *Empowering Education: Critical Teaching for Social Change.* Chicago: University of Chicago Press.

Sleeter, C. (1996). *Multicultural Education as Social Activism.* Albany: State University of New York Press.

Spring, J. (1991). *American Education: An Introduction to Social and Political Aspects.* New York: Longman.

Tejeda, C., M. Espinoza, and K. Gutierrez. (2003). "Social Justice Reconsidered: Toward a Decolonizing Pedagogy." In P. Trifonas (ed.), *Pedagogy of Difference: Rethinking Education for Social Change* (pp. 10–40). New York: Routledge.

Willis, P. (1974/1982). *Learning to Labour: How Working-Class Kids Get Working-Class Jobs.* New York: Columbia University Press.

Chapter 4

From Understanding to Application

The Difficulty of Culturally Responsive Teaching as a Beginning English Teacher

Melanie Shoffner, *Purdue University, Indiana*;
Matthew Brown, *South Carolina*

Beginning English teachers enter the classroom with the same responsibilities as veteran teachers (e.g., planning, grading, accommodating students' diverse needs) but with limited experiences, emerging knowledge, and developing skills (Lortie 2002). Overlaying these responsibilities is the relative isolation of new teachers (Rogers and Babinski 2002); the majority of an English teacher's day is spent as the sole adult in a classroom of adolescents, surrounded by the very people who often give rise to the questions and concerns percolating in new teachers' minds.

Aware of the challenges faced in the first years of teaching, English teacher educators work to address these issues in English education programs. Preservice English teachers take classes on young adult literature, multiculturalism, and child development; they write papers on literary theory, diversity, and motivation; they learn concepts like authorial intent, scaffolding, and the zone of proximal development. Well prepared in subject matter and pedagogy, new English teachers have a strong background with which to face the complexities of teaching, and leave their university eager to engage their knowledge and newfound skills in the secondary classroom.

What beginning English teachers often struggle with, however, is a different issue: the students before them. In their classrooms, they find some students grappling with issues far more important to them than well-scaffolded research projects or student-centered literature selections: "poverty, joblessness, low expectations, boredom, peer pressure, disaffection, lost opportunity, substance abuse, alienation, family disintegration, and, particularly for those who are poor or marginalized, the utter lack of prospects for the future" (Cochran-Smith 2003, p. 372).

New English teachers are somewhat cognizant such issues exist; experiences during student teaching and discussions in methods courses can prepare them to expect students to bring diverse issues to the classroom. Confident that they can teach regardless of student concerns, beginning English teachers often believe, despite teacher educators' efforts to alter their views, that "good teaching is transcendent; it is identical for all students and under all circumstances" (Gay 2000, p. 21).

Good English teaching, however, is more than a set of skills enacted on the students in a classroom, particularly when that classroom contains the diversity of students found in today's schools. It requires personal connection as well as professional competency, with effective teachers integrating both in the classroom (Shoffner 2009). This requires novice teachers to possess content and student knowledge, including an understanding of adolescents' social, emotional, physical, and intellectual development (Gomez, Allen, and Clinton 2004); an awareness of students' cultures, experiences, and needs (Banks et al. 2005); and a belief that students are individual human beings deserving of the opportunity to achieve on an academic and personal level (Cochran-Smith 2003).

Of singular importance, then, is the necessity for beginning English teachers to acknowledge and respond to the diversity of their students, taking into account "the different experiences and academic needs of a wide range of students as they plan and teach" (Banks et al. 2005, p. 233). Gay (2000) identifies this responsiveness as culturally responsive teaching; teachers use the "cultural knowledge, prior experiences, frames of reference, and performance styles of ethnically diverse students to make learning encounters more relevant to and effective for them" (p. 29). As culturally responsive teachers, English teachers can "read" their students in multiple ways, "cultivating [students'] cultural integrity, individual abilities, and academic success" (Gay 2000, p. 44).

At issue, however, is the ability of new English teachers—inexperienced in the profession, growing into their own identities as educators—to learn and enact that responsiveness at the beginning of their career. Teacher educators understand that the effective teacher develops over time, through intention, with experience (Darling-Hammond and Bransford 2005), yet beginning English teachers must still respond to the complex factors that direct their teaching and their students' learning when they first step into a classroom.

How can new English teachers push against their backgrounds, expectations, and beliefs to bridge the differences they face with their students? What happens when new English teachers face a classroom of students who are simply not like them? This chapter explores these questions from the perspectives of two educators, one a beginning secondary English teacher and the other an English teacher educator and former secondary English teacher.

Through personal narrative and reflective response, we explore the difficulties of developing into culturally responsive teachers and the tensions faced in that development. The resulting conversation allows us to investigate the disconnect of culturally responsive teaching as experienced in teacher preparation and the secondary English classroom.

CONTEXT OF THE AUTHORS

Matthew: I am finishing my second year as an English teacher at a predominantly African American high school in southeastern South Carolina. After graduating from Purdue University's English education program, I chose to look beyond my home state for this first teaching position. A middle-class White man born and raised in the Midwest, I wanted to see what other regions were like, what other people thought, how they spoke, and how they were different from me.

Ultimately I wanted a new experience. I chose South Carolina because it offered a challenge; with its poor reputation in education, I felt that teaching successfully there would allow me to do so anywhere. Before moving to the region, however, I admit that I knew very little about the state; my few visits in previous years had left an impression of a strong Southern accent and little else.

Melanie: A White working-class female from the South, I began my career in education as a secondary English teacher in a predominantly African American high school in central North Carolina. I am now an assistant professor of English education at Purdue University, preparing preservice teachers to teach at the secondary English level. Matthew was one of those preservice teachers three years ago and is now an educational colleague and a friend.

One element of teacher preparation is the concept of culturally responsive teaching, the enactment of which I continue to struggle to impart to my preservice teachers. I know from experience how important it is to incorporate students' backgrounds, abilities, and interests in the classroom, but it is difficult to make that knowledge relevant in a college classroom to preservice teachers so far removed from those students.

We do not pretend objectivity on the issue of developing as culturally responsive teachers. As secondary English teachers, past and present, our experiences support our interest, our backgrounds inform our understanding, and our subjectivities are shaped from the different facets of our identities. As

Glesne (1999) explains, "subjectivity is always a part of research" (p. 105), creating perspectives and insights that shape both exploration and presentation. Glesne (1999) believes, however—as do we—that when subjectivity is acknowledged and accepted,

> you learn more about your own values, attitudes, beliefs, interests, and needs. You learn that your subjectivity is the basis for the story that you are able to tell. It is a strength on which you build. It makes you who you are as a person and as a researcher, equipping you with perspectives and insights that shape all that you do as researcher, from the selection of topic clear through to the emphasis you make in your writing. (p. 109)

CULTURALLY RESPONSIVE TEACHING IN THE CLASSROOM

One of the most difficult realizations for many preservice English teachers is that they will be different from their students. They are older, ostensibly more mature, beginning a career; by virtue of their university degree, they have successfully navigated their past educational experiences; they are enthusiastic about issues of reading and writing; and they are often White, middle-class, and female. While the percentage of White women teachers is estimated at 85–90 percent in U.S. classrooms, "the students with whom they work have and will continue to become increasingly culturally, linguistically, and economically diverse" (Boyd et al. 2006, p. 334).

Imagine that difference magnified in the crucible of the classroom.

Melanie: I remember quite clearly the moment as a first-year teacher when I realized I was a White teacher in a classroom of Black students. It took some time for me to understand what that meant for my students, and I make no claims to have successfully navigated that issue even now, but it was a powerful moment of recognition.

I was not like them. They were not like me. For all that we shared, we were "different" and that meant something for my teaching and their learning. My ability to teach my students was dependent on my ability to see my students and I needed an understanding and acceptance of their culture, in all its forms, in order to do so.

Matthew: My experiences mirror Melanie's in many respects. My interactions, in and out of the classroom, have created the basis for some common ground with my students; we laugh about the same movies, enjoy some of the same music, even exercise together in the weight room after school. I feel like I am a presence at the school, someone the students interact with on a regular basis. Still, despite our commonalities, we are very different, and that difference is often difficult for me to overcome.

Although he does not speak for all beginning secondary English teachers, we feel Matthew's thoughts and experiences speak to the disconnect between understanding the concept of culturally responsive teaching and becoming a culturally responsive teacher. Like many beginning English teachers, he understands the concept of cultural responsiveness; he struggles, however, with how to move from the theory studied during preparation to the practice required for the classroom.

There is no easy answer to this disconnect. In my secondary English methods courses, I (Melanie) have tried to approach culturally responsive teaching with my preservice English teachers in numerous ways. I incorporate excerpts from the more theory-oriented works of Gay (2000), Nieto (1999), and Sleeter (2005), linking them to more practice-oriented works by Alsup and Bush (2003), Stairs (2007), and Thein, Beach, and Parks (2007).

I use former and current preservice teachers' personal narratives, individual experiences, and classroom observations to illustrate the connection of the theory to the practice. I include a classroom-based research project that asks preservice teachers to explore an educational issue of personal interest through theory and practice, those chosen issues often connected to culturally responsive teaching. I also attempt to model culturally responsive practices in my own instruction, supporting Boyd et al.'s (2006) imperative to "explicitly acknowledge and incorporate both [educators'] own and students' funds of knowledge" in the classroom (p. 343).

Once they enter the classroom, however, beginning teachers struggle to integrate cultural responsiveness into their teaching. Like so many concepts addressed during teacher preparation, culturally responsive teaching is most difficult at the praxis. As Matthew's narrative exemplifies, an English teacher's growth into a culturally responsive teacher is a difficult process. This difficulty in no way justifies teachers' dismissal of cultural responsiveness, but it does warrant consideration from both beginning English teachers and teacher educators. Simply put, we can teach culturally responsive teaching during university preparation, but we cannot ensure its enactment in the classroom.

This is not a situation particular to culturally responsive teaching, of course. Like all concepts, practices, and issues addressed during teacher preparation, once English teachers enter their classrooms, they are typically beyond the purview of teacher educators. At times, student-professor relationships extend beyond the university (such as my contact with Matthew and several others from his graduating class) and, in such circumstances, the teacher educator has the opportunity to support the beginning teacher's efforts with culturally responsive teaching in the classroom, by offering feedback, providing additional information, or serving as an objective sounding board.

Such relationships are grounded in personal choice, however, rather than institutional mandate. A formal support system between teacher educators and their former preservice teachers could assist beginning English teachers as they address difficult issues of teaching and learning, such as culturally responsive teaching, but English teacher educators would need to reconceptualize English teacher preparation in order to accommodate such long-term support.

Barring such a connection, beginning English teachers should develop the skills necessary to "rely solely on their own actions to solve problems, plan for the future, and grow as professionals" (McCann, Johannessen, and Ricca 2005, p. 137). Teacher educators must stress the importance of addressing problems, answering questions, and seeking perspective once English teacher enter the classroom. More importantly, they can teach preservice English teachers how to do so in the context of culturally responsive teaching by incorporating focused reflection into their preparation.

> As part of teacher preparation, preservice teachers will need to acknowledge both the limits of their personal knowledge as well as experience the privileges afforded them by virtue of their race and class. . . . While the demographic teacher population of the white, middle-class female will often have to cross more distinct boundaries, other preservice teachers who are more linguistically, culturally, racially, and socioeconomically aligned with an increasingly diverse student population will have to engage in making the familiar strange and the strange familiar. (Boyd et al. 2006, p. 336)

Matthew: A "Strange" Community

My school has a 90 percent free and reduced lunch enrollment, so the poverty level in this area is hard to ignore. I see where my students are living as I drive through the neighborhoods and the back roads. I notice when many of my students wear the same clothes several days in a row. When I drive down the main stretch of the town, which has a population of roughly 7,000, I am literally one block away from some of the most depressed and depressing neighborhoods I've ever seen.

It seems almost every other house has a caved-in roof, boarded or barred windows, and paint peeling from the exteriors. There are overgrown yards behind ragged chain-link fences, broken-down and rusted-out cars, and graffiti slapped across sheds, garages, and even some of the houses. These are all houses that my students live in. I often think to myself, "What is it about this place that makes people want to live here? What is it that keeps people here?"

I realize this is all my students have known, and sometimes I fear they don't know they can do something different with their lives. Even the ones who do want something different don't realize the difficulties of what they want. Each semester, I ask my students to respond to the journal topic, "What do you hope to do after high school?" Many of them respond that they want to go to college, although they aren't certain what they will do past that. To me, that says they know there is something out there they might discover and it's fine for them not to have the answers right now.

The majority of my students, however, tell me they want to be rappers, professional basketball or football players, or forensic scientists. They do have goals. I see that many do consider something different, but the majority of my students don't seem to realize how unrealistic their plans are considering their current academic performance or their athletic ability. They might be dedicated to their goals, but I don't see my students concentrating on how to accomplish them or what they might fall back on if their plans fail.

The South is very family-oriented. I notice constantly—in the school and the community—that so many people in this small town are related. Even through distant lines, the families are still able to trace the family tree. When everyone is so close-knit and the students know that I am not one of them, it makes it difficult to assimilate into the community. The lack of my own personal family ties to this area isn't the only thing separating me, of course. The things that I learned as morally sound or socially acceptable differ greatly from the things I see here and the things students share with me. Sometimes, it's a challenge to understand what the standard for values is here.

Students, of course, act differently in the school setting than they do outside it; popularity and teenage rebellion may not look the same outside school walls. I realize students don't always behave the same way in front of their parents as they do in school, so their questionable behavior may not be so easy to see. I'm always surprised at the transformation in my students during meetings with parents, however.

In my first year, I arranged a meeting with "Myron" and his mother to discuss his classroom behavior and academic performance. In class, Myron was nothing but troublesome; he constantly disrupted class activities, talked back when he was called out for violating expressed, posted, and reiterated classroom policies, and either refused to turn in homework or submitted homework copied from classmates.

When he came to the meeting, however, he was nothing but polite; he kept his eyes down, responded to every question respectfully and finished every response with "no, sir" or "yes, ma'am." Needless to say, his mother accused me of making up Myron's misbehavior and poor work; my reports of his classroom problems were completely inconsistent with what she knew and saw sitting beside her. In her eyes, Myron was simply misunderstood by his teacher.

Still, it seems to me that the values held by so many of the students are in stark contrast to those instilled in me. A fellow teacher overheard some male students bragging about how many girls they had gotten pregnant. Female students bring their two- and three-week old babies to football games and pass them around like novelties. In my first year, nine of my freshmen and sophomore students were pregnant or already had a child. I try not to judge, but it's still shocking to me that this appears to be the norm in this community.

In my first few months here, I had a conversation with a student about his older brother who had not finished high school. He was talking about how his brother had landed a job at a local gas station and that he was making good money. I asked him how much—out of curiosity for the economic situation people faced in the community—and he proudly responded with, "$8 an hour." I also learned that he was supporting a wife and two children on his salary.

I admire that this student looks up to his older brother, but I cannot imagine that seeing his older brother scrape by on that salary wouldn't motivate him to try harder, to finish high school, and make it possible to do better for himself. To me—and granted, I come from a different background—that would be all the incentive in the world to do better. That's a good salary if you're a high school student with few financial responsibilities, but I can only imagine that a 20-something trying to support a family on that amount is incredibly difficult.

Melanie: Reflection

Teachers can be so different from their students that their perspective seems mutually incompatible with their students' perspectives. Culturally responsive teaching indicates that, to function effectively as a teacher of diverse populations, secondary English teachers must accept different perspectives in the classroom: that of the teacher and those of the students. Neither party can bring enough to the classroom separately. As Boyd et al. (2006) remind us, there are limits to both knowledge and experience. Collectively, however, teachers and students can work together to cross those limitations and create a successful learning environment.

When Matthew looks at the community surrounding his school, he is quite aware of different perspectives. He sees issues of family, morality, and poverty creating the greatest divide between himself and his students. His personal knowledge and past experiences do not coincide with those of his students; to his eyes, there is a clear difference between what this community values and what he values. His statement that he is "not one of them" clearly articulates his place as an outsider in the community.

Yet how do issues of race fit into the divide? As a White teacher in a predominantly African American community, it would be disingenuous to believe race does not contribute to Matthew's alienation from the local community. He is quite clearly not one of them, being a White man recently arrived from the Midwest. Moreover, it would be naïve to believe that Matthew is not viewing these issues of family, morality, and poverty partly through a deficit lens, placing an "intrinsic worth" (Nieto 1999, p. 32) on his students' actions and choices.

When teachers judge a community, they are placing value on the choices made by that community's inhabitants; when the teacher is different from the community, it may be easier to place a negative value on those choices. As Matthew admits, he struggles to understand the values in his new community when they ostensibly support something he does not condone, such as teen pregnancy.

Boyd et al. (2006) believe the preparation of culturally responsive teachers can address the very issues facing Matthew. During teacher preparation, preservice teachers must examine the limitations of their knowledge and experience on their conceptions of teaching. They must also interrogate how issues of race and class—as well as gender, language, and other forms of identity—have contributed to known and unknown privilege.

However personal knowledge and privilege are addressed at the university, teacher educators are expecting preservice teachers to understand the influence of these elements without the context of their future classrooms, perhaps an unfair expectation. In my methods courses, for example, I use reflection journals, directed reading assignments, and class discussion to explore these elements with my secondary preservice English teachers. Based on his comments, did I do enough to prepare Matthew for his classroom?

Matthew appears cognizant that his personal knowledge has limits, accepting that his background may not have prepared him to understand his new community. Like many beginning teachers, however, he believes in the power of education to triumph over the issues faced by his students rather than the educational system's power to both construct and reinforce those same issues. I can understand Matthew's limited understanding as a beginning teacher new to the community.

As he noted above, he is an outsider to the area, still trying to make sense of community standards and values; at the same time, he is trying to construct his teaching experiences—classroom instruction, relationships with students, interactions with the local community—into a coherent framework for himself. Difference is hard to understand, however, especially when a new teacher is bound so tightly to a particular understanding. Matthew sees the community of his students through a specific lens, one that allows him to acknowledge the "strangeness" of the community around him but creates few opportunities to make that strangeness familiar.

The onus is on him, as the teacher, to step outside what he knows and place himself firmly in what he does not. For Matthew to combat the strangeness of his new community, he must purposefully (and humbly) try to learn from his students, his fellow teachers, and his community, and attempt to translate that learning into a more culturally responsive classroom practice. This could stem from something as simple as taking part in community activities and interacting with students in their own environment. Matthew mentioned attending a local church's fish fry one weekend with a fellow teacher. Besides expressing a newfound appreciation for hushpuppies, he mentioned the opportunity to interact with certain students outside the confines of the classroom.

I would not claim that Matthew developed any profound insights on cultural responsiveness from the evening's activity but, for once, he placed himself firmly in his students' environment. By interacting with them as individuals, rather than generic students, he has an opening to respond to that individuality in his classroom. Matthew must do more than recognize that opening, however; he must try to incorporate his emerging understanding in his teaching and accept that he may fail.

He might talk to fellow teachers, question former professors, seek out practitioner examples and explore educational texts; he might use reflection as a tool to examine his ideas and his efforts; he might ask students for feedback; he might immerse himself more fully in the community outside the school. In the end, however, Matthew must acknowledge his limitations and purposefully seek to move past them in order to do more than pay lip service to his efforts at culturally responsive teaching.

Students are not empty vessels, nor tabulae rasae, to be filled with knowledge. On the contrary, they bring with them rich and varied languages, cultural experiences, and practices . . . the rich experiences of children of diverse backgrounds often go unrecognized or undervalued. (Boyd et al. 2006, p. 337)

Matthew: Students as Individuals

There doesn't seem to be much planning for the future with the majority of my students. They live to be popular, and popularity comes from acting out in class, defying the teachers, and failing classes because it isn't "cool" to do otherwise. I understand that students are supposed to be thinking of themselves and what they want; their lives are theirs. They're trying to become independent, to get out from under their parents—I get that. It makes sense that they need to challenge teachers and exercise their individuality, at some level, but it's hard to understand the resistance my fellow teachers and I face from so many students every day.

A colleague of mine with 40 years of teaching experience says that students are only interested in the five Fs: fighting, food, friends, fashion, and fornication. It's an entertaining insight, but a walk through the hallways supports its truth to me. I see students without much money spending what they do have on expensive jackets, shoes, jewelry, tattoos, and hairstyles. Some students complain about not having money for school materials, but they're wearing $175 shoes.

These are the same students I see with new tattoos, designer clothing, expensive watches, and gold and silver grills over their teeth. One of my students loudly asserted that she didn't have the money to purchase a book for a weekly free reading activity. The week after, she came to class with a new tattoo stretching down the length of her arm.

Many students expect to be rewarded for the littlest tasks or receive praise for mediocrity. They expect to be rewarded at every turn and that reward is only good if it is something automatic and tangible. Obviously, those expectations run contrary to those of the faculty and administration. As educators, we expect good work; we expect students to think for themselves; we expect some level of moral and ethical behavior. Students may have expectations, but they certainly don't seem to agree with those held by the teachers.

Melanie: Reflection

If culturally responsive teaching rests on recognizing and valuing the differences students bring to the classroom, English teachers must see students as full individuals rather than empty adolescents and respond to the many elements that contribute to their individuality. This is a delicate task, requiring teachers to understand the many ways complex issues manifest differently in the lives of their students. Matthew recognizes many of the issues facing his students, but he interprets them through his own lenses of experiences, maturity, and belief, inscribing his understanding of the issues onto his students' practices.

For example, Matthew identifies money as an important issue for his students. Seeing the effects of local poverty on a daily basis, he accepts that his students may not have the funds to buy supplemental literature or poster board for class assignments. During university preparation, preservice English teachers are reminded—and accept without complaint—that they will need to have extra supplies on hand for those students who cannot afford their own. This acceptance is difficult for Matthew to offer, however, when his students' lifestyles seem to contradict their claims of poverty.

In fact, students' lifestyles contradict much of what Matthew holds in high regard. Through actions and words, he sees his students demonstrating that they care little for their education and more for their image. To his credit, he understands that much of their defiance comes from being adolescents; by challenging the status quo, his students are making sense of their world and finding a place for themselves.

However, what Matthew fails to understand is that his world is not the world of his students. By constantly evaluating his students' choices against his own, he dismisses the differences that have shaped his students' outlook on their education. As Apple (1995) explains, students have every reason to resist institutions that give differential treatment to and provide disparate opportunities on the basis of their race and class.

Matthew's views of his students' actions and behaviors—that they only value tangible rewards or lack respect for their teachers—are predicated on values and beliefs that create a "deficit syndrome" as explanation (Gay 2000, p. 23). With this viewpoint, students are understood by what they do not have and cannot do.

Gay (2000) explains that underachieving African American students are often credited with multiple "deficits": "lack of self-esteem; inadequate homes and prior preparation; poor parenting skills and low parental participation in the schooling process; lack of language development; poor academic interests, aspirations, and motivation; few opportunities for cultural enrichment; [and] high truancy and absentee rates" (p. 24).

These deficits are the qualities Matthew sees when he looks at his students, rather than the personal and cultural strengths, intellectual capabilities, and prior accomplishments they do bring (Gay 2000). In some respects, Matthew's focus on his students' deficits is reinforced by an educational system predicated on very specific ways of teaching and learning, ways that do not honor diverse student populations. "When a significant difference exists between the students' culture and the school's culture, teachers can easily misread students' aptitudes, intents, or abilities as a result of the difference in styles of language use and interactional patterns" (Delpit 1995, p. 167).

Culturally responsive teaching asks that English teachers recognize and respond to the influences and strengths of students' culture while acknowledging the individuality of each student. The difficulty, of course, is avoiding the stereotypes and value judgments often associated with individual views of culture. Teacher preparation seeks to upend those stereotypes, typically through classes on multiculturalism and discussions of diversity.

Interactions with parents and members of culturally diverse communities can also assist with dispelling stereotypes and broadening understandings of culture in students' lives (Delpit 1995). The opportunity to observe and student teach in diverse classrooms should also be a component of teacher preparation, with preservice English teachers engaged in focused inquiry during their practica on issues supporting culturally responsive teaching. The goal of all such activities must be to push preservice English teachers beyond generalized information about culture to consideration of its place in students' lives and educational experiences.

Once in the classroom, however, these former preservice teachers must enact their university-based (and emerging) understanding of culturally responsive teaching. They must use classroom curriculum and daily instruction to respond to students as the separate individuals they are rather than the generic mass of students they often appear to be. An English classroom provides a splendid platform for such responsiveness. Students' apparent interest in outward image and identity, for example (as Matthew identified through his students' tattoos and clothes), might be an entry point into works like Fitzgerald's *The Great Gatsby*, Morrison's *The Bluest Eye*, or Yang's *American Born Chinese*.

Matthew also noted his students' adolescent need for instant gratification and continuous rewards. He might approach these concepts indirectly through literature as diverse as Hansberry's *A Raisin in the Sun*, Anderson's *Feed*, Miller's *The Crucible*, or the speeches of Churchill, Gandhi, and Martin Luther King, Jr. Themes like respect, popularity, and independence are commonly found in literature—even more so in students' lives.

Matthew might respond to his students' understandable struggle with these issues by teaching the poetry of Gwendolyn Brooks, Walt Whitman, and Edwin Arlington Robinson, and the music of Johnny Cash, Mary J. Blige, or Lauryn Hill. By making an effort to see through the outer trappings and look beyond the constructed persona of students in the classrooms, English teachers have the opportunity to respond to their students and engage their minds, using a variety of traditional and alternative texts. "To recognize students' funds of knowledge requires unrestrained respect for them as well as ourselves" (Boyd et al. 2006, p. 338).

Matthew: Being "Educated"

Education does not seem to be a priority for most families here, which directly contrasts with what I expected. I expected that students would learn, that parents would be involved, and that I would make connections with all of them. During my interview at the school, the administration talked about the 95 percent graduation rate and the parents being nuisances because they were so involved with their students' lives. During my first year, however, roughly 80 percent of one of my freshman classes had a failing grade at the end of the first semester.

I teach in an area known as the Corridor of Shame, a stretch of schools and communities along Interstate 95 with low success rates and a high percentage of students scoring at or below basic on standardized tests in core subjects. The schools reportedly suffer from a lack of funding; claims are made that the schools do not have the appropriate facilities and resources to keep the children challenged and focused. That may be true in some cases, but we have a functioning building, with SMARTboards and digital televisions in nearly every classroom, a well-stocked library, computer labs, Internet access, and even laptops for checkout if the computer labs are full. Lack of resources isn't the reason for our students' failure.

I heard a State Board of Education member say recently, "These students want to learn. You can see it in their eyes that they want to learn. We need to provide the proper environment for them to reach their highest potential possible." The problem with comments like that is how detached the people making them are from what is really going on in the schools. Some are more involved in the schools than others, but more often than not they are secondhand recipients of their information. Regardless, facilities do not make schools successful; the quality of the teachers and the quality of the students' work do.

The major problem that I see is motivation. I looked up the breakdown of the freshman class recently; about 150 of 200 students in the ninth grade failed at least one core class. In my classes, it doesn't seem to faze students when they earn Fs and zeros for assignments. Students are held back a year and repeat classes two or three times, and it isn't an issue when they end up spending five or six years in high school.

I have students who leave multiple-choice questions blank on a test. They would rather take a zero than simply guess and give it a go. They aren't motivated when teachers tell them they can do better if they try, that they will have better futures if they apply themselves in high school. It doesn't seem to make a difference. It seems like, if it isn't handed to them, it's not worthwhile.

Melanie: Reflection

One of the concepts stressed in my methods courses is Valenzuela's (1999) concept of subtractive schooling, that schools may "take away" more from certain students than they purport to "add." Valenzuela's (1999) research explains that schools "are organized formally and informally in ways that fracture students' cultural and ethnic identities, creating social, linguistic, and cultural divisions among students and between the students and the staff" (p. 5).

To preservice English teachers who believe in the power of education, this is a contradictory idea, one that is often very difficult to grasp. How can their classrooms, which offer so much, take away from students who seem to have so little? They believe in education as a way to provide opportunity for students and equalize the disparity students must face outside school walls. With this perspective, preservice English teachers see their future teaching as transformative for the students in their classroom—as they should. Teaching is an act of change, requiring teachers to believe in their ability to reach students on some level in order to teach them.

Matthew has retained his belief in education as opportunity for his students. If they learn, if they apply themselves, they have the opportunity to change their lives. There is nothing subtractive about his classroom, in his view, because his teaching offers students options that do not appear to exist in their current lives. Working in tandem with this view of the classroom is Matthew's ability to teach (and reach) students. By making teacher-student connections, he should be able to support his students' learning and help them make changes in their lives. When his students appear to resist that learning, their actions read like a dismissal of education as an opportunity, implying Matthew's failure as a teacher to reach them.

When the teacher is so different from his students, however, it can be difficult for teaching to be a transformative act, simply because the concept of transformation is suspect on both sides. Change can bring addition as well as loss, imply positive as well as negative. As a teacher, Matthew sees the necessary materials in his school and his desire to educate students as positive factors; if they are willing to learn, students can move on to college, leave the community, and better themselves.

Students, however, may bring a different perspective to the situation, questioning the teacher's efforts from the viewpoint of loss. Does the effort to make them *better* imply that they are currently *not good*? Do school facilities, classroom resources, or teacher involvement support any of their current interests or future intentions? Is any value placed on what they—as individuals, as a community—bring to their education? Is there any point in playing by the teacher's rules when the world as they know it doesn't conform to the teacher's beliefs in fair play, equal opportunity, and social mobility?

When teachers regard students as deficient when they enter the classroom, it is extremely difficult to value students' languages, cultural experiences, and practices. When teachers see little motivation in students' eyes or actions, it is exceptionally difficult to recognize the worth of diverse backgrounds in the classroom. Culturally responsive teaching tells us we must acknowledge students' funds of knowledge and respect what they can bring to their own education. Yet the differences between teachers' and students' perspectives on education often create a disconnect that neither can easily bridge in the classroom.

With such a disconnect, it seems the effort at connection lies with the teacher. As adult and educator, the teacher must strive to look past the shading of personal beliefs and experiences and accept his students' differently colored reality. Matthew does not need to replicate his students' beliefs and experiences in order to validate the existence of such difference. He does, however, need to accept that his students may view their time in his classroom from perspectives on education, learning, and future opportunities that differ significantly from his own.

At its most simplistic, Matthew needs to filter what he sees and feels through his students' lenses rather than his own—rather than interpret their willingness to "take a zero" on a test as lack of motivation, for instance, he should consider and accept other reasons for a student's seeming apathy, from lack of study time to lack of comprehension to lack of self-worth to lack of agreement with the purposes of schooling. There is nothing simple about such an exercise in perspective taking, of course; by considering any situation he faces, Matthew may come to understand his students' perspective or solidify his own interpretation of events.

Like any educator, he needs support for his efforts to grow as a responsive teacher. That support might come through focused conversations with fellow teachers or intentional interactions with other educators; it might also come from graduate study at a university, personal study on the weekends, or professional study at a conference. Any efforts at support, however, must be grounded in an authentic wish to grow and act as a culturally responsive teacher; and that wish, in turn, must be established and nurtured during teacher preparation.

Personal awareness and empathic feelings about ethnic and cultural diversity without accompanying pedagogical actions do not lead to instructional improvements for students of color. Positive recognition of and attitudes toward ethnic and cultural diversity are necessary but not sufficient for dealing effectively with the educational needs and potentialities of ethnically diverse students. (Gay 2000, p. 209)

Matthew: Culturally Responsive Teaching

Being aware of who students are outside of school isn't the same for a teacher as being prepared to teach specific content. Granted, both are necessary, but a teacher who knows where the students come from and does something with that information will do more for them than a teacher who teaches English without any regard for students' home lives or after-school jobs.

To make learning meaningful to my students, I have to identify where the students come from, who they are, how they formed their opinions and attitudes, and make connections with that. The challenge is to do it in a way that is respectful, accessible, and effective. The complication I face is that because I know so little of my students, I find it difficult to answer so many of my questions: Why don't these students read? Why do so many of these students fail? Why haven't the parents taught them differently? Why do so many of them resist authority so much?

On the other hand, I wonder if I can ever know where they come from. Just because I see where they live and what they face doesn't mean I can respond to them in my teaching. I hate the idea of teaching a book by an African American author simply because my students happen to be Black; I feel that defeats the purpose of literature. At the same time, I wonder, when we are reading novels by White authors in class, if my Black students can identify with the characters in the stories.

I've taught a range of literature in my classes: *Romeo and Juliet, Macbeth, The Contender, Great Expectations, A Separate Peace, Flowers for Algernon, Across Five Aprils, Lord of the Flies*, etc. In only one of these stories was the major character a person of color. The students were very receptive to *The Contender*, but I don't think it had anything to do with the main character's race.

They couldn't really identify with his living in New York City or training to become a boxer. They did respond to the fact that he was raised by a single parent and came from a relatively poor background, though. There was also drug use in the novel, and some students verbally identified with those particular sequences. I found it interesting to see their reactions when we finished the novel; some students—those who typically have the lowest grades and the least interest in the class—responded so positively to reading it.

Recently I was preparing my tenth-grade class for the High School Assessment Program exam, which they need to pass to graduate from high school.

The topic was formal and informal language. Despite several textbook examples, they couldn't make the distinction between the two. While I was wondering what more to offer them, something clicked. I closed the book and walked to the board to give them one more example. While I was writing, I said, "Okay. This is language I hear every day at the beginning of class. I'm not trying to offend you or embarrass you, but I think this will help you understand." I wrote the following:

Formal Language:
   My friend, Tyrice, was wearing some clothes that made him look very stylish.
Informal Language:
   Tyrice, man, that nigga look fresh in his threads, 'bo.

I explained that, in everyday conversation, I expect to hear people using slang, but when it comes to speaking and writing formally, I—as well as other teachers, employers, and college admission committees—expect people to use standard English. That example finally worked. I felt like they made the connection because I used the language they know and use every day in the hallway, and they finished up the lesson with some good examples of their own.

Melanie: Reflection

Culturally responsive teaching is a complex practice with multiple character-istics guiding its enactment in the classroom; as Gay (2000) reminds us, that practice requires both recognition of diversity and pedagogical responsive-ness to that diversity in the classroom. Matthew can articulate the basic con-cepts of culturally responsive teaching: awareness of and respect for students' culture demonstrated through personal interaction and classroom instruction. He can also relate those concepts to his pedagogy: when he questions his stu-dents' connection to the literature he chooses for study, when he tries to bring his conception of relevant examples into his student learning.

Some may dismiss his pedagogical efforts as superficial—as, perhaps, does he—but they highlight an important point. Matthew may understand the definition of culturally responsive teaching, but he struggles to translate that definition into his own teaching. Perhaps the most telling point in Mat-thew's narrative is his realization that he knows enough to know he doesn't know enough about his students. He wants to connect his students' culture to the classroom; he understands the difficulty of making connections in meaningful ways; and he questions how to gain the information and apply it successfully.

Awareness of culture as an instructional issue is not enough, as Gay (2000) explains, but it is a first step if accompanied by action. Where Matthew falters—as do many beginning teachers—is the action accompanying his realization; while he asks compelling questions, he must try to follow his questions with equally compelling action.

Matthew's questions are indeed difficult. He concentrates on the "why" rather than the "how" or the "what," questioning issues that have created careers for educators and researchers as they examine possible answers. To take just one: why don't his students read? Is it an issue of ability, effort, time, engagement, choice, rebellion, or something else entirely? Would his Black students read if the literature included more Black protagonists, or addressed issues related to a Southern community, or dealt with themes connected to adolescence? Culturally responsive teaching means Matthew must consider all of these responses as pedagogical action, depending on none of them as answers.

Determining what action to take should lead a secondary English teacher back to culturally responsive instructional practices. From the use of literature circles to the study of young adult literature to the incorporation of performance, beginning English teachers have various means to respond to cultural difference in their teaching. They must be willing to try different methods, however, changing direction if necessary and working outside their comfort zone in order to meet the learning needs of their students.

They must also be able to sort through the multiple cultural, academic, social, and emotional issues at play in the classroom to enact those methods. This requires a great deal of flexibility and responsiveness from beginning English teachers—as well as support for their efforts and commiseration at their failings from teachers who value the goals of culturally responsive teaching.

PREPARING CULTURALLY RESPONSIVE TEACHERS

There is no simple response to the question of how to prepare beginning English teachers for culturally responsive teaching. Gay (2000), for example, recommends that teacher education programs should require preservice teachers to gain information about culture characteristics and contributions, pedagogical principles, and methods and material for ethnic and cultural diversity.

This knowledge should be complemented with learning experiences for teacher education students to critically examine existing paradigms of educational thought and practice to determine whether they can be modified to accommodate ethnic and cultural diversity, or if they need to be replaced. These analyses should be supplemented with supervised practices in designing and implementing replacement models. (p. 210)

She continues with suggestions for practicing teachers who are developing as culturally responsive teachers: staff development, instructional materials, constructive feedback, and recognition, additional activities comparable to culturally responsive teaching and techniques for dealing with opposition.

To a teacher educator, this is a daunting list of skills, knowledge, and actions for any teacher; to a beginning teacher, this is a seemingly over-whelming addition to the other skills, knowledge, and actions required for classroom teaching. Gay does concede the challenge and struggle of enact-ing culturally responsive teaching, as well as the complexity of integrating the care, competence, confidence, and conviction necessary for improving education for diverse students. Challenge and complexity are not reasons for dismissing the need for culturally responsive teaching, however, but an acknowledgment that the enactment of cultural responsiveness is a difficult and continuous effort.

In fact, the challenge of preparing teachers for the classroom is supported by teacher educators in the consistent reminder that learning to teach is a lifelong process; "teachers continually construct new knowledge and skills in practice throughout their careers rather than acquiring a finite set of knowl-edge and skills in their totality before entering the classroom" (Bransford, Darling-Hammond, and LePage 2005, p. 3).

Culturally responsive teaching, specifically, requires a breadth of knowl-edge and a depth of understanding of students, pedagogy, self, and com-munity that few teachers can assimilate in the early years of their career. Additionally, "if the information needed to teach well emerges during the practice itself, then learning how to think and act professionally is unusually difficult at the start of a teaching career" (Hammerness et al. 2005, p. 375). The difficulty of culturally responsive teaching is something that beginning English teachers can (and should) work toward in their classrooms, but we do them a disservice when we fault them for not achieving it immediately upon entering the profession.

Teacher educators can, however, create a foundation for beginning English teachers that allows them to develop and support the knowledge and skills needed to develop as culturally responsive teachers. Certainly, there are numerous ways to go about constructing such a foundation, but we focus on two specific approaches here. The first is the development of reflective prac-tice during teacher preparation, and the second is the continued connection between beginning English teachers and university instructors.

Reflection has long been connected to a wide range of benefits for prac-ticing teachers: the ability to question and consider issues of teaching and learning (Spalding and Wilson 2002); the development and refinement of dif-ferent perspectives (Loughran 2002); the consideration of multiple influences and contexts on classroom teaching (Liston and Zeichner 1990); and the acceptance of the emotional aspects of teaching (Shoffner 2009). A reflective teacher is one who is "aware of and questions the assumptions and values he or she brings to teaching [and] is attentive to the institutional and cultural contexts in which he or she teaches" (Zeichner and Liston 1996, p. 6), both features of culturally responsive teaching.

During teacher preparation, preservice English teachers need a range of opportunities to engage in reflective practice in order to draw clear connections between reflection and effective teaching. Moreover, preservice English teachers need specific opportunities to engage in reflection connected to issues associated with culturally responsive teaching.

Such opportunities might include collaborative reflection on case studies exemplifying issues of cultural responsiveness, individual reflection on readings addressing issues of student diversity and teaching, informal reflection (Shoffner 2008) on past experiences with and reactions to cultural difference, and/or formal reflection on approaches to teaching and learning that value and support multiculturalism. By building a foundation for reflection during teacher preparation, teacher educators are supporting the growth of reflective English teachers. This, in turn:

> signifies a recognition that the process of learning to teach continues throughout a teacher's entire career, a recognition that no matter how good a teacher education program is, at best, it can only prepare teachers to begin teaching . . . [and support] a commitment by teachers to internalize the disposition and skills to study their teaching and become better at teaching over time. (Zeichner and Liston 1996, p. 6)

Included in a list of suggestions to improve English teacher preparation, McCann, Johannessen, and Ricca (2005) suggest that teacher education programs maintain contact with beginning teachers after they have graduated and entered the classroom. Rather than an evaluative connection, teacher educators and beginning teachers should engage in conversations that focus on the teacher's experiences, needs, and general welfare.

In effect, McCann et al. (2005) support the importance of personal professional connections during the (often isolating) early years of teaching. This connection provides a forum for beginning English teachers to explore their efforts in culturally responsive teaching with supportive, knowledgeable, and interested others; questions and concerns about their classroom teaching are directed not to administrators or colleagues who may stand in judgment but to former instructors who played a role in developing their awareness of and responsiveness to cultural issues in the classroom.

This is by no means an easy role for teacher educators to play—for numerous reasons—but one that clearly indicates the importance of supporting beginning English teachers in their efforts to become culturally responsive teachers and the acceptance that learning to teach is a continuous and collaborative process. If beginning English teachers have "intelligent, positive, and supportive colleagues, in and out of school, they have brighter hope for the future and greater expectations for success" (McCann et al. 2005, p. 162).

We openly acknowledge the difficulty of developing as a culturally responsive teacher. Matthew's narrative often demonstrates that understanding the basic concepts of culturally responsive teaching does not guarantee the application of those concepts in pedagogy or belief. As a teacher educator—and Matthew's former professor—I could (and sometimes do) despair at the disconnect, but I see that as a simplistic reaction to a complex issue.

Beginning English teachers are still forming their understandings of education when they step into a classroom, adjusting to the complex factors that influence their teaching and their students' learning. For many, they are also pushing against societal and cultural backgrounds that create differences between themselves and their students. Despite the urgency of the issue, developing the skills, knowledge, and beliefs required of a culturally responsive teacher requires time, opportunity, and intent.

As Gay (2000) reminds us, culturally responsive teaching is effective only when teachers possess the requisite cultural knowledge and instructional skills, self-reflection and self-monitoring techniques, and institutional and personal resources to support their efforts. Rather than expecting beginning English teachers to enter the classroom with these attributes or to develop them as a matter of course, teacher educators must focus more specifically on the many issues surrounding culturally responsive teaching.

We see reflection and communication between teachers and teacher educators not as sweeping solutions to the many issues addressed in this chapter, but rather as practices that may mitigate the disconnect of culturally responsive teaching between teacher preparation and classroom teaching while supporting the efforts of beginning English teachers to enact such teaching in their own classrooms.

REFERENCES

Alsup, J., and J. Bush. (2003). *"But Will It Work with Real Students?": Scenarios for Teaching Secondary English Language Arts*. Urbana, IL: National Council of Teachers of English.

Apple, M. W. (1995). *Education and Power* (2nd ed.). New York: Routledge.

Banks, J., M. Cochran-Smith, L. Moll, A. Richert, K. Zeichner, P. LePage, et al. (2005). "Teaching Diverse Learners." In L. Darling-Hammond and J. Bransford (eds.), *Preparing Teachers for a Changing World: What Teachers Should Learn and Be Able to Do* (pp. 232–74). San Francisco: Jossey-Bass.

Boyd, F. B., M. Ariail, R. Williams, K. Jocson, G. T. Sachs, K. McNeal, et al. (2006). "Real Teaching for Real Diversity: Preparing English Language Arts Teachers for the 21st-Century Classroom." *English Education, 38*, 329–50.

Bransford, J., L. Darling-Hammond, and P. LePage. (2005). "Introduction." In L. Darling-Hammond and J. Bransford (eds.), *Preparing Teachers for a Changing World: What Teachers Should Learn and Be Able to Do* (pp. 1–39). San Francisco: Jossey-Bass.

Cochran-Smith, M. (2003). "Sometimes It's *Not* about the Money: Teaching and Heart." *Journal of Teacher Education, 54*, 371–75.

Darling-Hammond, L., and J. Bransford (eds.). (2005). *Preparing Teachers for a Changing World: What Teachers Should Learn and Be Able to Do.* San Francisco: Jossey-Bass.

Delpit, L. (1995). *Other People's Children: Cultural Conflict in the Classroom.* New York: Norton.

Gay, G. (2000). *Culturally Responsive Teaching: Theory, Research, and Practice.* New York: Teachers College Press.

Glesne, C. (1999). *Becoming Qualitative Researchers: An Introduction* (2nd ed.). New York: Longman.

Gomez, M. L., A. R. Allen, and K. Clinton. (2004). "Cultural Models of Care in Teaching: A Case Study of One Pre-service Secondary Teacher." *Teaching and Teacher Education, 20*, 473–88.

Hammerness, K., L. Darling-Hammond, J. Bransford, D. Berliner, M. Cochran-Smith, M. McDonald, et al. (2005). "How Teachers Learn and Develop." In L. Darling-Hammond and J. Bransford (eds.), *Preparing Teachers for a Changing World: What Teachers Should Learn and Be Able to Do.* San Francisco: Jossey-Bass.

Liston, D. P., and K. M. Zeichner. (1990). "Reflective Teaching and Action Research in Preservice Teacher Education." *Journal of Education for Teaching, 16*(3), 235–54.

Lortie, D. C. (2002). *Schoolteacher: A Sociological Study* (2nd ed.). Chicago: University of Chicago Press.

Loughran, J. J. (2002). "Effective Reflective Practice: In Search of Meaning in Learning about Teaching." *Journal of Teacher Education, 53*(1), 33–43.

McCann, T. M., L. R. Johannessen, and B. P. Ricca. (2005). *Supporting Beginning English Teachers: Research and Implications for Teacher Induction.* Urbana, IL: NCTE.

Nieto, S. (1999). *The Light in Their Eyes: Creating Multicultural Learning Communities.* New York: Teachers College Press.

Rogers, D. L., and L. M. Babinski. (2002). *From Isolation to Conversation: Supporting New Teachers' Development.* Albany: State University of New York Press.

Shoffner, M. (2008). "Informal Reflection in Pre-service Teacher Reflection." *Reflective Practice, 9*(2), 123–34.

————. (2009). "The Place of the Personal: Exploring the Affective Domain through Reflection in Teacher Preparation." *Teaching and Teacher Education, 25*(6), 783–89.

Sleeter, C. E. (2005). *Un-standardizing Curriculum: Multicultural Teaching in the Standards-Based Classroom.* New York: Teachers College Press.

Spalding, E., and A. Wilson. (2002). "Demystifying Reflection: A Study of Pedagogical Strategies that Encourage Reflective Journal Writing." *Teachers College Record, 104*(7), 1393–1421.

Stairs, A. J. (2007). "Culturally Responsive Teaching: The Harlem Renaissance in an Urban English Class." *English Journal, 96*(6), 37–42.

Thein, A. H., R. Beach, and D. Parks. (2007). "Perspective-Taking as Transformative Practice in Teaching Multicultural Literature to White Students." *English Journal, 97*(2), 54–60.

Valenzuela, A. (1999). *Subtractive Schooling: U.S.–Mexican Youth and the Politics of Caring.* Albany: State University of New York.

Zeichner, K. M., and D. P. Liston. (1996). *Reflective Teaching: An Introduction.* Mahwah, NJ: Lawrence Erlbaum Associates.

Vignette

Lotus

A Pedagogy of Listening

Jacqueline Deal, *Binghamton, New York*

It is late May and I am trying to teach my first period class. It's a small class to begin with, only six students, but today there are three. Of the three missing, Carla is chronically absent due to a barrage of debilitating medical conditions, Mel has been suspended since the beginning of the month for possessing drugs on school grounds, and I suspect that Ricky is sleeping off a hangover in the apartment he shares with the several high-school dropouts he sees as representative of the hopeless youth of our region. I say that I am "trying to teach my first period class" because it's not going so well today.

I know that there are interesting ways to talk and learn about poetry, but my three students aren't having it this morning. Instead, Mark is fluffing his hair with a pick, Jay is perfecting the art of passive-aggressive nonchalance, and although Gretchen is sincerely trying to work with me, she has asked me to repeat my question yet again. The proverbial pulling of teeth is boring me to death. I do repeat my question, but rather than wait for an answer, I turn to the stack of papers in front of me and start grading them. I do this because it is the one way I can think of to keep myself from screaming the chant that has been coursing through my head for the last twenty minutes: "I did not rack up $50,000 in student loans for this!"

I used to be a lot like these students. In fact, the last words spoken to me before I left high school were, "the next time we see you, you'll have two kids and no husband." I wish I could say now that I had the perfect words in response to the secretary who prophesied such a bleak future for my two would-be illegitimate children and me. But the truth is that I sat there, wordless, on my sixteenth birthday, waiting for the principal to finalize the details of my decision to quit school.

The secretary is a convenient stand-in for all that I saw wrong with the system I had been struggling with. She was smug, mean-spirited, and presumptuous. She assumed that because I was leaving high school, I was bound to fail. She didn't know that I cried when George shot Lenny in *Of Mice and Men*. Or that I had aced the *Julius Caesar* exam. She didn't know that I had two small nieces who loved me or that I worried about my dad a lot. She didn't know that I never thought of quitting school as "dropping out." I thought of it as going to college. But how could she have known? She didn't know me. She only knew what she had typed onto my "permanent record."

On days like this one in late May I feel a lot more like my old high-school secretary than an advocate for students on the margins. On the days like this, when I am angry and arrogant, the only thing that grounds me is to have a little laugh at myself and all my hotshot committees and conferences and papers. It is humbling to remember that my job is not to show my students how much I know about literature and writing, but to learn how to get to know my students.

Because at the end of the day, if I don't know my kids and what is going on with them, if I don't care about who they are and where they come from and where they're headed, I will never ever be able to teach them what I hope they will know before they graduate and move into the next part of their lives. Robert, a student from my debut year as an alternative high school teacher, gave me my first lesson on this matter.

Robert was a deep thinker and a talented artist; it was obvious to me that he should go to art school after graduation. I could picture him in a college classroom, feverishly taking notes while the professor lectured through a slideshow of postmodern classicism. I knew from conversations with Robert and his mother that he had struggled with addictions and had been involved in gang activities. In light of that, maybe I should have celebrated when his mother told me that, after many discussions with Robert, they had decided that he should join the Marines. Instead, I was horrified by the idea. I could not understand how she could encourage her bright, sensitive boy to become a Marine.

So I did what any good-intentioned, naïve, meddling teacher would do: I sat Robert down and told him that I respected his decision, but wondered if he fully understood what a dangerous situation he was getting into. Soldiers were dying in Iraq. Did he know that he could die? He looked from his hands to me. Then, with a level of confidence and poise I had rarely seen in him, he explained that the life he was living was most certainly going to kill him; the military would at least give him a chance at a future.

It was strange to find myself speechless. I had planned to . . . what? Talk Robert out of joining the Marines? Was I really so smug that I believed that

I knew better than Robert, his mom, and the countless other people in his life with whom he had talked his future over? I suppose so, because even though I supported Robert, I held on to my worries and disappointment for a long time. In fact, it wasn't until Robert was home on leave one summer and invited me to lunch that I finally understood just how wrong I had been about him. As I sat across the table and listened to animated stories from a smiling, healthy, young Marine, I knew that I was finally getting to know who Robert really was.

I wish I could say that my epiphanous moment taught me so well that now I am a wonderful teacher that always pays attention in just the right way and is able to bring the best out of each and every one of her students. But the truth is not so glossy: my experience with Robert simply taught me that it's not my job to have all the answers. The truth is that sometimes it is good and right to be speechless. Sometimes the best I can do is to serve as a quiet witness.

The students that I work with do not usually arrive at my school in good repair. Most of them have seen too much and many of them have adopted personae designed for survival. While the utility of these personae is clear, there are times when they threaten to sabotage a student's academic success. Take Greg, for example.

Here's the scene: Greg is polite. Polite and unreachable. He thanks me when I hand him his assignment and sits quietly while I go over the instructions. Once I feel sure that everyone is ready to begin, I take my seat and they start to write. Everyone except Greg. Greg sits with his paper in front of him and his pen in his hand. He looks at the table as if he is waiting for the words to come to him. I give him time to do this; I know that people need time to get warmed up.

After ten minutes or more I sit down next to him and ask if I can help. He tells me, "No, I just have trouble getting started." I make suggestions about ways that he might get started and ask if he thinks he can write just one paragraph, just one sentence. He tells me that he'll try. He seems uncomfortable having me so close, so I go back to my seat to give him space. I try not to look in his direction because I don't want to draw attention to the problem he is having.

When I finally chance a peek in his direction, he is still sitting in the same position and his pen has yet to touch the page. This happens day after day, and I can see that we are going to lose him. I suggest that he come in for extra help, which he does, but it changes nothing and after a while I start to lose heart. It gets pretty bad for me because I know that he is scheduled to take the NYS Regents exam and I'm sure he won't pass it—he has written nothing in my classes except for a few journal entries. I have failed him.

And I think that would have been true if not for two things. The first is that he passed his Regents exam with an 88. When I called to tell him the good news, I also told him that his secret was out: he could write and I knew it! The second thing that happened was that I asked all of my students to turn in their journals. I told them that they should select one page that they were comfortable having me read and mark it with a Post-It note. I promised that I would only read the one page and that I, in turn, would write a short reply. When I got to Greg's journal, I was surprised to see that he had written me a note on his Post-It: "You can read them all if you want." What follows is an entry that best illustrates how I finally came to understand that what Greg needed from me was not writing instruction, but an audience:

I grew up in a small apartment over a bar in West H_____. I lived there with my brother Frank, sister Denise, and other brother Larry. My biological mother, Patricia (I'm just going to refer to her as Patricia) was still a teenager. Patricia had my older brother when she was 14. By the time she was 18 she was on her own with me, Frank, + Denise. A year or two later she had Larry. So it was all of us in a tiny apartment with my mom, her boyfriend. Other people were there so much they pretty much lived there. Everyone there were druggies + my mom never had a job so we were poor. Us kids never had much at all to eat or anything like that. We were all neglected very much. My adoptive mother Karen, who is biologically my great aunt once told me a story that she could never tell without crying. My brother Frank has always had a rock/fossil collection. He must of been 7 or 8 at the time of this particular story. He was standing out on the sidewalk trying to sell his fossils so we could have something to eat. I remember Karen + other family members bringing over groceries from time to time. They also came + took us kids away from time to time so we could have time to be outside and do things that normal kids are supposed to do. Not just all be put in one room to sit around while the grown ups get high + try to ignore theyre kids crys. Most of my memories are dark smokey rooms usually filled with a few grown ups. I can remember Patricia telling us kids to go in the other room many times, + usually b/c she wanted to get high or she was probably buying drugs or doing god knows what to get them. Most the time she'd do drugs right in front of us kids. My uncle Carl is an alcoholic + was over at our place all the time. He was a scary man when he was drunk. I remember him swearing + threatening + just being a drunk asshole all the time. This next story was told to me by Frank my older brother because he was older then me + remembers it. One day some black guy came up to our house. He was a drug dealer who Patricia owed $ to. He pulled out a gun + picked up my baby brother then put the gun to his head. He wanted his $ + was saying he'd shoot the baby if he didn't get it. Eventually he put Larry down + my uncle Carl beat up that black guy + threw him through a window. There's many more stories of fights + people barging in to get there $. Once me + all my brothers and sisters were sleeping in my moms waterbed with her. It was during the day + she was passed out because some dude she owed $ to came in + trashed the place + cut a hole in the waterbed + she didn't wake up. I don't want to write anymore right now b/c not much time left.

Despite an overwhelming desire to respond in some heroic way, some way that might help Greg and his siblings and his mother, I have learned over the years to recognize my place. In this case, it was my job to be that quiet witness to Greg's story, to his life. I wrote him what I hope was a humble reply:

When I read this I was completely stricken. I mean, I had to set it down and just breathe. I know you're not looking for pity or anything like that, so I won't say something like, "I'm sorry." That, I think, would diminish/reduce your experience to something trite, and it's all just too big for such small words. What I will say is that I am honored that you trust me enough to share this with me. Thank you for that and thank you for being the person you've become. You are a *lotus*.

Admittedly, Greg's story is exceptional: he and I live in a region whose newspaper tolls the bell far too frequently. In recent history, our headlines have included the murders of no fewer than three children at the hands of their caregivers, a mass shooting at the American Civic Association, and countless jobs lost to our sinking economy. The sense of desperation is palpable. But I don't believe that there is a young person out there—from the students at my alternative school to the students attending the wealthiest private academies—that doesn't need an audience, someone who can listen without judging or trying to make everything better.

So here's the truth: I don't have any voodoo magic that makes my students do well. In fact, sometimes they fail or drop out or just squeak by and go on to do God-knows-what. But when I look closely, I see that they all have the potential to become lotuses: to grow up and out of the muck, reach for the light, break through the surface, and bloom into something beautiful.

Chapter 5

Reading *Romeo and Juliet* and Talking Sex

Critical Ideological Consciousness as Ethical Practice

Karen Spector, *University of Alabama*

We traveled the same route from campus to North End High School[1] that we had taken so often when Lisa Scherff and I co-taught a book writing project to a group of all Black and mostly poor ninth-grade English students. On this day, however, we weren't going to teach ninth graders, but rather we were going to sit down with their White teacher, Mrs. Stetson, and go over transcripts of her teaching that we captured during our research and had provided to her a month before.

This meeting with Mrs. Stetson was necessary from an ethical perspective, but it was going to be tough terrain to negotiate. How would we engage her in a discussion about her classroom practices, which from our perspective were low-level, culturally imperialistic, and even harmful, while remaining open to what she had to say? Would we fall into the cultural imperialism trap ourselves? We knew it was important to remember that the process of becoming (e.g., a teacher, a researcher, a student, a daughter) is open and ongoing for all of us. We knew we had to both inquire *and* listen.

Mrs. Stetson had, after all, graciously invited us into her classroom and allowed us to pursue our research with her and her students. Furthermore, we knew she genuinely cared about her students and was doing what she thought was best for them, even though she offered a brand of culturally relevant pedagogy that didn't fit within Ladson-Billings's (1990, 1994, 1995, 2002, 2006) call for high academic achievement, cultural competence, or sociopolitical consciousness. It was our professional responsibility to open up a pedagogical space with Mrs. Stetson in which our different perspectives would meet and be checked against one another.

When we arrived in the classroom during her planning period, we exchanged niceties and got caught up on the most recent news about our student participants: Agnes was doing well, due to deliver her baby before the end of the year; Laney had calmed down; King David was acting up; KiKi would be attending a summer program at a university a few states away. Then we began to address the teaching episode we call "Reading *Romeo and Juliet* and Talking Sex."

As Mrs. Stetson began reading, she started to laugh. "Gosh!" she said. "It sure takes me a long time to get class started, doesn't it?" I nodded affirmatively, sneaking a tense peek at Lisa as Mrs. Stetson was consumed with the transcript. After a while, I broke in.

"I want to draw your attention to a particular section, there on page 12," I said. "This is about *Romeo and Juliet*, right?"

"Right," she said, still reading.

"So it's about *Romeo and Juliet*. You ask the class, [reading from the transcript][2] 'Now not to be PREACHY but how many girls around here at any given time are pregnant?' And you move from talking to the students about the teenage pregnancy rate at North End High School to [reading from the transcript again] 'How many girls do you think are MARRIED?' Why do you do that?"

"My Baptist viewpoints, plain and simple," she said. "I just think that for this group of people. Because I'll tell you, their mamas aren't married. Now my mama [Mrs. Stetson's mother] said, 'Before you get married, you go to college.' My parents said, 'We'll pay for your wedding after you get your masters degree.' My husband and I both finished college before we got married. We got jobs, got cars, got a house, and then we had a kid. In that order. Around here, if you get one kid, you get welfare and you get food stamps. Around here kids get you money. And some think love. That girl who just left, she had a baby same time I had my first, and now she's pregnant again. I mean that's fine for me; I'm married and have a job."

Her response was candid. Teaching *Romeo and Juliet* was mediated by her "Baptist upbringing" and the authority of her parents ("Now my mama said" and "My parents said"), and her words at this particular moment contained traces of both, although they had become her own. As Mrs. Stetson's words entered into the "tension-filled environment" of our pedagogical encounter, they "weave[d] in and out of complex interrelationship" with my words, which contained traces of my own upbringing and affiliations (Bakhtin 1981, p. 276). I was getting a little closer to understanding her take on what the sex talk had to do with *Romeo and Juliet*.

Nervously coughing, I managed, "After I read this the first time, I was completely shocked that this kind of talk was going on in school."

"Why?" Mrs. Stetson asked. She had no guile, no apprehension at this point of how her words might appear to an outsider.

"Well, about the sex talk. And it obviously coming straight from your religious beliefs," I clarified.

"Well, the state says I should not talk about personal beliefs in school. But if I saved even one girl from being pregnant by saying that the condom works only 50 percent of the time, then it was worth it," she answered with strong and genuine conviction. And now her words were simultaneously meeting, recoiling, and merging with my words and the words of the state.

This was Mrs. Stetson's brand of culturally relevant pedagogy. She had worked at the school for 10 years, had seen a score of girls get pregnant and then drop out of school. She knew stories of intergenerational poverty and the hopelessness it engenders. She knew that many of her students had tough lives and her answer to combat these circumstances was that they should make better decisions (thereby placing responsibility on their shoulders alone). She reasoned that if they would do what she had done—finish college, get married, get jobs, buy cars, purchase a house, and then have a child—then their tough lives would be softened.

Mrs. Stetson was skilled in knowing her own cultural expectations. She was also skilled in knowing how these expectations seemed to differ from the life circumstances *some* of her students lived, the state's expectations, and now perhaps the researchers' expectations. All of this required reflection, but I will argue that she was not yet engaging in the *critical* reflection necessary to disrupt her cultural triumphalism (belief that her cultural values were superior to those of her students) so that she could engage in ethical pedagogical practices.

"Well, I'm still trying to get my mind around this, what this is. Quite frankly, Mrs. Stetson, most people reading that transcript would think you did something wrong," I said, no longer hedging. "Do you see that?" This was my attempt to open a space in which our different views could be encountered and reconsidered.

"Yeah. If the [department chair] knew [about the transcript], I'd probably get fired," she laughed nervously and looked around. "But it's still worth it, and I'd do it again." I left her classroom that day thinking that *she* didn't get it, and likely she was left thinking that *I* didn't get it.

On my next visit several weeks later, Mrs. Stetson said that she wanted to go back to school to work on her PhD because she wanted to investigate what the transcript showed, "You know, a White teacher in a Black school." She may still pursue that PhD, but at the end of the school year, she resigned from North End and accepted a position in an all-White district to the south. She chose to make a change; to what degree critical reflection and burgeoning attunement encouraged that change is unknown to me. But again, I think it is important to remember that the process of becoming is open and ongoing for all of us.

I struggled with *how* and even *if* I should write about Mrs. Stetson, the students, and myself. I am deeply troubled and saddened about what I learned during this project, but I have hope that teachers reading this chapter will see the importance of becoming critically conscious practitioners, attuned to their own and their students' cultural ways of being. I hope this chapter engenders dialogue within teacher study groups and preservice teacher classrooms about the ongoing, never finished process of coming to critical ideological consciousness that moves us all a little closer to the aim of ethical practice.

RESEARCHER, SITE, THE PROJECT

I am a White, now-middle-class, female professor who has taught in high schools serving poor and minority students. Lisa and I chose North End High School for this teacher research project because she knew it well, having provided free summer literacy enrichment programs there for several years. The school was struggling to make adequate yearly progress, and as members of the community, we wanted to support the efforts of the teachers and the principal however we could.

According to Orfield and Lee's (2006) definition, North End High School was an "apartheid school" (a school with 0–1 percent White students). The rate for free/reduced-price lunches, an indication of poverty, had remained around 78 percent from 2003–2006; however, for the most recent reporting period, the state board reported over 86 percent of the student population was approved for free/reduced-price lunches.

North End reported a 60 percent graduation rate, with a projected drop-out rate of 28 percent over the span of 2004–2008; however, in the most recent reporting period, the graduation rate plummeted to 46 percent. Only 53 percent of eleventh graders at North End passed the state high school graduation exam, down from 68 percent in the previous year.

These statistics paint a troubling picture of schooling at North End: segregated, high poverty, high dropout rate, low graduation rate, and low achievement. However, North End was staffed by a core of dedicated, long-term teachers—teachers who had seen the school transition from a more diverse student body to the present apartheid school when the county built new high schools and rezoned feeder neighborhoods.

The book-writing project we planned for this group of ninth-grade students was funded by a National Council of Teachers of English (NCTE) Research

Foundation grant and a University of Alabama College of Education grant. Basically, our plan was to have students write autobiographical pieces, music and movie reviews, and poetry, conduct research with community members, and take digital photographs. All of these compositions were gathered together for each student into a leatherbound book; students read their favorite pieces to an audience of their family members and teachers, and we publicly celebrated their achievements. Our practices were meant to tap into students' funds of knowledge and apprentice them into academic literacies in culturally relevant ways.

COMING TO CRITICAL IDEOLOGICAL CONSCIOUSNESS AS ETHICAL PRACTICE

People are always *becoming*, never fully closed off from negotiating new ways to mean, see, and be in the world. According to Bakhtin (1981), critical ideological consciousness is the process "of selectively assimilating the words of others" (p. 341) into our own. This entails being free to *select* the words that we will assimilate into our consciousness, which first entails being critically conscious of the ideologies that have been handed down to us (by religion, state, family members, teachers, and so forth) and the ideologies that we find internally persuasive (i.e., those that are half someone else's and half our own). So we move through our lives as unfinished ideological beings, testing our ways of being in the world against "various available verbal and ideological points of view, approaches, directions and values" (Bakhtin 1981, p. 346).

In *Art and Answerability*, Bakhtin (1990) argued that each human being occupies a unique and irreplaceable position in the world and this position creates an "excess of seeing" (p. 22). He wrote:

> I shall always see and know something that he . . . cannot see himself: parts of his body that are inaccessible to his own gaze (his head, his face and its expression), the world behind his back, and a whole series of objects and relations. . . . As we gaze at each other, two different worlds are reflected in the pupils of our eyes. (p. 23)

This excess of seeing brought about by each person's unique position in the world plays an important role in the unrepeatable nature of our actions and hence our ethical responsibility for them. So, for example, the preamble to the National Education Association's (NEA) Code of Ethics lists some of our responsibilities as follows: "[T]he educator, believing in the worth and dignity of each human being, recognizes the supreme importance of the pursuit of truth, devotion to excellence, and the nurture of the democratic principles" (NEA 2009). Principle 1 of the same Code of Ethics adds to our responsibilities. An educator:

> Shall not unreasonably deny the student's access to varying points of view. Shall not intentionally expose the student to embarrassment or disparagement. (NEA 2009)

Responsibility for upholding these and other ethical principles can be imputed to a person because one and only one person occupies that exact time and place. From a different position, the horizon of vision would be different, so the responsibilities might shift. When my gaze meets my participant's gaze, my excess of seeing makes me responsible for what I see since it is only I who experiences it exactly that way, shaded as it is with my own ideological consciousness and position in the world.

These ethical responsibilities are weighty concerns because, as classroom teachers, our pedagogical practices are informed by the ideological positions we take up for ourselves and open up for others. Deborah Hicks (2002) wrote about this dynamic:

> When I work with teachers who teach poor and working-class children, the first thing I often encounter is their expressions of anger: *these* children whom my lessons do not reach, and who fail their proficiency tests at such high rates; *these* parents who do not support my professional work or share my values; *this* community—and so on. What has to occur for things to change is not simply an intellectual shift, so that teachers have more information. This is not just the learning of new pedagogies . . . or even the learning of information about dialects, cultural practices, and injustices. Rather change also has to entail a moral shift, a willingness to open oneself up to the possibility of *seeing* those who differ from us. This is very hard work, but work that lies at the heart of teaching. (p. 152)

I agree with Hicks that we need to truly *see* students, not as monoliths that fit neatly under labels of "Black," "Hispanic," or "working poor," as if this information thoroughly defines a person—as if giving a Black kid a "Black" book is a masterful pedagogical move (though not necessarily a bad move either). Rather, when we look into the sea of faces staring back at us from the classroom, we see individuals who are all at different points in their process of becoming, just as teachers and researchers are, and we have an ethical responsibility to uphold the "worth and dignity of each human being" (NEA 2009). This holds for all people—not just those who are marginalized, but for privileged and unprivileged alike.

When we traveled to Mrs. Stetson's classroom to discuss the "Reading *Romeo and Juliet* and Talking Sex" transcript, I argue that we were engaging in a culturally relevant pedagogy. We were, after all, opening up a pedagogical space in which we could discuss our own excess of seeing in relation to Mrs. Stetson's teaching and in which we would try to understand what she was seeing that we could not. As the introduction to this chapter demonstrates, Mrs. Stetson's ideologies and my own collided in this pedagogical space.

And in a similar vein, I will explore the clashes in ideological consciousness that occurred in Mrs. Stetson's classroom when students read *Romeo and Juliet* and Mrs. Stetson gave her sex talk. I hope to highlight that these confrontations can be taken up in ethical ways, ways that acknowledge we are all in the process of becoming. The development of critical ideological consciousness—an ongoing process of critically selecting the words of others that we will blend into our own internally persuasive words—is what I claim to be culturally relevant pedagogy.

VIGNETTE: READING *ROMEO AND JULIET* AND TALKING SEX[2]

Students were excited to continue reading *Romeo and Juliet* out loud in class. Jermichael wanted to read the part of Romeo again. "No, someone different today," Mrs. Stetson said to the would-be Romeo. "Okay, King David, you're Romeo." The next 20 minutes were devoted to handing out the parts in Act 2, Scenes 1 and 2, quieting down students, answering the phone, and handling various interruptions.

Laney, reading the part of Juliet this day, became frustrated with the delays: "Can we start, please, Mrs. Stetson?"

"I'm ready," Mrs. Stetson replied, and after a few more interruptions, students picked up with *Romeo and Juliet* where they had left off the day before. They settled in and soon became uncharacteristically quiet, everyone following along in the textbook, even those who didn't have parts to read. Act 2, Scene 1 was finished, and they pressed straight through to Act 2, Scene 2. Mrs. Stetson sat at her desk, flipping through a catalog.

King David, possibly embracing the role of Romeo, got up from his desk and walked over to the lovely Juliet, bent down on one knee, and took her hand while reading his lines.

Noticing something was amiss, Mrs. Stetson looked up. "What are you doing? No King David. Sit down." Mrs. Stetson's voice had a tinge of disdain to it, I thought. "Romeo can't touch her. She's up in the balcony."

"My bad," King David confessed, and he slunk back to his chair to the titters of fellow classmates. The reading continued until the lovers parted at the end of Act 2, Scene 2. It was here that Mrs. Stetson stopped the reading, got up from her desk, and began giving verbatim notes.

"Write this down: 'Romeo is hoping,'" Mrs. Stetson began, "'to catch a glimpse,'" and here Mrs. Stetson paused so students could catch up. "'Romeo is hoping to catch a glimpse,'" she repeated and then paused again.

Seizing the pause as an opportunity, Jermichael offered to finish her sentence: "of Juliet naked?"

"Why would he want to see her naked?" Mrs. Stetson asked, criticism creeping back into her voice.

("Why *wouldn't* he?" I wondered.)

"I thought that's what he was doing standing outside her window. My bad," Jermichael apologized for his wrong assumption.

"What? No. You know that says a lot about culture today." Mrs. Stetson's voice was getting louder. "SEX is NOT all it's about." She continued, "If you are with someone just for sex, you're gonna get hurt; you're gonna get old. Now not to be PREACHY but how many girls around here at any given time are pregnant?

Agnes piped in humorously, "24/9," and students laughed.

Mrs. Stetson ignored Agnes and answered her own question. "Four in every classroom are pregnant at any given time. How many girls do you think are MARRIED?"

"These folks don't try to get married to nobody," Princess explained.

"North End is what it is," Mrs. Stetson sighed, and then went on to compare North End to the all-White high school she attended. She told the story of a girl from her school who got pregnant and had to be shipped off to North Dakota until after the baby was born because, Mrs. Stetson said, "it's a huge embarrassment to be pregnant . . . because it would be a huge embarrassment to have a child out of wedlock. Around here, having a baby and being on welfare is NOTHING." Even though there were pregnant girls in the room, Mrs. Stetson's invective wasn't followed by an uproar from the students.

Agnes simply gasped, "Oh my God!" Mrs. Stetson ignored her and went back to *Romeo and Juliet* for a moment.

"Now Romeo and Juliet have just met and supposedly they're in love, who knows. But when he goes to see her through the window, he's not worried about sex because when you're married, it's guaranteed. He knows he is going to marry this woman that he loves and because he is married SEX is something that comes with it. That is the FRUIT of marriage. I AM TALKING, Jermichael. You've talked enough. ZIP IT!

"Why do you have sex?" she asked the class.

Braving another response, Jermichael offered, "For pleasure?"

"What? No, not so much for pleasure," Mrs. Stetson was looking for something different.

"To make love?" Princess suggested.

"To make love. Right! Not to get jiggy with someone. You were drunk when you met them and you were sober when you woke up and guess what? They're UGLY and they STANK. Right? And you know people have said that and they've done that."

Agnes said, "So us ugly colored people up in here."

Nina said, "This ain't my mama. Don't talk about that."

"Uh uh. Because you need to know. Sex is something to be enjoyed once you're married," Mrs. Stetson replied to Nina.

"I'm uncomfortable talking about this," Princess quietly spoke.

"You know what? I'm not. I could be a sex ed teacher," Mrs. Stetson answered.

It was Agnes who spoke now. "I say it like this. My mama and my daddy say it ain't okay to have sex or nothing, but as long as you use protection and you ain't out doing everybody . . . you alright."

"Well, wait now. Condoms. LISTEN [she yelled at the students as they all started talking at once]. Condoms don't always work. LISTEN." Mrs. Stetson was trying to get her point across, but many students were talking loudly with one another.

Exasperated, Laney yelled, "Mrs. Stetson, can we please get back to *Romeo and Juliet*?"

"This is more important for ya'll than *Romeo and Juliet* ever thought about being," Mrs. Stetson replied, and then added, "SHHHH."

"I am not comfortable talking about this," Princess said, louder this time.

The uproar in the classroom continued for five more minutes, and then Mrs. Stetson went back to giving verbatim notes. "Romeo is hoping to catch a glimpse of Juliet. Romeo stands beneath Juliet's window." She paused and repeated, "Romeo stands beneath Juliet's window," and the students quietly copied down the notes.

ANALYSIS AND DISCUSSION

Two performances entered the pedagogical space of this classroom during this vignette, and I analyze them below: (1) King David embodying the love-struck Romeo; and (2) Mrs. Stetson's "that says a lot about culture today" speech and the exchanges that followed. For each, I will interpretatively consider the participants' excess of seeing and how the classroom practices were informed by the culturally mediated, ideological positions participants took up for themselves and opened up for others. I will conclude by discussing how critical attunement to the ideological becoming of the students and teacher would lead to more just, compassionate, and ethical practice.

King David Embodying the Love-Struck Romeo

From my perspective, which just included my excess of seeing, King David appeared to be physically embodying his role as the love-struck Romeo when he left his seat to hold Laney/Juliet's hand during the balcony scene. I viewed this as a laudable English language arts performance, as Shakespeare's plays were meant to be acted out, not read.

The intention that propelled King David to act out the balcony scene is unknown, for his excess of seeing was different than my own: he could have had a crush on Laney and thus seized this opportunity to hold her hand; he could have been performing for the benefit of one or more of his friends in the classroom; he could have been carried away by his role as Romeo, as I like to believe, trying as best he knew how to act out the scene; or his intentions could have been entirely different than any of these interpretations. Regardless, he made the choice to get up from his seat and take hold of Juliet's hand, perhaps reasoning that Mrs. Stetson would not even notice because she appeared to be busy reading a catalog.

But Mrs. Stetson did notice. What did she see in the "world behind his back" (Bakhtin 1990, p. 23) that I couldn't see? After all, King David's actions didn't disrupt the class, but her interruption caused King David to break character and apologize. Considering only her words and the way she intoned them with disapproval ("What are you doing? No King David. Sit down. Romeo can't touch her. She's up in the balcony"), it appears that Mrs. Stetson was bothered by the fact that Romeo couldn't actually touch Juliet in this scene, so that King David's performance was not an accurate depiction of the scene.

I don't think she was upset that he was merely out of his seat, because I witnessed many classes in which students stood up, danced to music, wandered around the room, and left the room without telling her, and these performances didn't appear to bother her. In exploring the ideological positions she took up for herself and opened or closed for her students, I begin to understand more deeply her response to King David's performance.

Mrs. Stetson controlled who orally read the various parts of the play, setting herself up as the classroom authority ("No, someone different today. Okay, King David, you're Romeo"). After she doled out the parts and dealt with several interruptions, she announced, "I'm ready," which was her permission for the reading to commence. Interestingly, she sat at her desk and flipped though a catalog rather than choosing to fully engage in the classroom activity. It was only when King David got up that her full attention was turned to the class, and then she positioned King David as someone who could be ordered ("Sit down") and herself as someone who should be obeyed, which he did.

Writing about education, Bakhtin (1984) argued that some pedagogues "know only a single mode of cognitive interaction among consciousness: someone who knows and possesses the truth instructs someone who is ignorant of it or in error" (Bakhtin 1984, p. 81). I don't believe that classrooms should be authority-less; rather, I agree with Matusov (2007) paraphrasing Morrison, who stated, "The teacher must gain control over the classroom in order to lose it through the development of internally persuasive discourse" (p. 233).

When Mrs. Stetson shut down the possibility for King David to imaginatively enter the play through acting out the scene, she failed to see him as a unique individual in the process of becoming. Rather, she unilaterally imposed her will and authority on him, perhaps without being conscious of what she was doing. Either way, if I had entered into a conversation with Mrs. Stetson about this part of the transcript, this may have opened up a space in which she could have critically weighed her choices and consciously decided how she would handle similar situations in the future. This would be a step toward more ethical classroom practice.

I began with this relatively innocuous example of how the teacher took up and closed down ideological positions in the classroom, but next I move on to an example that I view as outright harmful, "That Says a Lot about Culture Today."

That Says a Lot about Culture Today

Mrs. Stetson's sex talk was triggered by Jermichael's comment that Romeo wanted to see Juliet naked. First, I'll place Jermichael's comment within the classroom context. He and his peers were taking down verbatim notes from Mrs. Stetson about the scene that they had just read aloud ("'Romeo is hoping to catch a glimpse'"). Instead of patiently waiting for Mrs. Stetson to tell the students what the play meant, he offered up his own interpretation of the events.

From my perspective as an English educator, I viewed this as another laudable performance. Jermichael was actively interpreting the scene: this may have been a plausible explanation of why someone might be loitering in the dark outside of a woman's window. From Mrs. Stetson's position, and the excess of seeing it opened up for her, however, Jermichael's interpretation was an indication of the moral bankruptcy of the meaning he—and by extension the whole class—constructed ("You know that says a lot about culture today"). She saw "behind his back" a whole horizon of sexually energized Black females getting pregnant and living off of welfare ("North End is what it is. . . . Around here, having a baby and being on welfare is NOTHING").

Remember that these comments were directed to the entire class—a monolith of "poor Blackfolks"—and were precipitated by one student who offered up a tentative interpretation of Romeo's motive for standing outside of Juliet's window. This episode isn't explicable to me except when considered in the light of Mrs. Stetson uncritical acceptance of dominant ideologies passed down to her from authorities in her life (church, her parents, and perhaps other people from her all-White town).

Unlike the example of the "Love-struck Romeo," this sex talk caused some students to "talk back" (hooks 1989) to the ideologies Mrs. Stetson was authoritatively imposing on her students. For example, Agnes made a joke about the frequency of pregnancies at North End ("24/9"), an exclamation of shock at what she was hearing ("Oh my God!"), a protest against how Mrs. Stetson was characterizing her students ("So [we are] ugly colored people up in here"), and a plea for understanding ("I say it like this").

Agnes's joke, exclamation, protest, and plea can be seen as various attempts to voice her own internally persuasive words—words of others that have been selectively assimilated into our own words. Given the right circumstances, her words would meet and vie for position with Mrs. Stetson's words in the tension filled environment of the classroom, but in the first three cases, Agnes's words were simply ignored by Mrs. Stetson, an instance of excessive monologism (when only the words of authority are permitted).

In the fourth case, when Agnes tried to explain how she had been taught by her parents, Mrs. Stetson answered her by explaining why Agnes's parents were wrong ("I say it like this. My mama and my daddy say it ain't okay to have sex or nothing, but as long as you use protection and you ain't out doing everybody . . . you alright" to which Mrs. Stetson replied, "Condoms don't always work").

Bakhtin (1981) wrote that "the authoritative word demands that we acknowledge it, that we make it our own; it binds us, quite independent of any power it might have to persuade us internally; we encounter it with its authority already fused to it" (p. 342). Mrs. Stetson used her position in the classroom to authoritatively humiliate ("It's an embarrassment"), denigrate ("Around here being on welfare is NOTHING"), and characterize her students as alcohol-abusing, sexual deviants with poor personal hygiene ([making love is] "Not to get jiggy with someone. You were drunk when you met them and you were sober when you woke up and guess what? They're UGLY and they STANK. Right? And you know people have said that and they've done that").

Can anyone say that Mrs. Stetson was upholding the principles in the NEA Code of Ethics here? I think not. From her position, with only her excess of seeing, I argue that she was perpetuating words from dominant ideologies that she has uncritically accepted.

If she were to look around her room, she would see one or two pregnant girls, it's true, but to assume that these girls had drunken, one-night stands with ugly and stinky people is a clear breach of the NEA Code of Ethics: Educators "Shall not intentionally expose the student to embarrassment or disparagement" (2009). My words may seem harsh, I know, but all of us— Mrs. Stetson, her students, and me—are still in the process of becoming.

CONCLUSION

When considering Bakhtin's notion that each individual person has a unique vision or "excess of seeing" unknown to any other person, it quickly becomes mind boggling to imagine the number of different worlds being reflected in the eyes of the 20 students and 1 teacher as everyone shifts activities and positions. This vignette shows that Mrs. Stetson's view of the "world" was the dominant one being reflected in this classroom.

As a researcher, I can't know what exactly was behind the acts I saw— King David holding Laney's hand, Mrs. Stetson giving verbatim notes or a sex talk—but I can critically explore what ideological positions are taken up by teachers and students in classroom spaces and who is thereby empowered or disempowered by these positionalities.

As Hicks (2000) has argued, we can use the work of Bakhtin to "focus on how individuals intonate acts of living and knowing through the particularities of interpretation, feeling, and moral valuing" (p. 230). When I focus on the ways that Mrs. Stetson represented the lives of students and limited the free expression of their interpretations, I am deeply saddened and angry, despite the fact that I know Mrs. Stetson truly believes that she is doing what's best for her students, that she is practicing her brand of culturally relevant pedagogy. And who knows but that one or two people may have left the classroom on the sex talk day thinking, "You know, I am not going to have sex until I'm married." It's possible.

More likely, in my view, is that students—already marginalized because of their race and class, already marginalized by being zoned to all-Black schools for their whole K–12 education, already marginalized because they sit in classrooms where teachers like Mrs. Stetson uncritically foist upon them dominant ideologies that made segregated schools a reality in the first place—come to a deeper understanding of the structured inequality of schooling but remain powerless to change the situation. Powerlessness, perhaps, is passed along through a lack of access to mainstream funds of knowledge; for example, when Mrs. Stetson said that it was more important for her students to listen to her sex talk than to read *Romeo and Juliet.*

Culturally relevant pedagogy needs to be conceived of as an ongoing process of becoming critically ideologically conscious of the ways our idea systems position us and others in the world. Culturally relevant pedagogy is not a pattern to bring into the classroom, but a lifelong process. Just as I did as a researcher in this project, people may at times need to retrace roads they have traveled many times before in order to open up pedagogical spaces where different perspectives can be free to collide, merge, and recoil from one another.

I have come to new understandings about educating marginalized students and my responsibilities as a researcher in these situations. I struggled long and hard over whether or not I should write about this at all, but students like Agnes, King David, and Jermichael have taught me that not speaking out would be an abdication of my ethical responsibility.

I don't know how this project and my tough talk with Mrs. Stetson affected her practice. There are numerous reasons she could have left North End High School for the all-White school to the south, but I do know one thing. She began to consider what it meant to be a White teacher in a Black school ("You know, a White teacher in a Black school"). Since everyone is in the process of becoming, I view this as *a step* toward critical ideological consciousness.

Students like King David and his classmates already likely feel small in relation to the powerful structures of society, and my job as an educator is to create pedagogical spaces where King David and other students can imagine and accomplish ever-expanding possibilities for themselves. He, and likely others in his classroom, are well on their way to a critical ideological con-sciousness. He wrote this short piece as part of the book-writing project:

> My name is King David. I love my name. My name is from the king in the *Bible.* King David once defeated a way bigger person than anybody. And he did it with a rock and a sling shot. It sometimes makes me feel strong because if he can defeat a big giant, I can too.

Like King David, educators are facing giants—namely, our own uncritical consciousness—but we can take courage in the story that King David relates: giants can fall.

NOTES

1. All people and place names are pseudonyms, and I have altered many details to better protect the teacher and student participants.
2. See Appendix A for transcription notes and transcription conventions.

REFERENCES

Bakhtin, M. M. (1981). *The Dialogic Imagination: Four Essays.* M. Holquist (trans.). Austin: University of Texas Press.
————. (1984). *Problems of Dostoevsky's Poetics.* C. Emerson (ed. and trans.). Minneapolis: University of Minnesota Press.
————. (1990). "The Author and the Hero in Aesthetic Activity." In M. Holquist and V. Liapunov (eds.), V. Liapunov (transl.), *Art and Answerability: Early Philosophical Essays by M. M. Bakhtin.* Austin: University of Texas Press.
Hicks, D. (2000). "Self and Other in Bakhtin's Early Philosophical Essays: Prelude to a Theory of Prose Consciousness." *Mind, Culture, and Activity, 7,* 227–42.
————. (2002). *Reading Lives: Working-Class Children and Literacy Learning.* New York: Teachers College Press.
hooks, b. (1989). *Talking Back: Thinking Feminist Thinking Black.* Boston: South End Press.
Ladson-Billings, G. (1990). "Culturally Relevant Teaching: Effective Instruction for Black Students." *The College Board Review, 7*(15), 20–25.
————. (1994). *The Dreamkeepers: Successful Teachers of African-American Children.* San Francisco: Jossey-Bass.
————. (1995). "Toward a Theory of Culturally Relevant Pedagogy." *American Educational Research Journal, 32,* 465–91.
————. (2002). "'I Ain't Writin' Nuttin'': Permissions to Fail and Demands to Succeed in Urban Classrooms." In L. Delpit and J. K. Dowdy (eds.), *The Skin That We Speak: Thoughts on Language and Culture in the Classroom* (pp. 107–20). New York: The New Press.
————. (2006). "'Yes, But How Do We Do It?': Practicing Culturally Relevant Pedagogy." In J. Landsman and C. W. Lewis (eds.), *White Teachers/Diverse Classrooms: A Guide to Building Inclusive Schools, Promoting High Expectations, and Eliminating Racism* (pp. 29–42). Sterling, VA: Stylus.
Matusov, E. (2007). "Applying Bakhtin Scholarship on Discourse in Education: A Critical Review Essay." *Educational Theory, 57,* 215–37.
National Education Association (NEA). (2009). *Code of Ethics.* Retrieved from www .nea.org/home/30442.htm.
Orfield, G., and C. Lee. (2006). *Racial Transformation and the Changing Nature of Segregation.* Cambridge, MA: Harvard University.

Appendix A

I wrote the vignette based on field notes and classroom transcripts. I omitted: (1) word repetitions (e.g., "I, I know" turned into "I know"); (2) unheard fragments of talk (e.g., "not to get jiggy with someone [indecipherable]" turned into "not to jiggy with someone"); (3) the utterances of nonparticipants; and (4) some of the "noise" that makes reading a transcript difficult. I am not claiming that the noise and so forth are unimportant, but I am not focusing on those aspects of classroom talk for this chapter. For example, if the transcript read:

Teacher: SEX is NOT all it's about
Princess: yeah, you right
Student: [not a participant, didn't transcribe]
Teacher: if you are with someone
Agnes: ==you ain't nothing but a tramp [speaking to Princess]
Teacher: ==just for sex, you're gonna get hurt
Dante: huh huh

We represented it:

"SEX is NOT all it's about." She continued, "If you are with someone just for sex, you're gonna get hurt . . . "

Transcription Conventions
==means overlapping speech
ALL CAPS means emphasis

Chapter 6

"'Proper' Spanish Is a Waste of Time"

Mexican-Origin Student Resistance to Learning Spanish as a Heritage Language

Kimberly Adilia Helmer, *John Jay College of Criminal Justice, City University of New York*

> Bad behavior, from the point of view of the teacher's art, is as good a starting-point as good behavior, in fact, paradoxical as it may sound to say so, it is often a better starting point than good behavior would be.
>
> —William James (1899)

"Can I go to the *baño?*"

This question seems to occur quite often in this ninth- and tenth-grade Spanish class. With a nod, Beth,[1] the teacher, allows Isabel, the student, to leave the classroom even though it is the third such request from students that period. Often the students who leave class on similar errands don't return for 15 minutes or more even though the charter school is small, the restroom near. The students remaining in the classroom seem listless and bored. Their bodies slump in their chairs, their faces blank.

Peter rests his head on his desk, his long black hair falling over his crossed arms. "Why are we studying *this* in Spanish class?" he mumbles in English.

For Beth's first period class, "this" is how language maintenance, or maintaining a community's bilingualism, is a human right. In a Spanish class for 14 and 15 year olds, three weeks into the semester, Beth is still presenting material that is not engaging her students.

Linguistic rights as a human right probably "should" seem to be immediately relevant for a Spanish class designed for students with varying levels of Spanish-English bilingualism who are connected to the target language through family and/or culture, that is, a Spanish class for heritage language learners (HLLs) located in a school less than a hundred miles from one of the most contentious international borders in the world—USA-Mexico.

Relevant because all grew up with Spanish-speaking family members and, for some, have lost the Spanish-language fluency they once had before starting formal schooling in English-only classrooms. But the reasons for the lessons were not clear, though they probably should have been clear enough.

Students for the past week had been studying various views on Spanish-English bilingualism, including how language affects one's identity and how language discrimination affects one's self-worth. These issues "should" also be of interest to the ninth and tenth graders in this heritage language (HL) class since all are of Mexican origin and ethnicity and reside in a large southwestern city where immigration, migrant rights, and bilingualism are all "hot button" topics. Recently, with the passage of Proposition 203, bilingual education was all but outlawed in the state they live in, Arizona.

Yet, the students are not interested. They do not bridle against antagonistic politics or become engaged in political wrangling. For the most part, they do not protest the issues, or even seem to care about them.

The teacher's tone is level; her affect reasonable; the curriculum of her HL class well reasoned, socially responsible, and well intentioned.

"We are studying human rights," Beth explains to Peter.

But Peter is unresponsive to the teacher's answer to his query, even though his first language is Spanish; he frequently crosses the border to visit cousins, his mother emigrated from Mexico in her mid-twenties, and he and his mother live in the same desert that hundreds of Mexican migrant workers die in each year as they cross the treacherous strip of the Sonoran Desert known as "The Devil's Highway" (Urrea 2004). Peter lives in a place where human rights violations occur regularly and a large percentage of the population, legal and illegal, are bilingual to one degree or another. Arizona is also a state where, up until the mid-1960s, Mexican schoolchildren were corporally punished for speaking Spanish, the only language they knew (Combs 2006; Sheridan 1986).

Eventually, Isabel returns from the bathroom and Peter lifts his head from his desk; he begins to draw on his hand. And the Spanish class drags on. (From fieldnotes, September 2003.)

A SENSE OF PLACE: EDUCATING TO EMPOWER

In my two-year ethnographic study of the first two years of a start-up charter high school,[2] I studied Latino and Latina student engagement with and resistance to academic learning. As "City" High School had no prior history, I came into the project with my eyes wide open, eager to see how an innovative school takes shape as well as see how the school's educational philosophy of place-based learning was operationalized and enacted. As the founding principal explained to me, place-based learning situates school curriculum within the geographic, historic, ecologic, artistic, linguistic, social, and political boundaries of a school's neighboring—and students' varying—communities (see Gruenewald 2003a, 2003b; Haymes 1995).

Also, as a linguist and educational anthropologist, I was eager to investigate how the pedagogy of place would be applied to Spanish heritage language learning (HLL), a promising and sound approach to HL pedagogy not seen elsewhere. The newly hired Spanish teacher also impressed me. Beth had just completed her MA in border studies from the local university and, though neither Latina nor native Spanish speaker, she had advanced Spanish-language literacy skills and was well versed in Chicano history and border issues—content knowledge that would benefit students.

Thus, after meeting the energized young faculty of the soon-to-be-opened school, my intention was to capture an ethnography of best practices, to empirically record a curricular model that honored community through hands-on learning. What I did not expect to find was student resistance and reluctance to learn, especially in a classroom designed to develop increased Spanish language fluency and literacy for students directly tied to the target language linguistically and culturally, otherwise known as HL instruction.

However, despite the promise of this new school, from the first day I visited the Spanish HL class, I knew a major part of my study would shift from its focus on capturing ideal learning to getting to the bottom of student disengagement with formal language study. Sitting as a "student" in Beth's class, for I, too, am a Spanish HLL, but of Nicaraguan, not Mexican decent, I often found myself frustrated and puzzled by the students' lack of response to class content and their unwillingness to speak Spanish to their teacher.

Beth presented materials that urged students to critically examine Spanish-language discrimination, a topic that theorists and practitioners of culturally responsive pedagogy (CRP) (Cazden and Leggett 1981; Erickson and Mohatt 1982; Garza 2008; Gay 2000) and culturally relevant pedagogy (CRP) (Dutro, Kazemi, Balf, and Lin 2008; Esposito and Swain 2009; Ladson-Billings 1995, 2009) would approve. "Both" CRPs advocate that students of color develop critical stances that interrogate the social inequalities often rooted in larger social institutional structures.

It is argued that such critical awareness empowers students, yet these learners responded as if this type of inequality and discrimination had nothing to do with them or their communities. This seemingly uninterested student reaction flies in the face of theories explaining why students of color are dissatisfied with school. Hordatt Gentles (2007) posits that much of the research for understanding educational dissatisfaction is grounded in *cultural difference theory*, which claims that poor academic achievement stems from disparities between course content and students' cultural background. However, in this Spanish class, despite the conscious attempt to link content and cultural background, students seemed alienated rather than empowered and engaged.

Attempting to understand why Latino and Latina youth were turned off to topics designed to empower and engage is crucial, especially when considering that Latinos and Latinas have the highest high-school dropout rate in the United States while simultaneously being the fastest-growing demographic group in the nation (Carreira 2003; U.S. Census Report 2004; Waggoner 2000). In fact, Latino and Latina students make up 32.1 percent of our nation's K–12 public schools (Kohler and Lazarín 2007), while in large urban school districts such as Los Angeles, Miami, Houston, and Dallas, Latinos and Latinas make up over 50 percent of the student population (Hancock 2006).

To do nothing about student educational persistence, to quote President Obama's first address to the joint session of Congress, is "a prescription for economic decline" (Obama 2009), an economic decline rooted in the neglect of the intellectual, artistic, and linguistic potential embodied in students of color. As the above statistics suggest, educators and scholars must seriously study the factors fueling Latino and Latina educational dissatisfaction while working toward creating educational environments that foster engaged and sustained learning.

Culturally responsive/relevant pedagogy (CRP) attempts to ameliorate the disparities found in alienating, irrelevant curricula by connecting course content to the culture of students. Although there is not a single way to teach in a culturally responsive/relevant way, Ladson-Billings (1995, 2009), drawing upon her ethnographic work examining the practices of exemplary teachers working with African American elementary school children, describes how a CRP approach helps students to be "academically successful, culturally competent, and sociopolitically critical" (pp. 477–78).

Similarly, Esposito and Swain (2009) explain that the aims of CRP are to instill in students of color cultural pride, agency, and critical consciousness. Thus, CRP helps students to embrace their cultural identities while gaining the critical tools to understand, interrogate, challenge, and work to transform hegemonic ideologies, institutions, and practices that discriminate. Despite these characteristics and goals of CRP, as this edited volume shows, CRP is not a foolproof educational panacea for reaching students of color.

DOING RESEARCH AT CITY HIGH SCHOOL

Heritage language learning is complicated. HL classes are fraught with complexities—ethnic, political, pedagogical, social, and linguistic. And it is this complexity that is often not described in the extant literature on HLL, a literature that tends to focus (for obvious reasons) on the heterogeneity of students' language proficiency to the exclusion of their other, and perhaps more important, differences.

For instance, besides Spanish-language proficiency, the 14 students in this study varied considerably in terms of economic and social class and academic preparedness, not to mention personal style, musical tastes, and myriad other interests, abilities, and challenges. Yet, although their Spanish-language skills varied greatly, they had all been placed, through an interview process, in a Spanish class for HLLs. One means of understanding the complexities surrounding teaching HL students is to empirically study student resistance to and engagement with learning materials presumed to honor and respect cultural diversity, that is, a CRP approach to HLL.

Whereas other school researchers have shown that minority student poor academic achievement and high dropout rates are a result of negative institutional factors, such as underfunding, overcrowding, and overtaxed and/or underprepared teachers (see Alonso, Anderson, Su, and Theoharis 2009), the current study examines classroom-based factors. I look at the dynamic interactions between curriculum, pedagogy, and classroom social interaction to uncover classroom features that contributed to student disengagement.

Through the analyses of classroom fieldnotes and transcribed student interviews, I found that course content and how it was taught was important for students but, more importantly, that before any real learning could transpire, a foundation of trust and respect needed to be constructed—a foundation especially critical for HLLs, as the data will show. Through my observations in other classes, where these same students were class members, I found community building between teacher and students (and students and students) to be the critical first steps for creating a culture of learning.

Once these foundations were built, for course content to be most effective, teachers needed to pitch it to students in a comprehensible, well-scaffolded manner. Learners were most responsive to tasks and projects that were "real," that is, learning that came from personal or direct experiences, emerging from student interests—not material transmitted to students without acknowledging and tapping their own expertise and experience, and not material presented in standardized, decontextualized textbooks. Indeed, it was this sort of authentic, student-centered, real-world, place-based learning that drew me to the new school in the first place.

The Ethnographic Context: City High School

In 2003, City High School opened its downtown doors to 85 freshmen and sophomores who represented every zip code of the desert metropolis. The demographic profile of the newly enrolled student body was 45 percent Caucasian, 40 percent Latino or Latina, 6 percent African American, 5 percent Native American, and 4 percent Asian American; nearly half of these students were eligible for free or reduced-price lunch.

The three founding City High School teachers established their own small public school, a bold response to their dissatisfaction with their too-large, district-run high school that they believed could not sufficiently meet student needs. The three teachers sought to create a more personalized curriculum by connecting teaching and learning to the city's geography, history, politics, economics, and arts—a pedagogic framework, as previously mentioned, known as place-based learning (see Gruenewald 2003b; Lewicki 2000; Long, Bush, and Theobald 2003; Loveland 2003).

Gruenewald (2003a) suggests that a place-conscious education makes learning "more relevant to the lived experience of students and teachers" (p. 620). Because of these more personalized connections between classroom learning and student lives, a place-based framework responds to the gaps found between standardized ("placeless") curricula and the actual lives and backgrounds of students.

For example, as water is critical for desert cities, the City High School science teacher created a unit in which students learned about the water cycle that included a week-long visit to the city's water treatment plants; in humanities, students formed their own Museums of Place where they created poster board exhibits of their neighborhoods that included photographs, a neighborhood map, a transcribed neighbor interview, original poetry, relevant artifacts, and a history of their neighborhood.

Perhaps the best example of place-based learning is City High School's signature City Works program. Once a week students came to school for a half day to work with their year-long community partners in year-long or semester-long projects. Students also met for one period a week to continue their City Works work. Such partnerships included a science foundation connected with the local university, a historic theater, an art gallery, and a medical clinic. Place-based learning thus attempts to close gaps between "real life" and school curriculum, providing students with a more culturally responsive pedagogy that affords spaces for other ways of knowing and being.

Place-based learning resonates with and is complementary to CRP. The difference between CRP and place-based learning is one of emphasis, though both propose that teachers and students critically examine and question how, why, and at what costs dominant discourses construct societal cultures and spaces at the expense of its marginalized members. At the risk of oversimplification, one aspect of CRP strives to use learners' cultural ways of being and knowing as a vehicle for instruction as well as a source of content, while place-based learning takes as its starting point the varying contexts from which learners come—though both certainly can and do draw from cultural and contextual sources of knowledge.

Another important distinction is that CRP is an approach that consciously strives to work more effectively with students of color, while place-based learning does not have this specific mandate. However, as it is an approach that uses the students' culture/community as curricular content, it could very well be a form of CRP; it depends on student composition. Thus, Beth in the Spanish HL class approached her curriculum design within the context of place-based learning and an "unconscious" CRP: it was an unnamed and undeclared pedagogical orientation, but since her intention was to raise student critical consciousness, cultural competence, and academic abilities, the Spanish teacher's pedagogic goals were consistent with CRP practices.

Study Participants: Students and Teacher

I followed a group of 14 Mexican-origin students in two classroom contexts where they remained a cohort: a Spanish HL class (i.e., Spanish taught to learners who have ancestry in the target-language culture and possess varying proficiencies in Spanish) and a humanities class (a hybrid social studies–English course). Classes met the first and second periods of the day.

Even though all the HL students in the study agreed they were "Mexican"[3] as their ethnic identity, they still came from mixed ethnic and linguistic backgrounds; however, all of their mothers were of Mexican heritage. Students also varied in their Spanish-language proficiency; some were fluent Spanish speakers, while others mainly understood the language, but did not speak it. Despite the fluency of some, none had comparable Spanish-language literacy skills. Spanish was a *spoken* language, not a written or read language.

In addition to the students' varying ethnic/linguistic mixes, they also came from varying socioeconomic classes and educational backgrounds. Some lived in the city's tony foothills, in homes with their requisite swimming pools, while others lived in neighborhoods where drive-by shootings were a reality. At least half of the students had come from well-respected public schools and were well prepared academically; while at the other end of the spectrum, three students were known to have fourth-grade reading levels. The rest of the cohort fell somewhere in the middle academically and economically.

The teacher of the HL class was Beth, an Anglo woman in her late twenties. As a teen, Beth learned Spanish in school, and in her early twenties, she lived in South America. She taught high-school Spanish in her Midwestern hometown prior to beginning her graduate program at an Arizona university. As a graduate student, she taught Spanish at the university while also volunteering for a nonprofit group who worked to bring public attention to the plight of Mexican migrant workers. She was especially concerned about the undocumented Mexican nationals who die each year as they cross the scorching Sonoran Desert, primarily seeking work.

Shortly before this study began, Beth received her master's degree in border studies from the Latin American Studies program at the university. The founding teachers, though concerned that Beth was not Latina,[4] hired her because of her expertise with border issues. Considering the school's pedagogical framework of place-based learning, she seemed a logical choice to fill the position.

After spending a few weeks in the school, I revised my research question to center on understanding how "good" pedagogical intentions went wrong. I specifically ask why Spanish HLLs resisted "CRP-like" instruction that included topics such as Spanish-language discrimination, Chicano history, and Spanish-language skill building.

In the following section, I present classroom data that most exemplifies the themes that emerged to explain student dissatisfaction with their Spanish class. I present a "stretch" of elaborated classroom fieldnotes immediately followed by analysis/discussion so the reader can more readily connect the two. In the discussion, I also insert relevant excerpts from transcribed interviews and ethnographic information collected over the semester. I end this chapter with the study's implications and suggestions for HL pedagogy that is more sensitive to student needs while raising student awareness of the increased possibilities an expanded bilingualism can offer.

SPANISH FOR HERITAGE LANGUAGE LEARNERS— GOOD INTENTIONS GONE WRONG

The following classroom vignette and analysis, Segment I, comes from fieldnotes taken the second week of the semester. Though these notes were taken at the beginning of the semester, the overall ethos of the class did not change. Segment I comes from a two-hour lesson that represents a type of fractal of the issues and themes that arose from amassed fieldnotes taken during the first-semester Spanish class that contributed to student apathy-tinged resistance to classroom lessons. Below, the elaborated fieldnotes represent a day in the life of this class as well as show the seeds from which student discontent grew.

Segment I: Spanish at Hotel High: Foundations Built on Sand

(1) Clashes, Insecurity, and Teacher Ethos

"My friend is sitting there," Kathy protests.

I scoot over one seat. Chelsea arrives late and sits in the reserved spot. Kathy greets her in Spanish. I wonder if she does this to exclude me, not realizing that I, too, understand Spanish. This type of side conversation between students is the most Spanish that I have heard spoken by students so far. Students use Spanish to speak to one another "privately," like a secret language.

The renovations of City High School's downtown building were behind schedule. Thus classes for the past two weeks were being held at the downtown Ramada Hotel.

Beth reminds the students that today they will have a two-hour Spanish class.

"Why two hours?" Kathy asks.

"Beth told us on Monday," Olivia says, rolling her eyes.

"I want to hear it from *her*," Kathy spits back. Beth explains that the extended period is due to the humanities field trip exploring State Street, the street that runs parallel to the street where City High School will soon be welcoming students.

Beth finishes her explanation.

"*Satisfecha*, Kathy?" Beth says. The class laughs. Glaring at the laughing students, Kathy does not look satisfied.

Discussion

The primary point I want to emphasize in example 1, a phenomenon that repeated itself with different students over the course of the semester, is the pattern of hostile student interaction. Interstudent hostility represents one of the major reasons why students did not engage in their learning, as a safe environment for learning was never established. This pattern of hostility is shown between Kathy and Olivia in example 1 and again between Kathy and Josh in example 4 below.

These hostile student interactions created a negative classroom climate I found to be antithetical to the positive academic benefit of community-based knowledge construction found in exemplary CRP classrooms. In these classrooms students take responsibility for one another's learning and thus enable greater academic success for all students (Ladson-Billings 2009).

Observed student clashes occurred between two distinct groups: those who represented a more "Mexican" identity through dress and linguistic style (represented by Kathy, Chelsea, Luis, Paloma, and Marco) and those who did not (represented by Peter, Olivia, Isabel, Alec, Elizabeth, and Josh). Kathy was often at the center of these student clashes. Though Kathy had framed herself a "bully" outside of class, the data show many examples of Kathy being "bullied" in class. The bullying that she received revolved around her academic abilities. When she asked questions that others deemed "stupid," a fellow classmate would chastise her. When this occurred, she often lashed out with a curse or physical threat.

Only once in my fieldnotes did I record a teacher reprimanding this behavior directed at Kathy; this happened in Eve's humanities class around the same time period as this particular occurrence. Peter made a derisive comment toward Kathy to which she replied, "I'll slap your face." Eve ignored Kathy's violent threat and reprimanded Peter for stifling Kathy's right to ask questions. In Beth's class, the reprimands were typically directed at Kathy, not at the student who did the belittling. There were no attempts to build social peace between students and create a safe place for learning—that is, a safe place to make mistakes and engage in genuine inquiry.

Despite these negative student comments, Kathy wasn't completely discouraged from asking questions when she didn't understand something. For similarly "weak" students, they preferred to not participate in class—or they simply misbehaved. This was particularly true for Luis and Marco.

The other form of student hostility, not shown in example 1, occurred when a less proficient Spanish speaker would make a "mistake." This mistake always concerned the pronunciation of a Spanish word—that is, not sounding like a native-Spanish speaker. For example, a few days after reading Anzaldúa's (1987), "How to Tame a Wild Tongue," Beth asked students who the "zoot suiters" were. Josh responded, "The Pachucos." At his utterance, Luis and Marco laughed and repeated "Pachucos" in exaggerated Anglicized accents.

When pronunciation did not sound native-like, students would call this "speaking White" and rarely failed to humiliate the offender. The teacher never intervened. When this "teasing" transpired between friends (or non-friends), I detected embarrassment or humiliation on the part of the person being singled out for "talking White." Between friends, students showed this humiliation through timid smiles and shoulder shrugs, making eye contact with the "teaser." For the more mean-spirited criticism, students would usually tilt their heads down and avoid the gaze of the person criticizing.

For linguistic attacks, Juan, Marco, Chelsea, Paloma, and Luis, students who symbolically represented a more "Mexican" identity, generally delivered these pronunciation assaults. These students occasionally spoke Spanish to other Spanish-speaking friends in and outside of class—but generally not to Beth, their teacher. Their English also had traces of Spanish inflection, though English was (or had become) their dominant language.

The linguistic barbs they slung were aimed at students who did not outwardly represent a Mexican identity and had more limited Spanish-language proficiency, such as Josh and Alec. I want to emphasize, however, that there was no correlation between Mexican symbolic representation and Spanish-language proficiency. For example, Peter, Olivia, and Elizabeth were some of the most proficient Spanish speakers in the class, yet they did not outwardly express a Mexican identity through style.

Symbolically, the tension between the two groups presented itself spatially through student seating arrangements. When students were allowed to sit wherever they pleased, they separated themselves along these perceived ethnic lines—each group taking one-half of the room. Students were so disconnected from one another that several did not realize that all of them were of Mexican origin and some were fluent Spanish speakers. One would expect by the end of the semester that this sort of knowledge would have become self-evident, especially with only 14 students in a language class.

Indeed, Second Language Acquisition (SLA) theory recommends that language teachers create a highly interactive learning community among students, as interaction increases language acquisition and proficiency (not to mention that fostering friendships lowers nervousness that can impede and interfere with linguistic reception and production). The fact that this community was never established suggests that Beth was not well grounded in SLA theory and pedagogy, not to mention CRP literature advocating that teachers build caring communities of learners that foster the joint construction of knowledge and shared expertise (Garza 2008; Gay 2000; Ladson-Billings 2009). By not actively fostering classroom community, the tensions that impeded classroom learning never dissipated.

Though community building is good pedagogy for any classroom, it is especially true for the HL classroom, as language and identity are inextricably linked for HLLs—thus mandating that teachers construct a safe place for learners to use and experiment with the target language without losing face or a sense of self. Additionally, HLLs often see further acquisition of the HL as a means of bolstering or solidifying their ethnic identity (Kondo-Brown 2005), which is especially salient for the adolescent learner whose life stage includes the discovery and questioning of "self" (Tatum 1997) *while* straddling (at least) two cultures and languages. If there is a reluctance to participate in the HL language, the acquisition process is severely stalled, thus hampering essential identity needs.

The tensions and physical pressure of harassment between students was also observed outside of class. One morning as Peter was leaving his mother's car to enter school, he paused and, through the school's street-facing windows, he saw Kathy and her two Native American friends, a trio who referred to themselves as "the mean girls." After seeing the girls he told his mother that he didn't want to go to school because he was afraid of the "Mexicans." "But we're Mexican, too," Betty laughed. Peter reluctantly entered the building, avoiding the trio.

Peter's comment underscores the complex nature of identity for these students. Although Peter is Mexican, identifies as Mexican, and speaks fluent Spanish, he fears "Mexicans," though two of the "Mexicans" were Native American. Peter appears to be tapping into societal stereotypes that cast (southwest) gang members as looking a certain way, that is, indexing a "Mexican" identity that connotes danger and criminality. The increasing number of violent crimes inflicted by Mexican national drug cartel members in the Arizona-Mexico borderlands adds to this stereotype of "Mexican gang member."

Despite Peter's professed fear, he, more than any other student, attacked Kathy in class. Perhaps one explanation is that the classroom offered him some kind of protection where he felt free to hurl attacks where he otherwise would not have that freedom. Kathy, on the other hand, could more fully act out her anger outside of the classroom, away from any authority. Kathy's bullying behavior outside of class may result from a pattern of being picked on in class, or perhaps her in-class "bullies" represent "weaker" individuals who have a "safe" space in which they can retaliate against her.

These types of student antagonisms help to explain, in part, student reluctance to actively participate in class, as one "wrong move" could result in student harassment for being perceived as "stupid"[5] or non-Mexican. In the context of the observed HL class, student fear of failure may have been especially acute because of the great variation in academic ability/preparation and Spanish-language proficiency. No matter which way some (if not most) students would turn, there was the potential to "sound stupid" and/or momentarily lose their ascribed ethnic identity. Thus, silence was safe.

The stymieing ridicule for speaking Spanish with a non-native accent is directly related to the concept of *linguistic insecurity* (González 2001). Linguistic insecurity refers to feelings of inadequacy and/or shame when speaking a language that is no longer or has never been one's dominant language, but connects one to his or her ethnic identity group. HLLs, who identify with the target-language culture, may thus feel embarrassed or ashamed by their lack of linguistic proficiency in the language closely linked to their professed ethnic identity; and so, to preserve ethnic membership and face, the language is not spoken, but left for others to assume some level of proficiency.

This insecurity or "shyness" (Krashen 1998) is further compounded when members of the same ethnic group, who are more proficient speakers, ridicule or provide harsh corrective feedback. Krashen (1998) explains that this creates a vicious cycle whereby learners are inhibited to speak for fear of ridicule, thereby leading to "less [linguistic] input, and less input means less proficiency" (p. 41). Therefore, the reticence that students displayed in regard to public Spanish speaking can in part be attributed to linguistic insecurity. Ironically, by *not* speaking Spanish, the participants in the study preserved their Mexican identity; they did not dare to risk sounding "White" while speaking their HL.

Heritage language learning, unlike any other school subject, is a learning site where one's ethnicity (or essence) can be contested. One not only risks sounding "stupid," but one also risks ethnic identity negation in which one is betrayed by one's own talk. Thus, the less proficient speaker who may be studying his or her HL for identity needs can run the risk that their declared ethnicity may be questioned, ridiculed, or challenged. Heritage language teachers must understand that HLLs need protection and that a safe learning environment must be established if students are to use and thus acquire the HL.

At the end of example 1, the teacher's *satisfecha* [satisfied] also shows a tone of frustration or exasperation with Kathy, which perhaps fuels the students' laughter after its utterance. From attending teacher meetings, I know that Beth was experiencing a high degree of frustration with the lack of structure and discipline that she saw as a growing problem at the new school. At this time in the semester, the teachers were still in the process of constructing a discipline matrix to be uniformly used by faculty.

With no formal codes of conduct and consequences, coupled with the hotel's unorthodox learning environment, a genuinely chaotic environment took hold that the school never shook that first year. In meetings, Beth most actively voiced her concern about this, and it showed in her demeanor with students across all of her classes.

Beth's kind and light-hearted spirit that was her persona outside of class was not present in class. In class, Beth was serious; her voice and face showed evidence of strain, her brow was often furrowed. She rarely smiled or joked with students. Her serious and somewhat unfriendly teaching ethos persisted throughout the semester. Her teaching persona conveyed an uncaring stance that did not invite friendly interaction between her and her students. Cultivating an atmosphere of respect through caring relationships is particularly significant for Latino and Latina students (Garza 2008) as it is a critical source of motivation for Latino and Latina students who may feel marginalized by the schooling process (Perez 2000).

Ladson-Billings (2009) found that the ability to form positive relationships between students and teacher was one of the most important criteria for identifying exemplary CRP educators. Gay (2000) emphasizes that the actual sites for determining successful learning resides in the interactions between learners—and between learners and their teacher. The fact that this positive student-teacher relationship was missing adds another dimension to the explanation of student nonperformance.

So, in addition to student animosity toward one another, the same could be said for how students felt about their teacher to a certain degree. In focus group interviews, students commented that one of the reasons they did not like the Spanish class was because they could not relate to the teacher and preferred their other teachers—especially Eve, their humanities teacher.

The tensions between students, and students and teacher, never fully dissipated in the first semester. I argue that this lack of social cohesion and classroom community was a root cause for constructing a learning environment that did not promote active student engagement with classroom topics, language-learning tasks, or civil/helpful stances with one another and their teacher. Establishing a trusting, respectful environment may be the most crucial factor for ideal language learning, as unfettered language production is key for language acquisition; any kind of fear of failure or unease with classmates or teacher can thus spell disaster for the language learner.

Although a positive classroom environment that fosters positive interpersonal relationships is a necessary first step for any learning to occur, *what* was taught in class also played a role.

(2) Performance Strike!

After clarifying for Kathy the reason behind the two-hour lesson, Beth, speaking in both English and Spanish, explains to students the *Habits of Heart and Mind*—the school's educational rubric for creating and assessing student work within the overall framework of place-based learning. City High School's promotional materials describe these pedagogic practices as fundamental for cultivating lifelong learning through the development of good habits such as "examining multiple perspectives, using evidence, and collaborating with others."

Conceptually, the *Habits of Heart and Mind* is often found in the promotional materials and websites of progressive private and public (primarily charter) K–12 schools, though each defines the habits uniquely depending on the school's educational construct. At City High School, the habits include the following: *Action* (What can I do to make things better?); *Inquiry* (What do I want to know?); *Reflection* (What can I learn about myself?); *Expression* (How can I share what I think and feel?); *Evidence* (How do I know what I know?); and *Perspective* (Whose viewpoint should I consider?).

These habits guide teachers in the design of course units and projects, a construct that is shared throughout the entire school curriculum that also informs how teachers assign grades. They also provide a shared vocabulary for teachers, students, and parents to use for discussing student work and progress at semester-end conferences.[6]

During the second week at the new school, teachers introduced *Habits of Heart and Mind* in their classes and again in their advisories—classes where teachers advise, council, and bond with the same student cohort throughout the students' entire stay at the school. Tapping the habit of *inquiry,* Beth used it to segue into a small-group activity where they were to brainstorm what they would like to learn that semester in Spanish class.

Eve, one of the founders of the new school and the students' humanities teacher, suggested the idea of creating a student-generated "menu" of topics to form the semester's syllabus. Beth had sought Eve's advice due to her frustration with the students' grumblings over taking the compulsory Spanish class. Though example 2 is brief, I want to pause here to introduce another key factor that contributed to student dissatisfaction and reticence to participate in class.

Discussion

As mentioned above, an important aspect of the day's lesson was for students to brainstorm topics they would like to cover in first-semester Spanish. During the first week of classes, students had balked at the rudimentary verb conjugations they were asked to do. They rightfully considered this task to be "like, for fifth graders." In response, Isabel, Peter, and Olivia asked if they could instead take French. Elizabeth and Josh asked if they could take an advanced math class in place of Spanish. As these two classes were not available, Beth promised them that "things would get better."

It is interesting to note that these "complainers"[7] had come from Performing to Excelling public schools[8] and thus expected better; they also had enough agency to express their needs and offer alternatives. This is not to say that those who did not overtly complain came from underperforming schools;

it is just that those who spoke out had "good" schools in common. The remaining students did not loudly voice their complaints, but their lethargy and reluctance to actively participate in class spoke volumes.

This reluctance to participate is what Ira Shor (1992) calls *performance strike*. Performance strikes are informal, "unorganized mass refusal to perform well" (p. 20). Performance strikes emanate from student dissatisfaction with classroom tasks, which they find meaningless, impersonal, and autocratic. Often a strike manifests itself through "low motivation, low test scores and achievement" and "discipline problems" (p. 21).

Shor claims that such behaviors will persist if students are given irrelevant, teacher-imposed work that is disconnected from their lived experience. As long as students feel that they have no voice in their own education, active participatory learning will not occur. Thus, Beth's decision to have students select topics to study seemed like a sound plan to break the strike and give students voice and more control of their own learning.

But as I will explain in the discussion of the following excerpt (example 3), things did not proceed as expected, which contributed to the continued strike-like behavior exhibited in the first semester. This behavior consisted of reluctance to actively contribute to class discussions, read aloud, or answer grammatical or textbook specific questions. Example 3 shows the results of what students had decided to study.

(3) A Lost Opportunity

Speaking English, Beth asks students to: "Make a proposition on how you would like to improve your literacy, like reading *Motorcycle Diaries* or studying contemporary social issues." At this, Josh suggests that they study Proposition 200 on the upcoming Arizona 2003 November ballot, a proposition that would render it criminal to aid or educate illegal immigrants. With Josh and his sister Elizabeth's conservative views, I wonder on what side of the issue he falls.

Slowly, students form small groups. I sit with Chelsea and Kathy.

"What do we have to do?" Kathy asks Chelsea and me. She leans back in her seat, her arms folded across her chest.

"Pick any topic that you would like to study in Spanish class," I say. She looks at me skeptically.

"I don't know," Kathy says in a burst. Chelsea picks up her notebook and pencil, her actions volunteering her to be our note taker.

"Really, pick whatever you want," I say. I was feeling optimistic about Beth's new plan. I prod the girls to honestly write down what they are interested in doing and studying.

Eventually, all the small groups report back. Beth writes the students' suggestions on a flip chart propped up at the front of the room. The list includes Spanish-language rap, films, food, and *chupacabras*—literally, goatsuckers. Chupacabras are mythical, small, bear-sized reptilian beasts that suck the blood out of goats and other livestock; individuals report that they have spotted the creatures as far north as Maine and as far south as Chile. The urban legends surrounding the Chupacabra are of the same ilk as stories of Sasquatch, the Loch Ness Monster, and UFO sightings.

Discussion

Example 3, if studied as a snapshot, shows pedagogic promise. Instead of a teacher dictating what students will learn, Beth taps student interest, creating a democratic, learner-centered approach. As Spanish proficiency is not as strictly regulated through state norms or high-stakes tests, language teachers have freedom to create curriculum that best fits the needs and interests of their students. Here, students chose a menu of film, food, music, and popular folklore. Mexican music alone through its regional variation, rich lyrics, numerous forms (e.g., *Norteño, rock/rap en Español, ranchera, corrido, marcha,* Latin ska), or type of musical ensemble (e.g., *mariachi, banda, marimba, conjunto Norteño*) could form the basis of an entire course alone.

Indeed, through my school and classroom observations, I quickly realized that music was a passion for students, their ubiquitous music players a constant source of student-teacher contention. Thus, tapping into students' all-consuming interest would seem a logical choice for introducing learners to tough or uncomfortable topics. Considering the school's framework of place-based learning, border issues could be explored through coupling the writing of Gloria Anzaldúa (Beth's choice) and the music of Northern Mexico (i.e., *Norteño corrido*).

For instance, *Narcocorrido* [drug ballad], a controversial musical style rooted in the polka-based *Norteño* folk tradition, with its themes of drug trafficking, illegal immigration, and the poor and destitute, could serve as a relevant contemporary juxtaposition to Anzaldúa's earlier writing. By including music, the conversation becomes rooted in something students are more intrinsically interested in, with the potential thereby of deepening the conversation concerning the contentious border.

Song lyrics as Spanish-language texts are also rich linguistically and culturally. For example, the *narcocorridos* contain complex grammar, varied vocabulary, relevant themes, and strong rhetorical content, all of which can be unpacked in classroom exercises and discussion. Students could also examine similar lyrical content in Mexican rap, thus comparing and analyzing genre, style, intended audience, and impact. Though some may balk at using *narco-corridos*, the genre offers a means for confronting and discussing the border reality of human and drug trafficking that is increasingly becoming bloodier and deadlier.

In addition to the possible benefits of using music to teach, the HL class also had a resident music expert: mariachi violinist, Chelsea. Although Chelsea had been a member of a prestigious mariachi group and was well versed in the various forms of Mexican music, her expertise was never utilized during the course of the semester, nor was her musical background even discussed. In terms of film, the other expert was Olivia's mother, Marta; she could have been invited to show the documentary film she had shot in Oaxaca, Mexico, and to speak in Spanish of her filmmaking experience.

Though political topics or topics of Latino and Latina discrimination were not present in the students' list (despite Josh's suggestion), it is not to say that these topics could not also be covered, especially considering Beth's expertise and personal experience with such issues (and assuming the personal experiences that some of the students may have had). In order to respect student choice, while also including important critical course content, issues of discrimination could be amplified and complemented by music and/or film.

But the students' suggestions (and the group's own expertise) and propositions were never used. There was never any music, film, food, or *chupacabras*, save for a classic "Day of the Dead" film shown at Halloween. For the greater part of the semester, Beth had students use a standard Spanish-language textbook and a supplementary textbook designed for HLLs. Students worked on vocabulary lists and took vocabulary quizzes and, on occasion, the teacher taught historical content regarding Latinos and Latinas such as the heroism of Mexican soldiers fighting for the United States during WWII—their deaths granting their families citizenship.

Not following through with student stated interests was a lost opportunity and a serious breach of faith. Students continued to performance strike. Class morale got worse; students became more withdrawn and sullen and had occasional discipline problems. Not even the earlier "complainers" complained. No one even inquired about their "menu" of ideas; total apathy reigned.

Josh in particular took the uninspired class hard. His classroom comportment worsened each week. He often disrespectfully lashed out at the teacher, questioning her intellectual authority whenever he could. He and his sister Elizabeth left the school at winter break. Kathy, Juan, and Andrea also left. Luis was expelled.

Example 4 highlights the final issue that this classroom data offers: the challenging task of teaching literacy skills to HLLs. This type of student resistance stems from the difficulty of the learning tasks themselves.

(4) I Hate Writing in Spanish

Toward the end of the first hour of class, Beth, referring to the habit of Reflection, asks the class to reflect upon their linguistic strengths in writing—in Spanish.

"Do we have to write in Spanish?" asks Kathy.

"Yes," Beth says.

"Shit," Kathy says.

"No bad language," Josh scolds. Kathy glares at him.

"I hate writing in Spanish," Chelsea says. Beth assures students that she will circulate around the room to help them.

All but Kathy and Juan take out a sheet of paper to begin. To further exemplify the task, Beth mentions that Juan is an expert at mixing English and Spanish to form new words, like "kickiarando."[9] She also suggests that they think about the Spanish reading they have recently finished in order to assess their reading skill level and vocabulary knowledge.

"What if you know all the words?" Olivia asks. Beth walks over to Olivia and they speak quietly to one another. The rest of the students write.

"How do you spell *tiene* [he/she/it has]?" Kathy asks Beth from the last row. Beth leaves Olivia and comes over to Kathy. In response to Kathy's question, Beth reviews the Spanish sound system in order to help Kathy match her spoken Spanish phonetics to Spanish letters so as to help her with her spelling, much like one teaches a new reader/writer "to sound it out." Beth moves on to another student.

Discussion

In example 4, we see once more the somewhat hostile learning environment as demonstrated through Kathy and Josh's interaction. Again, the teacher doesn't intervene, thus abdicating her role of keeping the classroom safe. However, it is possible that Josh ventriloquizes or voices what Beth could scold ("No bad language"), and thus spares her having to play the "tough guy" in this instance, allowing students to monitor one another's behavior.

In this segment, some of the characteristics found in HL classrooms and amongst HLLs stand out. One characteristic is the English-influenced, innovative Spanish that some HLLs use. This is exemplified through Juan's ability to create neologisms. Only a relatively proficient Spanish and English speaker could do this. Juan's language use embodies the phenomenon of *language contact*—when two or more languages interact and influence one another.

Language contact can include lexical borrowing (i.e., when one language adopts a word from the other language, such as "rendezvous" borrowed from

French), code-switching (i.e., when bilingual speakers use both languages interchangeably in a single conversation), or the creation of innovative grammar and lexical forms, such as Pachuco Spanish (Anzaldúa 1987; Barker Carpenter 1974; Brito 1990).

Despite these linguistically interesting innovations, the tendency can exist for HL teachers to dissuade students from using linguistic forms resulting from language contact so that learners can better acquire "standard" Spanish. For example, instead of calling the midday meal *lonche*, a word derived from "lunch," students are instead taught *almuerzo* [lunch]. Some teachers also discourage code-switching.

A more complicated issue is the case where HLLs speak a nonprestige variety of Spanish, a Spanish they most likely learned from family members who lived in rural areas or had limited formal schooling. It is difficult for these learners to distinguish prestige and nonprestige forms (Valdés 1995) and thus they are prone to using inappropriate forms when the context requires a more formal register such as an academic exam. As far as I could discern, none of the students spoke stigmatized forms of Spanish but, as so little Spanish was spoken in class, it was nearly impossible for me to know.

Beth, to her credit, does not try to alter the way Juan speaks; instead she acknowledges and praises his linguistic versatility. The approach to use with students who speak nonprestige forms of language or who use lexical items born from language contact (i.e., "Spanglish") is to treat these forms as a linguist would, that is, non-judgmentally: no language or dialect is superior to another, and social context dictates form. A sociolinguistic approach that teaches students about language varieties (e.g., Mexican Spanish versus Iberian Spanish) and variation (i.e., language use often relates to age, gender, etc.) would help teachers avoid the risk of stigmatizing students and their linguistic communities.

Unfortunately, this may not be a common practice in today's Spanish-language classrooms, most likely a result of poor or limited teacher training regarding sociolinguistics and HLLs as well as strongly held linguistic teacher biases that privilege Iberian Spanish or dismiss or disparage the Spanish spoken as a result of language contact. In fact, native Spanish-speaking teachers can hold their students in contempt for not speaking "standard" Spanish (N. Lefkowitz, personal communication, March 23, 2009), a bias that may have its roots in economic and social class prejudices.

Example 4 shows another common phenomenon found within HLLs: asymmetrical language proficiencies. Both Chelsea and Kathy complain about having to write in Spanish. Their dislike of writing did not concern composition processes, against which many students may bristle, as what students were asked to do involved only simple declarative sentences.

Though the girls were proficient Spanish speakers—Spanish was Kathy's first language—their writing skills came nowhere near their speaking skills.

It appears that Kathy may not have Spanish literacy skills (i.e., not knowing the correspondence between produced sounds to alphabetic symbols). Because of this lack of awareness or formal Spanish-language schooling, it is not uncommon for HLLs to use their knowledge of the English language writing system to produce written Spanish, causing frequent misspellings.[10] This can also happen with the foreign-language (FL) learner, but this learner has most likely learned literacy linearly, with the sound system coming first. Foreign-language learners are also limited to what they can express in the target language, as their language competence at this stage is far less developed than HLLs.

Heritage language learners, on the other hand, can have a lot to *say*, but *writing* it down on paper is the problem. Thus, for most of these students, writing in Spanish is a challenge, especially when compared to their more developed speaking and listening skills. This frustrating and challenging aspect of acquiring Spanish-language literacy was most likely another contributing factor to students' reluctance to participate in classroom literacy-based activities.

As indicated in a student interview with Chelsea, there was also the perception that there was no need to acquire Spanish-language literacy, as their spoken Spanish was "good enough" to accomplish their communicative needs, consequently rendering "Spanish [class] a waste of time." This perception that Spanish literacy was not a relevant life skill fueled learner apathy. As Chelsea commented: "I mean, because it's not like I'm gonna go to Mexico to work and like write an ess—like an application and an essay explaining everything, you know."

Thus, it can be inferred that for literacy development to be meaningful for students, they had to directly experience its benefit and need. Textbook-style learning and nonrelevant vocabulary lists did not afford this immediate real world application of Spanish-language literacy development. Unlike content learning in the humanities class, students never used Spanish or course content to communicate or learn in real ways for authentic purposes or intrinsic needs or interests. For a school founded on place-based learning, with its proximity to the Mexican border and local Spanish-speaking communities, it is a wonder that relationships with these communities were not utilized and developed.

Finally, the examples of Kathy and Olivia show how HLLs can vary greatly in their reading, writing, speaking, and listening proficiencies, even when they are placed in the same class. Olivia (a third-generation Spanish speaker) had the most developed Spanish-language academic skills. Olivia had attended a bilingual elementary school before moving to Arizona; she had also attended a Mexican school in Oaxaca, Mexico, while her mother worked there. She often finished her work first and showed boredom. Especially toward the end of the school year, her boredom manifested itself as disruptive classroom behaviors that included side conversations, drawing on other people, and hurling items across the room (behaviors that never manifested in her other classes).

The above learner and classroom characteristics show how HL instruction is a complex juggling act. Behavior problems can arise from material that is too easy or too difficult. In sum, Beth faced myriad challenges: teaching fluent speakers to read, captivating students "who already knew it all," confronting students who held stereotypical beliefs regarding ethnic identity and in-group membership, providing learners with critical academic content, and creating a caring classroom, all while navigating a chaotic institutional environment. Beth had good intentions for this class, but too many negative forces and unwise pedagogical choices converged to make for an unsuccessful class.

IMPLICATIONS AND CONCLUSIONS: WHAT CAN WE LEARN FROM "BAD BEHAVIOR"?

Through the lens of resistance, or what William James in the opening epigraph calls "bad behavior," the complexities surrounding Spanish HL instruction became apparent. Student resistance or nonperformance brought into relief the personal, pedagogic, and linguistic factors against which students negatively reacted. In brief, the origin of student resistance had its deepest root in disrespect that contributed to the class's lack of community cohesion.

Students showed antagonisms toward one another and, at times, their teacher. Further contributing factors fueling student resistance to Spanish-language learning included the teacher's decision to not respect the students' requested input for thematic course content and the subsequent lessons that relied too heavily on textbook instruction, as opposed to place-based learning that included students' communities, interests, and expertise.

Although Segment I shows the failures of this CRP-like place-based Spanish class, adhering to a strict CRP–place-based approach may have helped to ameliorate the above factors. A foundation of exemplary CRP teaching as outlined by Ladson-Billings (2009), Gay (2000), and Garza (2008) is the creation of a respectful classroom community where students and teachers genuinely care for one another personally and academically and involve themselves in learning that is intrinsically meaningful.

Since HLLs may risk identity negation through their use of a non-fully acquired heritage language, a safe and respectful learning environment is essential if learning is to occur, especially if that learning is rooted in projects that students are legitimately concerned about. As the HLLs' exposure to Spanish has been through actual experience, a textbook approach to learning can feel contrived and false, especially when textbooks ignore language pragmatics (i.e., how a language is appropriately used in real life contexts) or favor non-local Spanish varieties that unconsciously disparage the students' HL, as they know it.

Imagined Communities

The concept of *imagined communities* (Anderson 1991), succinctly defined by Kanno and Norton (2003) as "groups of people, not immediately tangible and accessible, with whom we connect through the power of the imagination" (p. 241), is a useful construct to help explain the negative dynamics at play in the Spanish classroom. Because of the students' limited imaginings of who is a legitimate member of their ethnic and discourse communities—restricted by their limited lived experience—they were reluctant to accept others who did not fit their "imagined community."

Their behavior toward one another and their teacher suggests that students held a limited concept of who speaks Spanish and how it is spoken. Many held the native-speaker ideal in terms of fluency and accent as the only acceptable way to speak Spanish, leading them to censure one another and themselves. Without sufficient discussion, awareness raising, and broadened real-world experience, the limits of these HLLs' imaginations were never challenged or expanded.

Grounded in limited imaginings, student ideologies included beliefs that increased Spanish language development was "a waste of time," as they could not imagine a future where Spanish language literacy could figure. They viewed that only an oral, informal facility with Spanish was necessary for their present and future lives.

They could not imagine professional and personal communities in which their cultural and linguistic knowledge would be valued—spaces that might demand more sophisticated uses of language, both in English and Spanish. Students' incapacity to envision how fully formed Spanish language literacy would enrich their lives is a direct result of societal prejudices against Spanish-English bilingualism and bilinguals whose first language is not English. Societal bigotry is particularly harsh regarding those of Mexican origin, whose increased U.S. numbers are seen as threatening, both economically and socially.

The "limits of the imagination" also applied to the Spanish teacher. Beth's limited imagination shaped her view of Latinos and Latinas and their experiences. She primarily imagined this community through a border-conflicted political lens—not surprising, considering her degree in border studies and her political activism. Although her expertise is important for teaching students how to interrogate hegemonic practices, her narrow focus revealed a less nuanced understanding of the political, social, and linguistic variations that existed in the local Latino or Latina community. Whenever she strayed from the textbook, the themes she continually revisited centered on border conflict and Mexicans as victims—themes that students thought too restrictive and not fully descriptive of their actual experience.

The teacher's limited imagination also applied to how the HL course eventually reverted back to all-too-common foreign-language practices that include an over-reliance on textbook learning and rote memorization. Not all foreign language teachers embrace these practices, but it is a common critique of the field. In addition, Beth did not utilize the abundant community resources both inside and outside of her class, a surprising fact considering the school's pedagogic philosophy of place-based learning.

Hence, it behooves teachers of students of color to cultivate in themselves and in their students *practices of the imagination,* described by Wenger (1998) as "a process of expanding our self by transcending our time and space and creating new images of the world and ourselves" (p. 176). This process can begin through classroom-based discussions that then move into the actual world of experience. Through an *experiential community-based heritage language approach*, students are not instructed about themselves, as was the case in the present study, but students learn about their community through hands-on projects.

An example of an experiential community-based approach (though not in an HL class) occurred in a third-year City Works class that studied illegal Mexican migration into the United States. Through field experiences, students studied the intricacies of the Arizona-Mexico border first hand. They met with community activist groups on both sides of the debate, filled water tanks stationed in the desert for Mexican crossers, witnessed the destruction of desert habitats resulting from illegal crossings, met with local politicians, and read political briefings on the issue.

At the annual City Works Student Showcase, it was apparent from student presentations that the class experience greatly complicated their views on the migration debate. The issue was no longer black and white as it is often framed, but an issue fraught with complexity that will not be readily resolved. Although not all schools have the luxury to have such courses, it is still in their capacity to offer course content relevant to school communities, invite expert community members to speak to students, go on field trips, and assign out of class work that involves hands-on experience.

Spanish-language literacy development needs to be contextualized and embedded in real-world experiences that are completed for authentic purposes such as volunteering with Spanish monolingual children or elders, shadowing a Spanish-English court interpreter, or writing an immigration narrative of a family member. Reading and writing thus is not an end in itself, but a necessary means for effective communication, especially if that communication holds meaning for the student. Through authentic practice, students will understand how developing their Spanish-language literacy can be useful to them and may realize that classroom learning can develop skills that are not readily developed through casual conversation.

To conclude, the present study does not mean to suggest that only Latinos and Latinas can teach other Latinos and Latinas, but it does suggest that teachers have a responsibility to develop their practices of imagination by understanding who their students are, as well as opening their imaginations of what learning is. Foreign-language teaching has for too long relied on published materials and textbook learning. Language and culture are much too complicated and varied for this type of pedagogy to prevail.

For any language class, but in particular the HL class, the real world is the classroom; hence, teachers need to broaden their repertoires of what is considered academic. Through authentic real-world projects, teachers' imaginations also widen as they and their students learn about their communities together with the goal of knocking down the walls of their imagined ones.

NOTES

1. Participant names have been changed. Students at the new school called teachers by their first names.

2. I still attended school events in its third year, but I was not a daily participant-observer.

3. Students did not use the hyphenated Mexican-American to describe themselves. They simply said Mexican. For the ethnic description of parents, "Mexican" refers to parents who were born in Mexico and Mexican-American refers to second and subsequent generations of individuals with Mexican ancestry.

4. A Latina native Spanish-speaking teacher was originally hired for the position, but as she was a PhD student at the time, she declined the offer as she realized the job would entail too much work. Beth had been the runner-up for the position and gladly accepted the offer.

5. For decades, "second language" has been commonly used in the field of applied linguistics. Nonetheless, this nomenclature masks the fact that for some "second" language learners, they are acquiring third or more languages.

6. Advisory teacher, parent(s)/guardian(s), student, and another individual of the student's choosing attend conferences. For example, students can invite another relative, a classmate, another teacher at the school, the school secretary, a researcher, etc. This format highlights the importance of community in one's learning.

7. With regard to example 1 above, these students were also students who did not symbolically represent a Mexican identity. There may be a correlation between agency and social identity, but this was not a focus of the study.

8. The local school district rated public schools (in this case, K–8) based on students' averaged standardized test scores on three testing instruments (AIMS, Arizona Measure of Academic Progress, and an English proficiency test). Based on these scores, schools receive either Failing, Underperforming, Performing, Performing Plus, Highly Performing, or Excelling labels.

9. This is how I have the word written in my notes, but I am not certain of its correctness. Its form however, suggests "to kick it" or "kick back" plus "-ando," the morpheme that indicates the progressive tense, similar to "-ing" in English.

10. Young monolingual Spanish learners will also make similar spelling errors such as confusing letters that have a similar sound (e.g., /b/ and /v/). Therefore, with HLLs, it is uncertain if their literacy challenges are also a result of arrested Spanish literacy development.

REFERENCES

Alonso, G., N. S. Anderson, C. Su, and J. Theoharis. (2009). *Our Schools Suck: Students Talk Back to a Segregated Nation on the Failures of Urban Education.* New York: New York University Press.

Anderson, B. (1991). *Imagined Communities: Reflections on the Origin and Spread of Nationalism* (Revised ed.). London: Verso.

Anzaldúa, G. (1987). *Borderlands/La Frontera: The New Mestiza.* San Francisco: Aunt Lute Books.

Barker Carpenter, G. (1974). *Pachuco: An American-Spanish Argot and its Social Functions in Tucson, Arizona.* Tucson: The University of Arizona Press.

Brito, A. (1990). *El Diablo en Texas/The Devil in Texas.* Tempe, AZ: Bilingual Review Press.

Brito, I., A. Lima, and E. R. Auerbach. (2004). "The Logic of Nonstandard Teaching: A Course in Cape Verdean Language, Culture, and History." In B. Norton and K. Toohey (eds.), *Critical Pedagogies and Language Learning* (pp. 181–200). Cambridge: Cambridge University Press.

Carreira, M. (2003). "Profiles of SNS Students in the Twenty-First Century: Pedagogical Implications of the Changing Demographics and Social Status of U.S. Hispanics." In A. Roca and M. C. Colombi (eds.), *Mi Lengua: Spanish as a*

Heritage Language in the United States (pp. 51–77). Washington, DC: Georgetown University Press.

Cazden, C., and E. Leggett. (1981). "Culturally Responsive Education: Recommendations for Achieving Lau Remedies II." In H. Trueba, E. Guthrie, and K. Au (eds.), *Culture and the Bilingual Classroom: Studies in Classroom Ethnography* (pp. 69–86). Rowley, MA: Newbury.

Combs, M. C. (2006). *The 1C Americanization Program, Proposition 203 and Structured English Immersion* (SEI). Unpublished lecture. University of Arizona.

Dutro, E., E. Kazemi, R. Balf, and Y. S. Lin. (2008). "What Are You and Where Are You From?": Race, Identity, and the Vicissitudes of Cultural Relevance. *Urban Education, 43*, 269–300.

Erickson, F., and G. Mohatt. (1982). "Culturally Organization and Participant Structures in Two Classrooms." In G. Spindler (ed.), *Doing Ethnography of Schooling* (pp. 131–74). New York: Holt, Rinehart, & Winston.

Esposito, J., and A. N. Swain. (2009). "Pathways to Social Justice: Urban Teachers' Uses of Culturally Relevant Pedagogy as a Conduit for Teaching Social Justice." *Perspectives on Urban Education, Spring*, 38–48.

Garza, R. (2008). "Latino and White High School Students' Perceptions of Caring Behaviors: Are We Culturally Responsive to Our Students?" [Electronic Version]. *Urban Education OnlineFirst*. Retrieved from uex.sagepub.com hosted at online .sagepub.com.

Gay, G. (2000). *Culturally Responsive Teaching: Theory, Research, and Practice.* New York: Teachers College Press.

González, N. (2001). *I Am My Language: Discourses of Women and Children in the Borderlands.* Tucson: University of Arizona Press.

Gruenewald, D. A. (2003a). "Foundations of Place: A Multidisciplinary Framework for Place-Conscious Education." *American Educational Research Journal, 40*, 619–54.

———. (2003b). "The Best of Both Worlds: A Critical Pedagogy of Place." *Educational Researcher, 32*(4), 3–12.

Hancock, S. D. (2006). "White Women's Work: On the Front Lines in Urban Education." In J. Landsman and C. W. Lewis (eds.), *White Teachers/Diverse Classrooms: A Guide to Building Inclusive Schools, Promoting High Expectations, and Eliminating Racism* (pp. 93–109). Sterling, VA: Stylus Publishing.

Haymes, S. (1995). *Race, Culture and the City: A Pedagogy for Black Urban Struggle.* Albany: State University of New York Press.

Hordatt Gentles, C. (2007). "Critical Pedagogy and Authoritarian Culture: Challenges of Jamaican Migrant Teachers in American Urban Schools." In R. P. Solomon and D. N. R. Sekayi (eds.), *Urban Teacher Education and Teaching: Innovative Practices for Diversity and Social Justice* (pp. 129–46). Mahwah, NJ: Lawrence Erlbaum Associates.

James, W. (1899). *Talks to Teachers on Psychology: And to Students on Some of Life's Ideals.* New York: Henry Holt and Company.

Kanno, Y., and B. Norton. (2003). "Imagined Communities and Educational Possibilities: Introduction." *Journal of Language, Identity, and Education, 2,* 241–49.

Kohler, A. D., and M. Lazarín. (2007). "Hispanic Education in the United States." *NCLR (National Council of a La Raza) Statistical Brief, 8,* 1–16.

Kondo-Brown, K. (2005). "Differences in Language Skills: Heritage Language Learner Subgroups and Foreign Language Learners." *The Modern Language Journal, 89,* 563–81.

Krashen, S. (1998). "Language Shyness and Heritage Language Development." In S. Krashen, L. Tse, and J. McQuillan (eds.), *Heritage Language Development* (pp. 41–49). Culver City, CA: Language Education Associates.

Ladson-Billings, G. (1995). "Toward a Theory of Culturally Relevant Pedagogy." *American Educational Research Journal, 32,* 465–91.

———. (2009). *The Dreamkeepers: Successful Teachers of African American Children* (2nd ed.). San Francisco: Jossey-Bass.

Lewicki, J. (2000). *100 Days of Learning in Place: How a Small School Utilized "Place-Based" Learning to Master State Academic Standards.* Washington, DC: Rural School and Community Trust.

Long, V., W. S. Bush, and P. Theobald. (2003). *"Place" Value: The Rural Perspective. Occasional Paper.* Arlington, VA: National Science Foundation, Appalachian Collaborative Center for Learning, Assessment, and Instruction in Mathematics.

Loveland, E. (2003). "Achieving Academic Goals through Place-Based Learning: Students in Five States Show How to Do It." *Rural Roots, 4*(1), 6–11.

Obama, B. (February 24, 2009). *Remarks of President Barack Obama: Address to Joint Session of Congress.* Retrieved from www.whitehouse.gov/the_press _office/Remarks-of-President-Barack-Obama-Address-to-Joint-Session-of -Congress/.

Perez, S. A. (2000). "An Ethic of Caring in Teaching Culturally Diverse Students." *Education, 121*(1), 102–05.

Sheridan, T. E. (1986). *Los Tucsonenses: The Mexican Community in Tucson 1854–1941.* Tucson: The University of Arizona Press.

Shor, I. (1992). *Empowering Education: Critical Teaching for Social Change.* Chicago: The University of Chicago Press.

Tatum, B. D. (1997). *"Why Are All the Black Kids Sitting Together in the Cafeteria?": And Other Conversations about Race.* New York: Basic Books.

Theoharis, J. (2009). "'I Hate It when People Treat Me Like a Fxxx-Up": Phony Theories, Segregated Schools, and the Culture of Aspirations among African American and Latino Teenagers." In G. Alonso, N. S. Anderson, C. Su, and J. Theoharis (eds.), *Students Talk Back to a Segregated Nation on the Failures of Urban Education* (pp. 69–111). New York: New York University Press.

Urrea, L. A. (2004). *The Devil's Highway: A True Story.* New York: Little, Brown and Company.

U.S. Census Report. (2004). Retrieved from www.census.gov/population/www/ socdemo/school.html.

Valdés, G. (1995). "The Teaching of Minority Languages as 'Foreign' Languages: Pedagogical and Theoretical Challenges." *Modern Language Journal, 79,* 299–328.

Waggoner, D. (2000). "The Demographics of Diversity in the United States." In R. Gonzalez (ed.), *Language Ideologies: Critical Perspectives on the Official English Movement* (pp. 5–27). Mahweh, NJ: Lawrence Erlbaum Associates.

Wenger, E. (1998). *Communities of Practice: Learning, Meaning, and Identity.* Cambridge: Cambridge University Press.

Chapter 7

Bodies before Me

Stephanie Jones, *University of Georgia*

> The little working-class girl presents, especially to education, an image which threatens the safety of the discourse of the innocent and natural child. She is too precocious, too sexual . . . she is deeply threatening to a civilizing process understood in terms of the production and achievement of natural rationality and nurturant femininity.
>
> —Valerie Walkerdine (1997, p. 4)

This is a tale borne out of the unspoken, absent, and unimaginable. For sure, many undergraduate students in my class one May morning likely left our meeting wondering what had happened and what relevance it had to them learning to be a teacher.

This is a tale about civility, or refinement, and the project of educational institutions to chisel away—through punishment or exclusion—all that might be read as common, vulgar, or working class in teachers and children. This is a tale about unspeakable bodies in woman-filled spaces where those who have been successfully refined and perform civility find comfort and reward, and those who come from the other side of the tracks work diligently to mimic their classmates and attempt to take up the subject position privileged in such spaces.

This is a tale about a little working-class girl who grew to be a woman professor who is always on the verge of being swallowed whole by an institution she owes both everything and nothing to, and the day she realized how much the institution had become a part of her body in the classroom. And finally, this is a tale of educational and social theory bound up in bodies, minds, and language that pushes, prods, kicks, and pokes at oppressive practices until a small opening sucks oxygen inside and allows—if only momentarily—a way of thinking and doing that is more responsive to the bodies before us.

PROUD CRITICAL PEDAGOGY

It was a warm spring morning when I gathered my teaching materials (books, quotes on transparencies, dry erase markers, envelopes sealed with students' first-day answers to questions about teaching and research, and copies of our collective class poem, "where we're from") for the last class meeting of the semester. I was completing my first year at a new university and quite proud of the ways I had grounded this undergraduate course for teacher education students in all that was critical and aimed toward social justice. "We've never had a course like this before!" was one of my favorite group-consensus comments earlier in the semester, and I felt my critically focused scholarship was one reason I seemed "attractive," even if a bit dangerous, during the interview process the previous spring.

Here I was, finishing up my first year after having done most of what I set out to do: immerse students in readings and discussions that might promote new ways of seeing the world (including Dorothy Allison, Paulo Freire, bell hooks, Gloria Ladson-Billings), and use those readings to observe young children closely and create curricular investigations to meet the particular needs, interests, and desires of children. Many of my students had constructed incredible curricular responses to the children they were learning about and experienced success when working with those children in the classroom.

I was sure my course evaluations would not be a detriment to the promotion and tenure process, but because I was submitting my dossier for promotion and tenure, my department chair had just reminded me that he and others were "counting on the course evaluations." Course evaluations.

I had planned a celebratory last class meeting complete with breakfast, a collective reading of our class poem, sharing the students' strengths-based case studies of marginalized children in their field placements, and an inspirational lecture about the difference one teacher can make in the life of a child and his or her family. Such a culminating event would surely fill the classroom with hope and excitement. And, just maybe, my hope and enthusiasm would also influence the course evaluations my students would be completing at the end of the class. I was wishing my department chair had never mentioned "counting on" those course evaluations. It was seriously messing with my mind.

Things were moving along smoothly until a student shared an experience that brought all my best-laid pedagogical plans tumbling down.

BODY TALK AND NOMOS IN THE KINDERGARTEN CLASSROOM

Classroom management systems of all sorts can be found in elementary classrooms: stoplights with children's names on clothespins affixed to the "appropriate" light (red, yellow, green) based on each child's behavior during the day; wooden sticks earned by individual children as they behave in a way rewarded by their teacher; names of the "bad kids" on the whiteboard; and many other kinds of practices less associated with classroom management than with pure punishment and humiliation (kids sitting in corners, out in the hallway, in another teacher's classroom, on the bench during recess, etc.). Kids find themselves in precarious disciplinary positions for various reasons, too, but mostly because they don't incorporate the *nomos* (Bourdieu 2000) of the classroom or school—the unspoken rules of the game that immediately privilege some and place others at a disadvantage.

Bourdieu describes nomos as, "the principle of vision and division constitutive of a social order of a field" (Bourdieu 2000, p. 143), and he writes of the *habitus* (or embodied way of being) that incorporates a nomos as one that "generates practices immediately adjusted to that order which are therefore perceived, by their author and also by others, as 'right,' straight, adroit, adequate, without being in any way the product of obedience to an order in the sense of an imperative, to a norm or to legal rules" (Bourdieu 2000, p. 143).

In other words, some students are perceived as those who "get it" and others as those who "don't"—and those who seem to get it are rewarded in the system without recognizing how their bodies and minds have been actively shaped by the institution to seem as if they "fit" into the order without even trying. And, it goes without saying (because it is a part of nomos), that the institutional order is never questioned.

Therefore the same children are punished over and over and the same children are rewarded over and over without teachers challenging the nomos of the school or questioning why and how the school norms are what they are. Since Bourdieu conceived of habitus—or the ways of a body—as specifically *classed*, in that the social class conditions of one's experiences produce certain ways of being in the world that are recognized and approved of by those living in similar class conditions, then it is fair to say that social class plays a significant role in whose habitus does or does not incorporate the nomos of elementary classroom spaces that is grounded in middle-class scholastic reason.

So after a long discussion about various disciplinary measures my university students witnessed in their observations, one student reported that a kindergarten child had been suspended from school.

"What on earth for?!" I stopped my cat-like pacing in the front of the room.

"For saying 'coochie'," she said.

I was ready to pounce and the students seemed to know it was coming when the pacing started again, with quicker steps and wilder gestures, "For saying 'coochie'?! A kindergartener?! Let's talk about that."

We didn't talk about it, however, since I was outraged and didn't let anyone else get a word in edgewise as I used the child's suspension as an example of concepts we had been working through all semester long: classism and racism in schools, curricula, and classrooms. "What's wrong with the word coochie? So this young boy was referring to the body and used a word he knew to verbalize his thoughts. Why is it punishable?"

I went on with questions and concerns: What if a White, female, middle-class good-girl said coochie in school? Would she be suspended—or do you think her middle-class parents might get a phone call from an embarrassed teacher who wants to inform them about the "slip" in her habitus and perceived deviance from the nomos? This young boy was African American and received free lunch at school—does his gender, race, and class have something to do with the harsh punishment for saying *coochie*?

Could it be that a young, Black, working-class boy is always already perceived as vulgar within the nomos of schooling and therefore in need of harsh punishment to correct such deviant language practices and thoughts and force him in line with the unspoken rules of which he is only beginning to decipher? Whereas a White, middle-class girl who is typically a teacher-pleaser is always already perceived as fitting into the nomos of school, slipping into the context like a glove, and therefore in need only of a raised eyebrow or subtle reminder of the unspoken rules of refinement and civility in school that she already understands completely?

Pacing, pacing, pacing.

The blue carpet disappeared with each step as I walked the length of the whiteboard in the front of the classroom and small groups of students sitting around five tables stared at me.

I stopped talking and walked back and forth across the front of the classroom shaking my head and sighing. Speechless at this point, I quickly considered a lecture on Basil Bernstein's studies about social class and language use that might be helpful here, or a lecture on the perceived vulgarity of working-class and poor folks' language practices by the bourgeois in Pierre Bourdieu's studies of social class and varied social practices.

Anything to remind these students—on the last day of their course with me—that middle-classness rules school spaces, a reason why working-class and poor children of all races and ethnicities are often pushed out of educational institutions (the irony of such a lesson didn't strike me until after class—that I preach against middle-class school spaces and yet I was pacing inside an institutional space ruled by middle-classness and filled mostly with White, middle-class girls; a space perpetuated by me, a former working-class girl who may have been "deeply threatening to a civilizing process" in classrooms during my childhood, and who was getting ready to cross that threshold again as a professor). And once the pushing out begins, all the best-laid plans by parents to encourage upward mobility in the game of social economics in society begin to come crashing down.

"What would you have done?" a single quiet voice asked me from the far back corner as my mind raced with the pedagogical possibilities in this critical moment.

My pedagogical decisions in this moment were tricky, of course, because so many of the young, White, middle-class (or working-class but doing their best to "pass" as middle-class) women sitting in front of me had done so well in school they had decided to *willingly* subject themselves to *more school about school*, and a career spent inside elementary school buildings. The population is skewed in teacher education classes—most of the students looking at me *had* been and continued to be rewarded by the system and had *not* been suspended such as the little boy whose story provoked this pedagogical possibility.

And though we had discussed systematic marginalization of certain groups in school ad nauseam, how do I really convince a roomful of young women who have mostly loved school that school *as it is* isn't meant to work for working-class and poor kids? My own academic trajectory was much more perilous than many (though not all) of theirs: skipping school, vocational school, barely figuring out how to graduate from high school, not going to college right away, dropping out of college, and so on (e.g., Jones 2009).

The gulf between us on this issue about social class and schooling felt like such a wide one, particularly since many of the young women in front of me had been rewarded by schools that expected them to be submissive, quiet, attentive, docile "teachers' pets" (Luttrell 1997; Walkerdine, Lucey, and Melody 2001), in exchange for credentials providing cultural and symbolic capital for access to middle-class economic opportunities (Bourdieu 1980, 1984). And still, in my teacher education classroom, they were still just as anxious to take up similar subject positions perpetuating the academic reward system for those who will perform the teacher's pet.

They wanted to know what *I* would have done, but not a single person spoke out about competing perspectives of what *might* have been done differently. My sighing, silence, and pacing must have carried on much longer than I thought and someone (or perhaps the entire class) wanted to break the awkward pause.

All eyes were on me. Some squinting, others wide open.

Bodies were still.

Too still, in hindsight, given the wild gesturing and frenetic pacing I had been performing.

"Hmmm. Well. I might have looked at him and said, 'I think you are referring to the part of the female body that some people call the vagina.'"

A deafening silence fell across the room.

I hadn't thought it was possible for the room to be quieter than it had been ten seconds prior to my response, but it was.

I stopped walking and looked closely at the 30 young women's faces.

Some of them were flushed.

Some just bright red.

There were giggles.

Lots of toothy smiles.

I was out of my league here and couldn't tell what was going on for a moment until it occurred to me that some of them may be embarrassed to say vagina.

Could that be right? How could it be? I mean, we were sitting in a room filled with women who presumably have vaginas, and there were no identifiable or self-identified men in the classroom who might otherwise make some women uncomfortable with talking about body parts that are used for sex identification or intercourse. So what was the problem?

NOMOS AND BODY TALK IN TEACHER EDUCATION

I *could not* knowingly let them go out into the world afraid of saying "vagina" when they would be teaching young children who will be talking about bodies at some point and who will be looking to their teachers for confident guidance in feeling good about their own bodies as well as those of others. It is the punishing of "body talk" that further pushes bodies underground, into closets, and into repression.

The discursive histories of—especially—women teachers have provided trajectories of being classed and gendered in particular ways that ignore the body altogether and repress productive discourses of the body. Speaking of the body becomes vulgar, and therefore taboo and unrefined. So I shouldn't be surprised at their hesitation or embarrassment around talk of the body, but these young women will be teachers soon.

But those damn course evaluations.

Promotion and tenure.

"We're counting on these course evaluations," he said.

Shit.

Nope. Couldn't do it.

Course evaluations or no evaluations, I would not let this go.

"Wait a second. You all aren't afraid to say vagina, are you?"

Giggles began quietly at first and some young women laughed out loud.

The once still bodies were now moving, fidgeting, pushing their chairs out from the table, pulling their chairs in closer to the table.

"Okay then. We're going to say it here all together. I'll help you. One. Two. Three. Va—. Come on, you can say it with me."

No one was taking the bait.

"Alright. Everyone up here," at this point I was really glad we'd worked at getting to know one another all semester, "in a circle with me."

Students slowly got up and walked toward the front of the classroom and willingly stood in a circle with me, but only three or four of them say "vagina" after my three count.

I laughed a little and look at the woman near the windows who was wearing a "baby doll" style maternity blouse over a basketball-sized belly, "Now two of you are pregnant in here—you're not telling me you're afraid of saying 'vagina' too, are you?"

The "fear" I reference was likely different for different women in the room: a fear of embarrassment, a fear of being perceived by a professor as a sexual being, a fear of using language not typically used in a school setting, and so on. But perhaps all the possible fears are grounded in cultural prohibition where families, peer groups, schools, and other institutions have routinely prohibited talk about the body in explicit or unspoken ways. And to engage in talking about the body under such prohibition would mean marking oneself as too "precocious" or "sexual," and aligned with all that is perceived as vulgar and common in the working classes.

After more laughter one student rushed over to shut the door (hmmm . . . why did she do that?) and I asked everyone to close their eyes, "No one will see you. But I'm asking you to please say the word out loud. We'll say it three times together on the count of three. Okay?"

Nods, eyes closed.

"Everyone's eyes are closed now. Even mine. Ready? One. Two. Three."

"Vagina. Vagina. Vagina." We chorused together loud and strong and opened our eyes—Eve Ensler (2007) would applaud a first bold step.

It was like a ton of bricks crashed to the ground from our backs and we sighed, laughed, nodded our heads, and looked around the circle.

"Nice job. I knew you could do it. Now you know where we're going next," I announced, "we'll close our eyes and on three we'll say penis three times together."

"One. Two. Three."

"Pee-nis. Pee."

"Come on. You can do it. Everyone's eyes are closed. This is a word for a body part, you all. Like knee. Foot. Penis. It may be filled with all kinds of meanings from our society, our upbringing, popular culture, and so on, but the word refers to a body part, and you must be able to say this to your students if necessary or *they'll* also grow up thinking something is bad about it. There is nothing bad about this."

This last statement was from my critical feminist perspective, of course, and I'm well aware both in the moment and in subsequent analyses that these words may be perceived as bad or inappropriate to some of the young women who have been raised in a particularly Christian Evangelical region of the country where homosexuality is still perceived a sin; where sexuality, period, is not something one discusses; where niceties and southern hospitality frame etiquette and "yes ma'ams" and "no sirs" create an image of innocence, naiveté, and ultra femininity.

In effect, to speak of one's body might be considered vulgar. Thus, this particular brand of southern religious young woman is not only expected to behave in standards proposed by the church or their version of the Bible, but these expectations are also entwined with social class and the airs of a particular (middle- and upper middle-) class status.

Bourdieu writes of the body being "in the social world but the social world is in the body . . . when the same history pervades both habitus and habitat, dispositions and position, the king and his court, the boss and his firm . . . history communicates in a sense to itself, gives back to itself its own reflection" (2000, p. 152). In this moment of pedagogical wrestling, the young women's historicized bodies met a social world in the classroom that did not reflect their experiences of schooling or even of social etiquette and "appropriateness" for the contexts in which they have likely lived. Rather, their histories and habitus bumped up against a space that privileged talk about the body— in fact, mandated talk about the body.

Contrary to Bourdieu's assertion that in many cases privileged citizens "are led to live in a world that is not radically different from the one that shaped their primary habitus, there is an unproblematic agreement between the position and the dispositions of its occupant. . . ." (2000, p. 157), the young "privileged" women in this class, for this moment, were forced to live in a world quite different from the one that shaped their primary habitus, even if they resisted the practices of this new world.

"Ready. One. Two. Three."

"Penis. Penis. Penis."

This time voices were stronger and louder as we stood side by side in that large circle of 31 women. We all opened our eyes and I pursed my lips together and nodded my head at them.

Nice job.

I confessed to the group that I'd never participated in such a lesson in any of my teacher education classes before—not surprising, given the historically regulated spaces of teacher education to produce docile, passive, "feminine," and refined subjects (Apple 1987, 1989; Beauboeuf-Lafontant 2005; Miller 1996; Spring 1994), but nevertheless unsettling for a self-identified feminist educator. And following a group reading of our collective class poem from the semester, I thanked them for teaching me and learning along with me across the semester, and asked for a volunteer to distribute, collect, and deliver the course evaluations.

And I walked out of the room hoping the words "penis" or "vagina" would not find their way to the student comment section—at least not before I was tenured.

THE CARRYOVER OF K–12 NOMOS INTO TEACHER EDUCATION

What is the nomos of teacher education classroom spaces? While many of us work to introduce readings, assignments, and discussions that represent perspectives that have often been ignored in the past, does the nomos of teacher education spaces still hold tight to classed and gendered ways of being that are rewarded in K–12 education? Is the nomos of teacher education one of refinement and cultivation—both reflective of upper middle-class and specifically gendered practices?

Some of you may have heard the word "coochie," said it yourself when you were younger—or perhaps you still do—and some of you will have had no idea what "coochie" is. Instead, you may say "va-jay-jay," "private part," or if you're really bold in this world that marginalizes and punishes such language use, "pussy." These are all common words used to refer to the vagina when somehow saying vagina is beyond one's capability or inclination.

But what would make someone uncomfortable with saying vagina? Haven't we come a long way, Baby? I mean, we're post-second wave feminism, right? Girl Power and All That? But maybe it wasn't simply that the 30 young women sitting in front of me weren't *capable* of verbalizing the word "vagina," but rather they weren't capable within the *space* of formal education.

I'll go out on a limb here and say that coochie (and other words referring to a woman's vagina) has been constructed as a vulgar word. Vulgarity is positioned in opposition to high class, which is refined in particular ways to be perceived as high status by others. Bourdieu would say women in the upper middle class create bodies for others (1984), knowing present society's expectations of a high-class woman, how she might dress, sit in a chair, stand next to her man, and extend her hand for a greeting. She would know how to tilt her head just right, open her mouth only slightly, and speak in soft consensual tones and stunted sentences.

A "classy" lady knows how to be such and she alters everything from her wardrobe and head nodding to her waistline and portion sizes (e.g., Bourdieu 1984). And, most likely, a classy lady wouldn't be talking about coochies, va-jay-jays, vaginas, or pussies in spaces where class refinement is not only privileged but expected and unspoken—through nomos.

School is one of those places.

So just as I was stunned at my students' inability to say vagina or speak about the body openly, I am also guilty of perpetuating the refined space of schooling in teacher education classes; guilty of immersing my university students in the same middle-classed space that a young Black boy found himself in as a kindergartner; guilty of holding tight to the nomos of K–12 schooling where a working-class boy who says coochie is suspended and similar language by someone who is already perceived as middle-class is ignored or subtly "corrected"; guilty of creating a university space where mostly White, middle-class women self-select participation; guilty of upholding unspoken rules about the prohibition of body talk; guilty.

Exactly where we have full classes of women, we fail to educate them as women, we fail to see them as women, we fail to recognize the wounds they've endured after 20 or more years of living in a society that encourages the love of children (which these women embodied) and discourages the love of oneself (which these women also embodied).

Just where a feminist pedagogy grounded in women's daily experiences could take root and help grow young women who can be more comfortable within their own skin, more confident in their own body, and begin to reject the classed and raced expectations layered onto unhealthy body and beauty standards constructed in a patriarchal, heteronormative, media-saturated world; just when we might be able to suggest alternative readings of gender, class, race, and ways of being with and talking about one's body, we sit these young women in chairs—at tables—and treat them as receptacles for more phallic filling.

You see, even the female-dominated teacher education is grounded in masculine discourses. We speak of mathematics, science, and social studies—all dominated by men—and language and literacy. Even our critical theories have emerged from overly confident (and sometimes angry) privileged men in the field. So no wonder we haven't explored the necessity or potential power of engaging women's bodies in teacher education.

Vagina monologues in early childhood teacher education, here we come.

If many teacher education programs are filled with students who (1) liked K–12 school enough to subject themselves to a career spent in similar institutions, (2) performed well enough academically to be accepted into (in my case) a flagship university with competitive academic standards, and (3) perform well enough in teacher education classes to reach student teaching, it is very likely that many teacher education students' habitus find themselves "at home in the world [field of schooling] because the world is also in him [sic], in the form of habitus, a virtue made of necessity which implies a form of love of necessity, *amor fati*" (Bourdieu 2000, pp. 142–43).

NOMOS, INTERRUPTED

Nomos is interrupted, or reconceptualized, through the privileging of different kinds of practices—embodied and discursive. In this one instance, the use of vulgar language was not only acceptable, but required as a part of being in the space. No one got an out, and while I offered many bodied ways of saying the words (at one's table, in a circle, with all eyes closed), saying the words "penis" and "vagina" in the space of the classroom was mandatory. Surely a reclassifying of such language use from vulgar, inappropriate, unladylike, and so on into "appropriate" or "professional" words that a teacher can use and teach a child, instead of subjecting him to symbolic violence by suspending him from school, is in order.

The production of subjectivities in schooling occurs within the limits of discourse, and the official discourse of schooling is one of refinement and high status, not one of common vulgarity such as speaking of the body (until you listen in on hallway and playground talks—new spaces constructed outside nomos). Schooling and formal education is traditionally thought to be the work of the *mind,* assumed to be disembodied, making it irrelevant whether one is a female or male, White or Black, poor or wealthy, straight or gay, able-bodied or dis-able-bodied.

A discourse of disembodiment saturates schooling where students sit still and quiet waiting patiently for the input of information to be transferred to them (a la banking education, Freire 1970)—but the irony of such a discourse is that it is lived and performed through *bodies* and it always privileges the phallus, the original man, masculinity. The privilege is unspoken and unwritten, but privilege nonetheless.

When women's bodies are privileged it must be spoken overtly, or no one will recognize it as a woman's space. The discursive limits of K–12 education are carried on and repeated in undergraduate teacher education, where many young women enact subjectivities they have performed much of their life, and others are attempting upward mobility and engaged in performing class-passing, therefore working hard to refine their speech, filter their words, shift their accents, shed their vulgarity.

And we, as teacher educators, don't ask anything different of them.

EMBODYING AND REFUSING INSTITUTIONAL NOMOS

Bourdieu writes of a subject becoming the institution to which the subject owes everything:

> The further one moves away from the ordinary functioning of fields towards limits, which are perhaps never reached, where, with the disappearance of all struggle and all resistance to domination, the space of play rigidifies and shrinks into a "total institution," in Goffman's sense, or—in a rigorous sense this time—an *apparatus,* the more the institution tends to consecrate agents who give everything to the institution (the Party, the Church, the Company, etc.) and who perform this *oblation* all the more easily the less capital they have outside the institution (the holders of "in-house qualification," for example), and therefore the less *freedom* with respect to it and to the specific capital and profits that it offers. The *apparatchik,* who owes everything to the apparatus, is the apparatus personified, ready to give everything to the apparatus that has given him all he has. He can be safely entrusted with the highest responsibilities because he can do nothing to advance his own interests that does not thereby satisfy the expectations of the apparatus. Like the oblate, he is predisposed to defend the institution, with absolute conviction, against the threats posed by the heretical deviations of those whom a capital acquired outside the institution authorizes and inclines to distance themselves from the internal beliefs and hierarchies. (2000, pp. 158–59)

I used to be the little working-class girl Walkerdine (1997) writes about, poor to be more precise, and likely read by teachers and middle-class friends' families as too precocious, too sexual. I worked hard to chisel away all that might be read as common, vulgar, or working class so that I might class-pass, or be read as middle-class by others. This work was about making my body different for others to read differently, as more civilized and refined.

But now that such work has been done, I labor to undo it, trying not to embody the institution that inflicted so many wounds on me and others like me. I owe everything to the institution for upward mobility, and yet I owe nothing to the institution that for more than 30 years insisted I become a part of the nomos that excludes, marginalizes, threatens, punishes, ignores, and abandons those who refuse it. The same institution continues to inflict wounds on generations of students, including the one that got this whole story up and running: the one who was suspended for saying coochie.

Now I am the institution, and even in my "critical" and "feminist" pedagogies, I perpetuate the nomos of K–12 education that rewards teachers' pets, quiet docility, and eager-to-please female students (even if they *are* taking up critical stances). In doing so, I fail them, and I fail their future students, and in the end I fail my vision of why I would want to prepare future teachers to begin with.

So I attempt to re-class and re-gender teacher education spaces, shaking up the expected middle-class feminine civility that bounds education protocols as I work to threaten a "civilizing process understood in terms of the production and achievement of natural rationality and nurturant femininity" (Walkerdine 1997, p. 4). I want nothing to do with making the 30 young women in front of me more deeply regulated as ultra feminine, desexualized, and hypercivil or refined.

More civilizing work will only position them to see the common, working-classness of their future students and families as pathological, deficient, lacking, indeed vulgar, regardless of how many culturally sensitive texts I introduce them to and how often we discuss the use of funds of knowledge (e.g., Moll, Amanti, Neff, and Gonzalez 1992) and culturally relevant pedagogies (Ladson-Billings 1995). After all, it is in the *un*spoken and absent spaces where the rules of the educational game are sedimented, where nomos becomes reality and reason for privileging some and punishing others.

So this is about the vagina, and it's about body talk, and it's about gender, and it's about feminism, and it's all tied up with class and the refinement or vulgarity that is "appropriate" or otherwise in schooling spaces. Why must one perform such narrow constructions of middle-classness to be a teacher? Why must schools expect refined, rigid, discursive, and embodied practices from children and teachers, rather than full-bodied curious beings living in the world in diverse, interesting ways?

Don't *talk about* the use of profanity to express various emotions and promote the idea that language diversity is good, rich, productive, and so forth while speaking in a regulated, upper–middle-class way—*cuss* for crying out loud. Don't *talk about* (in the same ol' refined teacher education discourse) sex and sexuality as important things for teachers to consider, read novels and short stories with explicit sexual content (e.g., *The Brief Wondrous Life of Oscar Wao*, or *Trash*).

Move around the room, perform skits, role play uncomfortable situations between students and teachers, watch films that challenge patriarchy and heteronormativity, assign autoethnographic writing around issues of gender and sexuality (e.g., Vavrus 2009), deconstruct heterosexist, misogynist advertisements and television shows (Jones 2006), talk about vaginas and penises—use the *words*. Shake up the embodied discursive world of teacher education so we don't produce the same repressed, rigid teachers who will move on to K–12 settings and construct similarly repressive spaces.

Like Vavrus (2009) and others, one goal of my teacher education pedagogy is that future educators will create more inclusive, validating, open spaces in future classrooms. However, this constant focus on the *future* may position us to miss the *present*. A focus on the present (with the assumption that it will inform the future in generative ways) will force us to see the people right in front of us and help them along on their journey to become whole people, healing the wounds inflicted on us and them along the way.

Neither "vagina" nor "penis" showed up on my course evaluations. Instead, several comments such as the following did:

> "This was the best teacher I ever had! She opened my mind to a whole new way of seeing the world. . . ."
> "This was a great, intellectually stimulating course. . . . I wish we would be able to continue these discussions in [our next course]."

And I was officially promoted and tenured at my institution.

In my revisioned teacher education space, I won't have to worry about potential consequences for the words "penis" or "vagina" appearing on my course evaluations either (I certainly wasn't worried about issues of race, class, ethnicity, language, and social justice appearing on those evaluations—what does that say about such critical pedagogies becoming a part of nomos?), and I can teach the minds *and* bodies of the young women, and few young men, before me, and we'll play and make education together differently, and I'll fight more heartily to escape the gaping mouth of the institution that has swallowed me in the past, spit me back out, and is always on the verge of swallowing me up again.

REFERENCES

Allison, D. (2002). *Trash*. New York: Plume.

Apple, M. (1987). "The De-Skilling of Teachers." In F. Bolin and J. M. Falk (eds.), *Teacher Renewal: Professional Issues, Personal Choices* (pp. 59–75). New York: Teachers College Press.

———. (1989). *Teachers and Texts: A Political Economy of Class and Gender Relations in Education*. New York: Routledge.

Beauboeuf-Lafontant, T. (2005). "Womanist Lessons for Reinventing Teaching." *Journal of Teacher Education, 56,* 436–45.

Bourdieu, P. (1980). *The Logic of Practice.* Stanford, CA: Stanford University Press.

———. (1984). *Distinction: A Social Critique of the Judgment of Taste.* Cambridge, MA: Harvard University Press.

———. (2000). *Pascalian Meditations.* Stanford, CA: Stanford University Press.

Diaz, J. (2007). *The Brief Wondrous Life of Oscar Wao.* New York: Riverhead Books.

Ensler, E. (2007). *Vagina Monologues.* New York: Villard.

Freire, P. (1970). *Pedagogy of the Oppressed.* New York: Seabury Press.

———. (1998). *Teachers as Cultural Workers: Letters to Those who Dare Teach.* Boulder, CO: Westview Press.

hooks, b. (1996). *Bone Black: Memories of Girlhood.* New York: Henry Holt and Company.

Jones, S. (2006). "Lessons from Dorothy Allison: Social Class, Critical Literacy, and Teacher Education." *Changing English, 13,* 293–305.

———. (2009). "Jagged Edges: A Psychosocial Exploration by One Who 'Made It.'" In J. Van Galen and V. Dempsey (eds.), *Trajectories: The Education and Social Mobility of Education Scholars from the Poor and Working Class* (pp. 55–86). The Netherlands: Sense Publishers.

Ladson-Billings, G. (1995). "Toward a Theory of Culturally Relevant Pedagogy." *American Educational Research Journal, 32,* 465–91.

Luttrell, W. (1997). *School Smart and Mother Wise: Working-Class Women's Identity and Schooling.* New York: Routledge.

Miller, J. (1996). *School for Women.* London: Virago.

Moll, L., C. Amanti, D. Neff, and N. Gonzalez. (1992). "Funds of Knowledge for Teaching: Using a Qualitative Approach to Connect Homes and Classrooms." *Theory into Practice, 31*(2), 132–41.

Spring, J. (1994). *The American School, 1641–1991* (3rd ed.). New York: McGraw-Hill.

Vavrus, M. (2009). "Sexuality, Schooling, and Teacher Identity Formation: A Critical Pedagogy for Teacher Education." *Teaching and Teacher Education, 25,* 383–90.

Walkerdine, V. (1997). *Daddy's Girl: Young Girls and Popular Culture.* Cambridge, MA: Harvard University Press.

Walkerdine, V., H. Lucey, and J. Melody. (2001). *Growing Up Girl: Psychosocial Explorations of Gender and Class.* New York: New York University Press.

Closing Vignette

The Distance of Formality

Working within (and through) Propriety

Aaron M. Kuntz, *University of Alabama*

Moving from the cultural comforts of the Northeast to the uncharted waters of the South was full of anticipated challenges. I grew up in the Northeast and did my entire graduate work at schools there. Consequently, my knowledge of the cultural South was limited to a few short visits in the distant past as well as the ever-present media biases found in movie portrayals and books that represented a land never fully recovered from the Civil War. And yet, I was happy to transition to a faculty position that seemed a perfect fit for my research and teaching aspirations.

I was confident in my teaching abilities in the classroom, potential to collaborate with students and colleagues on a variety of emergent projects, and the promise of continuing my own work in a collegiate environment. At the same time, I recognized I was moving into a cultural zone that I had never previously encountered—that geographical change brought with it a variety of newfound daily practices, interactions, languages, and interpretations that often resulted in what we collectively term "culture shock."

Any amount of life change brings with it a degree of anxiety, most often articulated as an inability to properly predict what life's new circumstance will bring. In response to new contexts we develop new coping mechanisms, ways of engaging with unfamiliar circumstance through newfound practices. As such, my family and I were braced for significant change as we packed into an overstuffed minivan and followed the moving trucks south.

Though I have encountered numerous challenges throughout my tenure here in the South, the one that most affects me on a daily basis was unanticipated and, on the surface anyway, relatively benign. I came to my current position intent on engaging in and with local communities as an involved scholar, someone whose academic work remained grounded in the practicalities of community needs.

Several of my mentors in graduate school modeled ways to link their academic endeavors with the local communities in which they resided: going to local schools to speak about cultural literacy and media violence; lending an engaged voice to educational issues as they played out in surrounding schools; working with displaced immigrant populations at town cultural centers; and inviting their graduate students into their offices and homes as future colleagues. These faculty mentors were seemingly integrated into multiple and varied communities, seamlessly merging academic work with social awareness. They were known to me as Gretchen, Sharon, Joe, and Rick, and I valued the ease with which I connected with both their academic and daily family lives.

When I ventured south, I encountered a unique cultural phenomenon that maintained a formal distance on account of my academic achievements. Quite simply, wherever I went I was known as "Dr. Kuntz." To me, such formal salutation kept me at arm's length from fully engaging in local activities and I quickly became frustrated at my inability to move beyond the "Dr." title. Upon first glance, invoking my educational title may seem an insignificant recognition of educational achievement, though its incessant repetition in a variety of venues I interpreted as an othering, a separation of the speaker's world from what I represent.

This first occurred when I stopped in to see my daughter's elementary school principal before we moved to our new home. I introduced myself as "Anna's dad," and this identity was quickly exchanged for the soon-to-be-familiar "Dr." moniker after the principal learned of my new position at the university.

Similarly, in the graduate classes I taught I began by introducing myself by my first name before asking those seated around the seminar table to do the same. The students resisted. Men and women who were ten years my elder, who had countless years of experience in the classroom, insisted on calling me "Dr. Kuntz." I often responded to such formality by naming it as a rhetorical—and unnecessary—distancing, a learned practice of foregrounding the power hierarchies inherent in educational systems.

I then went on to note the need to disrupt such patterns, to situate ourselves on even ground as colleagues who believed in the value of studying and enacting progressive, community-based education. Students would nod silently at my remarks, the subject would change, and inevitably they would greet me the next day as "Dr. Kuntz."

Upon reflection, my eagerness to establish more familiar relations with those with whom I worked resulted in an artificial binary that overlaid the informal-formal split with the close-distant pattern of meaning. My experiences conducting my graduate work in the Northeast taught me that close working relationships were part and parcel with informality; we called everyone by their first names, regardless of prior experience or faculty rank. My own naiveté caused me to assume that a similarly patterned relationship would occur in the South.

Additionally, the use of formal salutation no doubt played in my own anxieties as a Northern transplant, already distinguished by cultural differences from the setting in which I now lived. I valued my graduate school mentors because they easily merged into their local contexts. I interpreted the use of "Dr. Kuntz" as recognition that I was never fully integrated, never fully connected to my newly local communities. In a sense, resisting the "Dr." prefix was my own attempt to negotiate the anxieties of cultural difference, a strategy to close the distance that comes with feeling an outsider. In short, it was more about me than anyone else.

What I came to learn was that my articulated insistence that students and community members address me by my first name made many of them uneasy. Indeed, through asking others to take on and share my value of informality I, at the same time, invoked the very power-laden relationships I was trying to disrupt, to value my culturally idiosyncratic experiences over their own.

The fact is that I was—still am—culturally distant from many of the graduate students and community members I encountered: a Northern Yankee in the South; a White man in a community irrevocably marked by a history of racial inequity and patriarchy. We share a campus that houses "the mound" (the foundational remains of a dormitory destroyed by an aggressive Northern army) and the "school house door" (the site of George Wallace's public pledge to block educational integration).

My own academic training has taught me that identities are both multiple and mutually constituted. This is to say that "who we are" depends quite a bit on the social, historical, and material contexts in which we are immersed. As I moved south, I anticipated that the student-faculty patterned relationship would follow intact. I assumed that initial greetings of "Dr. Kuntz" would fall away as students and local community members got to know me better. The more we work on collaborative projects together, I surmised, the easier it will be to drop the formal distinctions that separate us from one another. What I hadn't anticipated was the strong pull of what some might call "Southern propriety" and others might simply term "politeness."

This is not to say that all Southern universities, faculty, and students operate under the conditions of formality, or that I simply read my experiences moving from the Northeast to the South along the lines of Southern propriety. As someone engaged in poststructural theory I work against such problems of essentialism. Instead, this transition has revealed the many ways in which cultural ways of knowing that are often taken for granted and treated as commonsensical break down when geographical and cultural distances are crossed. In my academic work I strive to examine daily practices, the means by which individuals engage in and give meaning to those activities practiced on a daily basis.

It took me some time, but I eventually came to realize that the daily practice of invoking one's academic rank or accomplishment was not so much a distancing that stood in the way of connection, but rather in many cases a cultural practice of placing relations. The way in which we are "placed" or "displaced" within multiple contexts reveals much about the social processes that in many ways produce us—such instances require unpacking.

As I look back now on my initial transition to the South, I'm struck by the multiple ways in which I sought to establish working relationships with students and in local communities based on notions of displacement. I sought to displace my educational role in order to more closely connect with those with whom I worked. I also sought to displace my own representations as a White Northern Yankee working in the Deep South.

Yet this element of displacement, in turn, required the students and community members with whom I worked to undergo a displacement of their own—a disruption to their own learned cultural codes and familiar ways of interacting. And, of course, a key part of critical thinking requires a degree of interruption to patterned ways of knowing. Yet, what soon became clear to me was that my request for informality invoked the very power relation that I hoped to disrupt in my own work. I inhabit a power-laden position as a result of my faculty status and I soon became uneasy calling upon that status in the hopes of replicating the informal relations of my own graduate school experience.

Further, my time here in the South has caused me to reevaluate the relational meanings invoked throughout my graduate school experience in the Northeast. In truth, the power relations between me and my mentors in graduate school were no different than those I now experience as a faculty member at my present university in the South; they were perhaps simply hidden behind a veil of informality. Thus, there is the potential for such informality to, in many ways, be a bit dishonest—to falsely claim that the difference between faculty and student had been more fully mitigated by the circumstance of informality.

Consequently, neither the informality I experienced in the Northeast nor the formality of the South were more "real" or equated to better relations. Instead, they simply represent similar power relations in similar educational institutions differently; a difference brought about in many ways by sociohistorical location.

In the end, I don't want to misrepresent or simplify the multiple placements involved in my transition to the South. I don't think everyone views my Northern accent solely in relation to the Civil War, nor my white skin as a direct connection to a history of racial oppression. Yet I cannot ever fully distance myself from such histories, nor should I—I am, in very real ways, tied to such discourses.

As a consequence, I have begun to offer my own cultural placings up for analysis in the classes I teach. I teach critical qualitative inquiry and emphasize skills of cultural analysis. By foregrounding the multiple identities I present as a Northern transplant, I encourage students to unpack the layers of identity, to consider the implications of cultural markers, local and global contexts, and history on our daily practices. I aim for an explication of the subtle ways in which history and immediate context mark us. It is, as the saying goes, more than navel gazing and less than therapy.

Index

About the Editors

Lisa Scherff is an associate professor of English language arts at the University of Alabama. A former high school English and reading teacher, she earned a Ph.D. in reading education, with a graduate certificate in educational policy, from Florida State University. Scherff's research focuses primarily on the opportunity to learn in secondary English, the teaching of young adult literature, and teacher preparation and induction, and has been published in journals such as *English Education, Teaching and Teacher Education*, and *Research in the Teaching of English*. She and Leslie Rush (University of Wyoming) are the coeditors of *English Education* (2010–2015).

Karen Spector is currently an assistant professor of English language arts and literacy at the University of Alabama. She taught high school English in Florida and Ohio to diverse students before earning her Ed.D. in literacy from the University of Cincinnati and beginning her career in higher education in 2005. Spector's working class background has shaped the way she sees the world and has thus also shaped her research and writing interests, which include social class, narrative, and response to literature. Her research has been published in journals such as *Research in the Teaching of English, Journal of Adolescent & Adult Literacy*, and *Changing English*, as well as in several books, including *Trajectories: Social and Educational Mobility of Education Scholars from Poor and Working Class Backgrounds*, edited by Jane Van Galen and Van Dempsey.

About the Contributors

Dawn Abt-Perkins is professor of education at Lake Forest College. A former chair of the Conference on English Education, the College Forum, and the Assembly for Research of the National Council of Teachers of English, she has published extensively on teacher preparation and cultural diversity, including *Making Race Visible: Literacy Research for Cultural Understanding* (co-edited with Stuart Greene), winner of the Meade Award for outstanding contribution to the field of English education.

Ruth Balf is currently a professional development consultant for mathematics initiatives in the Puget Sound area. She spent many years teaching at the elementary school level.

Matthew Brown currently teaches 11th and 12th grade English at Manning High School. He graduated with a degree in English Education from Purdue University in 2007. Following graduation, he moved from his hometown of Fort Wayne, Indiana, and now resides in Manning, South Carolina.

Jacqueline Deal teaches 11th and12th grade English for the Evertech and New Visions alternative education programs at Broome-Tioga BOCES. She has a long-term and personal relationship with alternative education: After taking her GED, she went to college and later to graduate school. In 2008, Deal joined the National Writing Project; she now serves as a "Teacher Consultant," working with K–12 teachers in finding ways to use writing to learn in all disciplines.

Elizabeth Dutro is associate professor of literacy studies at the University of Colorado at Boulder, where she pursues research on the emotional dimensions of schooling and issues of race, class, and gender in the school experiences of children and youth. Her scholarship received the Alan C. Purves and Frank Pajares awards and has appeared in numerous venues, including *Research in the Teaching of English, Theory into Practice*, and *Journal of Literacy Research*.

Kimberly Adilia Helmer is assistant professor of English at John Jay College of Criminal Justice, The City University of New York (CUNY). She is an applied linguist specializing in linguistic and educational anthropology. Her research interests include heritage and second language acquisition, ethnic identity construction, and second-language/second-dialect issues in composition.

Stephanie Jones is associate professor in the College of Education at the University of Georgia. Her research interests include critical feminist pedagogies in elementary settings and teacher education; issues of gender, race, social class, and poverty in education and society; and critical literacies. She is author of *Girls, Social Class, and Literacy: What Teachers Can Do to Make a Difference* and co-author of *The Reading Turn-Around: A Five Part Framework for Differentiated Instruction*.

Elham Kazemi is associate professor of mathematics education at the University of Washington. She is interested in how schools nurture the intellectual and social lives of both children and adults. She studies how teachers, over the long term, transform their classroom practices through collaborative work focused on understanding children's mathematical ideas.

Aaron M. Kuntz is assistant professor of qualitative research methods at the University of Alabama. His research interests include critical geography, academic citizenship and activism, materialist methodologies, and critical inquiry. He received his doctorate in education from the University of Massachusetts, Amherst.

Kysa Nygreen is assistant professor in the Teacher Education and Curriculum Studies Department at the University of Massachusetts, Amherst. Her teaching and research focus on issues of race, class, culture, and equity in education; urban schooling; critical and anti-racist pedagogies; participatory action research; and educational ethnography.

Eileen R. C. Parsons is associate professor of science education at the University of North Carolina-Chapel Hill. She investigates the role of context in science learning and the science, technology, engineering, and mathematics (STEM) participation of groups underrepresented in the sciences. Specifically, she uses critical theory to examine how racial and cultural influences impact opportunity, access, and attainment of people of color in STEM and STEM-related fields.

Melanie Shoffner is assistant professor of English education at Purdue University, with a joint appointment in the Departments of English and Curriculum & Instruction. Before earning her Ph.D. from the University of North Carolina at Chapel Hill, she was a high school English teacher in North Carolina and Arizona. Her research interests include reflective practice, secondary English teacher preparation, and beginning English teachers' issues of practice.

Steven Wall is a doctoral student in the Culture, Curriculum, and Change program at the University of North Carolina-Chapel Hill. He is currently working on projects investigating the development of professional identity in pre-service educators, the structural modeling of science identity, and the role of technology in developing interest and improving achievement in science in multicultural classrooms. He has taught in the United States, Sub-Saharan Africa, and the Far East.

Victoria M. Whitfield teaches high school English in Tuscaloosa, Alabama. She is currently pursuing her Ph.D. in Curriculum and Instruction, with emphases in literacy and language arts, from The University of Alabama.